WHAT'S IN YOUR WEB?
Stories of Fascial Freedom

PHIL TAVOLACCI, MSPT, PT

BALBOA.
PRESS
A DIVISION OF HAY HOUSE

Balboa Press books may be ordered through booksellers or by contacting:

Balboa Press
A Division of Hay House
1663 Liberty Drive
Bloomington, IN 47403
www.balboapress.com
1-(877) 407-4847

Because of the dynamic nature of the Internet, any web addresses or links contained in this book may have changed since publication and may no longer be valid. The views expressed in this work are solely those of the author and do not necessarily reflect the views of the publisher, and the publisher hereby disclaims any responsibility for them.

The author of this book does not dispense medical advice or prescribe the use of any technique as a form of treatment for physical, emotional, or medical problems without the advice of a physician, either directly or indirectly. The intent of the author is only to offer information of a general nature to help you in your quest for emotional and spiritual well-being. In the event you use any of the information in this book for yourself, which is your constitutional right, the author and the publisher assume no responsibility for your actions.

Any people depicted in stock imagery provided by Thinkstock are models, and such images are being used for illustrative purposes only.
Certain stock imagery © Thinkstock.

Printed in the United States of America.

ISBN: 978-1-4525-7697-8 (sc)
ISBN: 978-1-4525-7699-2 (hc)
ISBN: 978-1-4525-7698-5 (e)

Library of Congress Control Number: 2013911393

Balboa Press rev. date: 7/23/2013

TABLE OF CONTENTS

Acknowledgements vii

Foreword By John F. Barnes, PT xi

Introduction xv

Section One: Phil's Fascial Journey 1

Chapter 1   The Lecture on the Floor................................3
Chapter 2   Invisible Kid Scars...11
Chapter 3   Appendix Explosion...................................... 20
Chapter 4   Ice Pick in the Back..27
Chapter 5   Sword to the Neck..33
Chapter 6   Depression.. 44
Chapter 7   Déjà vu 52
Chapter 8   Shoulder This Storm 63
Chapter 9   Pain, Pain, Go Away 73
Chapter 10   Aha! MFR!.. 84
Chapter 11   The Path Unfolds 97
Chapter 12   And the Journey Continues 112

Section Two: MFR Therapists' Stories 119

Chapter 13   Ann Devlin-Low, BA, MAT, LMT 121
Chapter 14   Derek Metzler, MPT 143
Chapter 15   Kathy Monkman, BSN, LMT 158
Chapter 16   Francis 'Chino' Ramirez, DPT, MS, CPT 166
Chapter 17   Kathleen Troust, DPT 183
Chapter 18   Debbie Walden, MR, RMT 190
Chapter 19   Garth Whitcombe LMT 204
Chapter 20   Ann Udofia, PT, DPT 214
Chapter 21   Drucilla J. Likens Pape, OTR/L............................... 221
Chapter 22   Nancy Murray, BSN, RN, MA................................. 238
Chapter 23   Cathy Covell, PT 249
Chapter 24   Sandy Whitcombe, LMT 267
Chapter 25   Laura Probert, MPT 277
Chapter 26   Wendy Isom, LMBT 290
Chapter 27   Linda Aileen Miller, LMT, EAV 307

Afterword 325

Myofascial Release Resources 329

Acknowledgements

First, I thank my incredible partner of fifteen years, Jeff, for his encouragement and support in writing this book. Thank you, Jeff, for keeping me grounded, semi-sane, and on track as I navigate this eventful life of mine. I love you.

I would also like to thank my wonderful family-- Roberta (Mom), Peter (Dad), and Mike (Brother) Tavolacci. I believe that when we all enter this physical world, our spirits choose which family is right for us. I chose the right family without a doubt. I love all of you very much.

Words alone cannot express how much John F. Barnes, PT, has impacted, transformed, and altered the trajectory of my life, both personally and professionally. Thank you so much John for being who you are and standing for what you know to be true and authentic. Your courage, strength and persistence in your development of genuine healing work are astonishing. I feel so blessed to have been personally taught by you and treated by you. You are a gift to this planet.

"Thank you" is also not enough for the generous and open-hearted individuals who made written contributions to this book. This book would not be what I envisioned it to be if the contributing therapists and clients did not add their unique experiences and brilliant insights. So, a million THANK YOU's to the book contributors!

I would like to thank each and every one of my patients that I have treated since becoming a physical therapist in 1998. Every single one of you has taught me something that has allowed me to evolve, expand, and grow – as a therapist and as a human being. It has been a privilege to facilitate your journeys towards happier and healthier lives. You have been crucial contributors in my journey towards peace, health, and knowledge!

The Universe has blessed me with the most amazing colleagues since starting my wellness clinic, **TAVO Total Health**, in 2004. I would like especially to thank my three Myofascial Release colleagues- Kathleen Troust, Ann Udofia, and Tanya Colucci. It has been such a fantastic journey over the past several years with the three of you skilled, compassionate, and dedicated therapists. Thank you for all you've done and for being a part of my clinic and my life.

I would like to thank three specific friends and colleagues who recently published their own first books, and thus, gave me more conviction that I too could actually write and publish a book. Thank you Linda Aileen Miller (author, *Who is That Woman?*), Honi Borden (author, *The Day I Became a Superhero*), and Laura Probert (author, *Living, Healing, and Taekwondo*). All three of you are great authors, genuine healers, and inspiring beings.

I also would like to profusely thank my Office Manager Extraordinaire, Kristen Cortiglia, for her tremendous assistance with this book. Thank you, Kristen, for helping me to organize and stay on track during this book writing journey. Thank you, especially, for not making me feel stupid when I'd ask computer questions like, "Now how do I get this to go over into that little storage thingy over there [aka flash drive]?" Clearly I couldn't have done this without you!

I also thank Lynne Heneson for editing the first half of this book- my autobiographical segment of the book. This was not an easy task since I have an addiction to commas and have no idea where hyphens and semicolons truly should be parked! Thanks, Henny!

There are countless other individuals that have been pivotal in my journey. I thank you all for your impact on my life. I'm going to take a leap of faith and optimistically declare that future books will allow more acknowledgements.

Foreword
By John F. Barnes, PT

My friend, Phil Tavolacci, MSPT, PT is an incredible person and therapist. You are about to embark upon a journey; a profound journey. With his wonderful new book, Phil is going to take you into the fascinating world of Myofascial Release. Myofascial Release will open you up to a larger, new world; one very different from what you thought reality was. The power of our instinctive, intuitive wisdom has always been there, but was unavailable to most of us. Myofascial Release helps treat all aspects of the human being in a totally safe and effective way.

The fascial system has been ignored in most therapists and physicians education. Many of the problems that you and many others have encountered, whether it be pain, headaches, restriction in motion, etc., may be coming from restrictions in the fascial system.

Trauma, thwarted inflammatory responses, surgery, and emotional upheavals in one's life can restrict the fascia. When this occurs, the fascia can exert enormous crushing pressure on pain sensitive structures- up to approximately two thousand pounds per square inch.

It is also important to recognize that fascial restrictions do not show up in any of the normal testing- CT scans, X-rays, myelograms, blood work, etc. Therefore, myofascial problems have been misdiagnosed or completely ignored for eons.

The good news is that there is hope! Myofascial Release will help you to find your "true self" and lead you to a more healthy, joyful, and fulfilling life. The individuals who are in Phil's book are also incredible Myofascial Release therapists who have faced their own fears and have had the courage to go into them so they can evolve and help their patients and clients.

It would be helpful to add an excerpt from my book, *Healing Ancient Wounds; the Renegade's Wisdom*.

"As a patient/client, when you are being treated by a Myofascial Release therapist you are encountering a very unique individual, one that has extensive and very special training and talents, a person who has expended a considerable amount of time developing their skills and awareness. They have done everything that they will be asking you to do and feel. We believe that you can only take your patients as far and as deep as you are willing to go yourself!

When you are with a Myofascial Release therapist you are in the hands of someone who has internal strength, courage, integrity, and incredible awareness. You will sense the gentle, yet powerful feel of their essence when they are near you and as they touch you. Allow their presence and the luminescence in their eyes to inspire you and reconnect you with your essence.

We know that you have these attributes also, and we will help you reach your full potential! We will help you reach your goals as long as you are willing to help yourself. As in life, you will get out of Myofascial Release what you are willing to put into it!

Your Myofascial Release therapist's formidable skills, inner calm and confidence will help you peel away myofascial and emotional barriers that have blocked the full expression of your true self, to rediscover your own tranquility, strength, mental clarity and awareness. Re-igniting your 'spark of life' will return you to a natural, joyful, healthy and pain-free active lifestyle!"

The "inner journey" is not the most important journey, it is the only journey!

Sincerely,

John F. Barnes, PT, LMT, NCTMB
President of the Myofascial Release Treatment Centers and Seminars
www.MyofascialRelease.com

Introduction

I believe in the power of authentic storytelling. Some of the most profound lessons I have had in my lifetime have come from stories. The stories that I find most powerful are those that honestly, boldly, and accurately relay life experiences. This book is a book of such stories.

My intention is to accomplish three basic goals:

(1) Give the reader a basic understanding of the body's miraculous fascial system and the power of authentic Myofascial Release (MFR), as taught by John F. Barnes, PT

(2) Share the varied experiences of multiple individuals, so readers are likely to resonate or "connect with" at least one or two shared experiences

(3) Give readers **hope** that whatever challenging issues they are experiencing might potentially be transformed by accessing and treating their fascial system

This book is not an academic or clinical book. It is written with the public as the target audience. It is meant to be a first step, an introduction, an awareness raiser. It is meant to be read and then shared with people. Many readers might be motivated into action and seek out a John Barnes trained MFR practitioner to begin exploring what's in their own fascial web.

The book is split into two sections. Section One is autobiographical. I share key components of my journey from chronic pain and depression, to my current state of pain-limited living and happiness. I say pain-limited living because it would be inauthentic to say that I am completely pain free. But, I think most would agree that going from chronic, daily, eight out of ten (8/10) pain to infrequent two out of ten (2/10) pain is a quantum leap! The beginning of each chapter in this first section, except Chapter 1, starts with basic information about fascia and MFR. Each of the chapters in Section One ends with a written contribution from one of my clients. Each client's story is written in their own words with little, if any, editing.

Section Two of the book is comprised of fifteen "What's in Your Web?" experiences shared by varied amazing John Barnes trained MFR therapists. Most chapters in this section end with one or two of their clients' "What's in Your Web?" stories. As with my clients' contributions, these stories were written by the clients themselves, and very little, if any, editing has been made to their stories.

The term "Myofascial Release" (or MFR) is used differently by different practitioners around the world; this can be a great source of confusion to the public. When I speak about MFR throughout this entire book, I am speaking very specifically of MFR as taught by John F. Barnes, PT. Many therapy schools and continuing education courses teach what they label as MFR, but it is quite different in many ways than John F. Barnes' specific method.

I am extremely excited that this book has found its way into your life.

Since you are reading this right now, the time is likely right for you to embark on a journey. Your journey, like you, and like your fascial web, is completely unique. It is one of a kind. There is no one else on this planet that has the same exact journey as you. Maybe one day I will be fortunate enough to hear **your** "What's in Your Web?" story!

.

SECTION ONE:
PHIL'S FASCIAL JOURNEY

Chapter 1

THE LECTURE ON THE FLOOR

I was writhing in pain on the floor of my soon-to-open, first-ever, leap-of-faith, teeny-tiny wellness clinic.

"Oh NO! Not again! Not NOW!"

It was a Sunday in August of 2004. The clinic space I was about to occupy was a small suite within a large medical building in Chevy Chase, Maryland. Since it was a Sunday, the building was closed and deserted. I saw and heard no one as I carted painting materials up to the space on the twelfth floor of the building.

After being a physical therapist for six years, I was beyond excited to start my own physical therapy and fitness business. In just a couple weeks, I would see my first patient at **TAVO PT & Fitness** (later to become **TAVO Total Health**). Coupled with the excitement, however, was intense fear and anxiety.

The thoughts of fear and anxiety were relentless: How are you going to get patients and clients? Why are you starting a business where you know absolutely no one? How are you going to financially survive? All you've got is a treatment table and some rinky-dink exercise things –how are you going to help anyone?

After I finished the few trips back and forth to my car to get everything I needed, I decided that painting the treatment room would be task number one. The treatment room was only roughly 100 square feet and had no windows. I picked a cheery bright yellow paint to give some illusion of natural light in the room.

I popped the top of the paint can. I bent down to pick up the little wooden stir stick and **WHAM!!!!**

Excruciating pain ripped through my lower back. Within two seconds I was face down on the floor, writhing in pain. The pain was so intense it was difficult to breathe. It was, by far, the worst episode I'd experienced since I first injured my lower back in 1989. I saw that my cell phone was about two feet from my head. I tried to crawl to my phone but every attempt at motion caused the pain to intensify.

Panic set in. I knew from past experiences with my spine "going out" that I could be out of commission for hours or even days. I tried one more time to get to my phone. It was impossible. For four long hours I lay on that floor in agonizing pain.

But, those four hours on the floor were completely pivotal to the transformation that was about to unfold in my life. Let me explain.

At this point in my life I was thirty-two years old and dealing with more chronic spinal pain than the majority of my patients twice my age. There were days when I would simply turn my head and kick off a two-week long neck spasm with stabbing pain into a shoulder blade. There were other days where my mid-back was so tight and painful that I'd have to excuse myself from a treatment session to pop my ribs and vertebrae back into place with a foam roller or with tennis balls. There were other days where my lower back had so much pressure within it, it felt as if it would explode if I made a movement it did not like.

This was my daily life. I will go into greater detail within the book, but for now I want to get back to the lessons that unfolded during those four hours on the floor.

The voices in my consciousness now had me as a very captive audience. They had four hours to give me the lecture of a lifetime. Of course, I cannot recall the specifics of everything that was "said" but I could never forget the core messages, insights, and questions. I will do my best to convey what transpired in that chunk of time on the floor.

The Lecture on the Floor

So, here you are again.
You help so many people, Phil, when are you going to help yourself?
Are you not important?
Do you not deserve to have a better life?
Do you even love yourself, Phil?
No, really, do you?
You are starting your own physical therapy
business and you are basically crippled!
When are you going to wake up?
WAKE UP, PHIL!!!
W A K E U P!!!
What's it going to take to get your attention?
Do you want to be in a wheelchair by the time you are forty?
It's time.
Now.
It's time for you to help YOU!
It's wonderful that you help people… now help YOU.
We will give you some credit – you have
tried some things to help yourself.
You became a therapist and fitness trainer.
You have taken many classes.
You have read lots of books.
You have tried therapy and massage.

This knowledge and experience has helped
you become good at what you do.
But it hasn't helped you one bit to GET BETTER YOURSELF.
You've been searching.
You have been searching, we know.
Do you remember…
You were talking to Laura[1] about the work
you were doing with your patients.
You said that it felt like you were being
pulled deep into their muscles.
Even though you were only putting light pressure into their bodies.
You said it was strange that these people
seemed to be getting better quickly,
Even though it felt as if you weren't doing much.
Do you remember?
Laura said "It sounds like you are starting to naturally do
myofascial release – you need to take a John Barnes class!"
Do you remember?
This IS what you need to do, Phil!
This is a piece of your puzzle!!!

[1]   Laura, referenced above, is Laura Probert, MPT.
Right before starting my own clinic I served as a
Director in one of Laura's three clinics in Northern
Virginia. Laura has written a fantastic chapter in
this book- Chapter 25

The lecture ended and, almost instantly, I was able to move. I still had
a great deal of pain but I was no longer pinned down in a heap on the
floor. I crawled to my cell phone and called for help.

The lecture sunk in on a cellular level. I really got it. I listened. Of
course I also thought I'd just spent four hours in crazy-land! Where
were these voices coming from? I should clarify that there weren't

actually audible voices. Nothing could be heard in my ears. These were like telepathic messages zapped directly into my consciousness.

Within a few days, when my back pain subsided, I did some research on MFR. I borrowed my friend Laura's MFR book, written by John F. Barnes. As I started reading the book I recall feeling my body start to buzz. This is the first time I recall having this sensation, but it's now a common sensation for me when I am encountering "my truth." When something crosses my path, and I literally start to buzz, I know it's something that is relevant to me and my journey! When something resonates for me, I buzz.

I knew that I needed to take one of John Barnes' introductory MFR courses. My challenge was that I just left a well-paying salaried job to leap into the gaping unknown of starting my own clinic. I was so stressed about being able to pay my bills and the overhead of my new clinic, how was I going to pay for an MFR course? I knew it HAD to happen as soon as possible so I pulled out my credit card and signed up for my first class. I took my very first MFR class in Miami, Florida in April 2005 and it was like stepping into another dimension of reality!

I experienced more pain reduction and increased mobility in my body at my first MFR course than I had experienced in fifteen years. One of the most amazing revelations was that probably ninety percent of the seminar attendees were first-time students of MFR, like I was. How is it possible that I could get such great results by working with therapists who were just now learning how to do these techniques? Over the course of the three-day seminar I had multiple "Aha" moments. So many things just clicked into place. And I buzzed, and I buzzed, and I buzzed.

One of Phil's clients shares...

Cameron

It's hard to put into words what my web is without explaining how unaware I was that such a thing even existed before being introduced to MFR. I started getting frequent migraine headaches when I was thirteen years old. I quickly went from being a normal, athletic teenage girl with friends, a social life, and good attendance to the token sick kid that was always bailing on friends, activities and school because she wasn't feeling good. Doctors replaced friends, and a dark bedroom replaced any place I would rather be.

As most people who suffer from headaches do, I turned to countless neurologists for answers. Instead of answers, however, I got drugs – and a lot of them. My medicine cabinet became an arsenal of pharmaceuticals. And while some of my so-called weapons helped to decrease the frequency of my headaches, the negative side effects always outweighed the benefits. While I may not have had a headache, I was nonetheless still confined to a bed as a result of the drowsiness and sheer confusion from whatever my prescribed cocktail was at the time. This is essentially what initiated a long downward spiral.

By the time I turned sixteen, I was no longer participating in any sports or athletic activities. During a good week, I would make it to school at least three out of five days, and good weeks were rare. My energy level was non-existent, and my grades suffered as a result, not to mention my self-confidence. While I tried to live as normal a life as possible, there was nothing normal about a young adult that couldn't function due to severe headaches. I developed debilitating insecurities, and anxiety began to control both my body and my life.

As a result, my body became increasingly weaker to the point that I couldn't stand for prolonged periods of time without experiencing immense amounts of back and neck pain. Naturally, this pain would make its way up to my head and trigger a migraine. During the times when I didn't have a migraine, my body would be anticipating the onset of one. I was constantly on edge, and my muscles were always tight. Essentially, I got stuck in a vicious cycle of chronic pain and migraine headaches.

By the age of twenty-three, I had developed alarmingly bad posture. My shoulders were rounded and my neck jutted forward. I could not stretch my arms to their full capacity without crying out in pain. I reached a point in which simple, daily activities became my Everest: taking a shower, getting dressed, walking down stairs, everything. My body ached tremendously and I felt breakable. This feeling of constant pain became my new sense of normal.

I finally reached a point where I decided to give up on modern medicine and, instead, began to pursue more natural methods of healing, something I wish I had done from the very start of my headaches. It was very clear to me that I needed to seek hands-on treatment for my physical pain. This is when I was introduced to MFR. It really wasn't up until this point that I realized my body did not have to feel this way.

MFR didn't reduce my symptoms immediately, but it certainly gave me a sense of hope. Phil explained MFR and described the concept of the body's web. The fundamentals were simple: everything is connected. And while I couldn't appreciate this concept at first, it became clear over-time.

At the beginning of each session Phil would automatically start by assessing the misalignment of my hips. He would then release the tissue restrictions around my hips accordingly. I initially thought that working on my hips was odd and unnecessary as my pain was in my head and neck. The techniques that Phil used, however, echoed throughout my body and I began to understand both the meaning and significance of my fascial web. As soon as my hips were realigned, my whole body felt straighter, more connected. It was as if my hips were setting a precedent for each and every limb. I began walking straighter and standing taller. My legs were actually functioning better and more gracefully, even though I had never previously recognized any fault in them. Every limb seemed to take on its own new life, instead of being tied down to another. Eventually I began to move freely and was no longer forced to turn my entire body in order to look sideways.

As the pain in my body began to subside and my movement began to improve, my headaches also became less frequent. My hips finally started to maintain the correct alignment, allowing Phil to focus on the tangled web that still existed in my head, neck and shoulders. The base of my skull felt like a brick and it took a while before I even felt Phil working in certain areas. Slowly but surely, the tangled web in my upper body began to release and unwind.

These releases are hard to put into words. The way in which my muscles reacted to MFR was as if they completely let go of all of the tension they carried and simply melted into Phil's hands. Once I was able to identify where my body was releasing, I naturally became more attentive to where it was not. In other words, I became self-aware. I think this is one of the most important benefits that I received from MFR: a conscious recognition of my own web that has allowed me to be proactive in maintaining its proper alignment.

Chapter 2

INVISIBLE KID SCARS

John F. Barnes, PT, begins his first book, *Myofascial Release, The Search for Excellence*, with the following powerful description:

> The fascial system surrounds, infuses with, and has the potential to influence profoundly every muscle, bone, nerve, blood vessel, organ, and cell of the body. Fascia also separates, supports, connects, and protects everything. This three-dimensional web of connective tissue is alive and ever-changing as the body demands. Thus it is a network for information exchange, influencing and influenced by every structure, system, and cell in the organism. Like air and gravity, its influence is so all-pervasive that we have tended to take it for granted.

I recall when I first read that paragraph and immediately flashed back to my Gross Anatomy class in the summer of 1991. The fascia must have been all that slimy, shiny, slick stuff that we had to sift through to get to the REAL object of our dissection and study: the muscles, bones, nerves, and blood vessels. In thinking back, I could recall that the fascia was absolutely everywhere! Why were we just hacking and yanking this important tissue and discarding it without examining it? Of course I wasn't thinking that back in 1991. I was just eager to learn what I thought all anatomy students and potential therapists needed to learn. I was excited to learn everything there was to know about muscles, bones, nerves, and blood vessels.

I realize, of course, that not many people outside of health and medical schools have the opportunity (or desire) to dissect a deceased human body. However, most people who have prepared meat for a meal, be it chicken, or beef, or pork, for example, have seen and felt fascia.

If you are not a vegetarian, the next time you are about to handle a raw chicken, please allot a few extra minutes to really examine the miraculous specimen within your hands. First, super-slowly peel the skin from the underlying meat and look closely at what is connecting the skin to the meat. This is fascia. Then, before using any utensil on the chicken, gently pinch the outer slimy covering between your thumb and first finger and try to tease it away from the meat. This is fascia. Keep pulling and exploring – see where it takes you and what it is attached to. Then, cut into the chicken and visually scrutinize the inner landscape of the tissues. Use your fingers to slowly pull a segment away from a bone. Notice the glistening, shiny, likely-translucent tissues that separate the muscle from the bone and one muscle from an adjacent muscle. This is all fascia. And, from a structural and fascial standpoint, please understand that we humans are designed much like that chicken!

Now, this fascial exploration can also be done with an Orange. Yes, fruits, vegetables and really anything that is living (or once lived) have a fascial system as well! Let's use an orange, however, for ease and example. Grab an orange, pierce the skin with your fingernail or knife and begin to slowly peel the orange skin away from the fruit. That fibrous white tissue that connects the skin to the fruit is fascia.

Now pull the orange open so it is in two halves. Look closely at how the fibrous white tissue separates each of the slices from each other. The fascia is dividing the fruit into segments, that we call slices. Now pull one slice away from the rest of the orange. Peruse the thin outer layer of the slice that is defining the borders of the slice. This is fascia. Slowly break the slice in half and bring your eyes very close to the inside of the orange slice. Can you see that there are a multitude of little elongated capsules, made of fascia, that encase the "juice" of the orange? Just like in the chicken, the fascia of the orange is everywhere and serves many purposes and functions.

I believe that the first significant tangle within my fascial web began when I was six years old. This first influence on my web was not a physical trauma or event, however. It was more like a psycho-emotional unfolding.

Up until my sixth year of age, I had a very "normal" life. My mom, Roberta, and my dad, Peter, were great parents and providers for me and my only sibling, Mike. Mike and I are two years apart in age, with Mike being the elder brother. We lived in a small middle-class suburb one hour north of New York City called Yorktown Heights, NY. My father worked full-time in customer service for a large company and my mother worked part-time as an assistant for a local electrician.

My brother and I played sports, enjoyed school, had tons of friends – a normal, happy, all-American kid's life. Something strange started, however, when I was six and Mike was eight.

Mike began making weird movements that he said he couldn't control. His eyes began to blink forcibly and frequently. His neck began to twitch. His shoulders started to jump involuntarily. He also started to have uncontrollable vocalizations. He would clear his throat repeatedly and make bizarre sounds. He also had to impulsively touch whatever was near him – the walls, the furniture, and people.

What in the world is happening to my brother, I thought incessantly?! Does he have a disease? Is he possessed? Is this contagious? When am I going to start twitching and grunting? Is this something temporary that he will outgrow? What in the world is going on here?

Over the next couple years my brother saw a multitude of doctors, allergists, therapists, and counselors. None of them knew exactly what was going on with Mike. All the while, his situation was deteriorating. He couldn't walk more than eight or ten steps without having to bend down and touch the floor. He would have to extend his right elbow violently at least once every few minutes. I learned quickly not to stand to the right of Mike, or I would have the air knocked right out of me! He had a phase where he'd have to turn his head and spit, regardless of where he was.

Mike started having bursts of rage. I recall coming home from school and seeing a new picture on the wall, oftentimes in an abnormal place. I'd peek behind the picture and see that Mike had punched another hole in the wall.

Mike would also get a word or number or phrase stuck in his head and have to repeat it over and over: "two and two…two, two, and two… two, and two and two." One that really freaked me out was "Phil, 'm Phil…Phil, 'm Phil, 'm Phil, Phil." I recall yelling, on occasion, in child-like frustration, "No! I'm Phil! You are not me! You are Mike! I AM PHIL!!!"

Finally, after two years of misdiagnoses and countless opinions, in 1980, Mike was diagnosed with Tourette's syndrome (TS) at the age of 10. Although the diagnosis gave a name and some clarity to the situation, it didn't change the challenges that came with the disorder. The unfortunate "fact" was that there was no known remedy or cure.

So, how did this all have an impact on me? How did this alter **my** fascial web, so to speak? Let me do my best to explain.

As a young boy, I believe *I subconsciously decided to deem the following as TRUTHS*:

(1) Mike is your older brother, and there is such a thing as genetics, so you are next.

(2) You must become like an adult right now. Your parents have so much to deal with, so you need to start doing everything for yourself.

(3) People are mean and hurtful to people they do not understand. You, Phil, must work hard to BE NORMAL. Do not stand out, or you too will be mocked and ridiculed.

As a young boy, I lived in constant fear of getting what Mike had. Any little involuntary twitch of my body or sound I made brought on panic. This was a fear and panic that I never showed, however. I couldn't allow people to divert their attention to me and my needs when my brother clearly needed 100% focus.

The diagnosis did little, if anything, to calm my fears. "It's genetic." "There is no cure." "We don't know very much about this disorder." These were not revelations that gave a small boy any reason to stop being fearful.

I became fiercely independent and overly busy as a young boy. I became an overachiever in school and in sports. I did my homework and frequently, assisted Mike with his homework. I was a straight-A student who craved extra-credit opportunities. I became a raging perfectionist. One example is that my handwriting had to be perfect. My Mom and I still joke to this day about how I'd place two fingers between written words to ensure that the words were properly spaced! I used to win "Penmanship Awards." I think you get the picture.

Of course, to the now-adult Phil it is crystal clear that I was trying to exert control over whatever I could possibly control. The independence, overachieving, and perfectionism were necessary to counteract the absolute lack of control inherently created by Tourette's syndrome.

One of the harshest and most damaging lessons that stemmed from my brother's illness was the daily observation of how cruel and hurtful people can be. Not only did I see children make fun of my brother on a daily basis, but I also witnessed adults--"who should know better." When you directly observe a police officer or a school teacher blatantly and cruelly mocking your sibling, it wounds to the core.

With what I now know about the fascial system, it is evident that this prolonged childhood situation impacted me on every level. The constant worry and anxiety, the observation of cruelty towards my brother, the perfectionism and overachieving--all created a "stuckness" in my connective tissue system. Bracing patterns were born. Hair-trigger reactions to certain stimuli took root. Of course, I don't have any objective evidence to support the claim that my fascial system began to constrict. There are no scans or imaging devices that can observe the tightening of a whole-body, web-like, ever-changing system. I know because I simply KNOW. I know because as I write this, I buzz.

One of Phil's clients shares...

Cheryl

In February 2008 I was an active, sixty-two year old, tennis-playing, retired school teacher living in Washington, D.C. By some fluke or fate, I contracted a bacterial infection of the blood called Group A Streptococcus which caused Toxic Shock Syndrome. This rare and often fatal microscopic bug produces toxins that circulate through the bloodstream and soon triggers a defensive response that redirects blood flow to the vital organs at the expense of the extremities. I don't remember any of it but my limbs began to turn black, and then gangrene set in. In order to save my life, emergency amputations were performed to remove both of my arms and both of my legs-- below the elbows and knees.

For six weeks, I was in a drug-induced coma in the ICU. I managed to contract nearly every hospital infection there is and survived other complications, including pneumonia, MRSA infections, staph infections, pulmonary fluid buildup, and renal failure.

At this point I had lost all strength in my body. I was unable to lift my arms or legs off the bed, sit up without support or feed myself, bathe myself or perform virtually any other daily life skill.

Doctors told me that for every day you spend in a hospital bed your body needs four days or more of physical therapy to regain body strength. Every motion was a challenge. I had started to make progress when I developed a hematoma, a blood clot caused by a leaking blood vessel, in my right upper leg. It was excruciatingly painful. A hematoma can sometimes resolve without surgery but that was not the case for me. So I faced yet another surgery, consuming another two weeks of recovery time. When I returned to rehabilitation after the hematoma surgery, I could no longer lift my right leg or move it from side to side. I started from scratch once again.

My husband and I had raised our two children in a two-story house in Northwest Washington DC. We both realized that the stairs in our house would be too much for me. So my husband found a one-story apartment about a mile away that seemed to fit the bill.

I needed to let go of my former life where I played tennis five days a week, traveled extensively, could dress myself, and lived an independent life. Now I had a new life with new challenges. I needed to set small achievable goals like walking short distances and stepping up and down curbs with my prosthetic legs. I would not learn to walk in a day. I would fall. There was nothing I could do but take one small step at a time and believe me, my steps were ever so small, a couple of inches long, and ever so slow.

My prior life experiences helped me to cope. Tennis had shown me how to train and discipline myself to do exercises in order to beat my opponents. Teaching special and elementary school children for twenty years taught me to be patient. Growing up with my difficult mom taught me to be tough, perseverant and resilient. My dad had a fun-loving spirit, sense of humor, and optimism--all attributes which served me well while healing. He frequently told me, "You're a lucky girl." I am.

My husband, Paul, and my two beautiful children and my friends kept up my spirits and gave me the support to keep practicing the basics of walking, standing and doing everyday activities.

Life works in mysterious ways. I knew that I needed one-on-one specialized physical therapy and started looking for a therapist who could work with amputees. Totally by chance I found the perfect person right in my new living complex!

My new physical therapist, Phil Tavolacci, taught me the basics: to walk, climb stairs, negotiate ramps and uneven surfaces; even to get on and off escalators. Wherever I go, I think of him. "What do you feel like doing today?" He would say. Translation, "Shall we do the

stairs? Or jump? Or get on and off the floor?" All the exercises I knew
I needed to do but didn't want to do. Even when I walk on sand or fall
and pick myself up, I think of him. He taught me the skills I didn't
even know I needed to learn. He was ever so patient and funny. He
would kid me about walking down the hall like a drunken sailor.

In addition to all the mobility-based PT stuff, Phil also integrated
MFR into my plan of care. It was like spraying WD40 on rusty
hinges! Initially MFR treatments were focused on healing the scar
tissue from my amputations and the hematoma surgeries. Subsequent
sessions delved into regions of tension throughout my whole body,
especially my legs, which allowed me to walk faster and further--
three miles on a good day!

Now I drive a specially modified car, cook in a standard kitchen
and travel extensively. My husband and I just returned from an
incredible eight-week trans-American journey. It is very clear to me
that I would not be functioning as well as I am, physically, mentally,
and emotionally, if I didn't receive the skilled combination of physical
therapy and MFR with Phil. I may have "lost" my limbs, but I've
gained a great awareness of my body and a heightened sense of how
powerful and resilient I am.

These past five years have been a rough ride with many bumps and
scrapes along the way but when asked "how do you feel about all that
has happened?" I can only say, "It is what it is." Nothing will bring
back my hands and feet no matter how much I miss them. I just need
to hold my head up high, not care what strangers think, and keep
climbing those stairs, step over step!

Chapter 3

APPENDIX EXPLOSION

Fascia, also commonly known as "connective tissue," is comprised of three basic components: Elastin, Collagen, and Ground Substance. Elastin, a fibrous substance, allows the fascia to be stretchy, flexible, and expandable. When you think of elastin, think "elastic." Collagen, another fibrous substance, allows the fascia to be supportive, strong, and structural. Collagen gives fascia its fortitude and integrity. Blended in with, and in between, these fibrous elements is the ground substance. It is the gel, or goo, so to speak, that gives the fascia great fluidity, in its normal state.

In areas of the body where the fascia needs to be highly mobile, like beneath the skin, at the shoulder joint, or within the abdomen where all the organs reside, there is a higher concentration of elastin. In areas of the body where fascia needs to be more sturdy and supportive, like within the skull or surrounding the pelvis, there is a higher concentration of collagen. Basically, the proportion of the fibers is dictated by the needs of the body region.

When fascia is healthy and in its "normal" state it is a beautifully functional blend of stability and flexibility. However, when fascia is damaged or traumatized, it morphs structurally and its function becomes impaired. Traumatized fascia becomes dehydrated, dense, less mobile, and compressive. It is speculated that fascial restrictions exert two thousand pounds per square inch of pressure on whatever structures reside within the region of the restriction. Simply imagine two thousand pounds (one ton) of pressure pinching a nerve, or compressing a knee joint, or chronically squeezing the brain!

Fascia surrounds, and therefore influences, every single cell of the body. The fascial system is one continuous, uninterrupted three-dimensional web-like structure, from the top of the head to the bottom of the feet. Everything literally sits within the body's fascial system. Fascia is so pervasive that if it were possible to view a person's fascial system in isolation, it would be like looking at an intricate hologram of the individual. It would be so detailed, even in the face, that one could be recognized by their fascial system alone.

I was thirteen years old and being wheeled into an operating room. The nurse pushing the gurney looked me in the eyes, cocked her head slightly, and then softly and clearly said, "There is a chance you might die today."

What? Did I hear what she said correctly? I might die? Today? At thirteen years of age from abdominal pain?

Well, ok, I thought. This is certainly a surprise but I guess it's a possibility. I did already feel like I was dying over the past few days! I guess some people don't even get thirteen years to live, so, ok.

I began having intense abdominal pain the day after my family had tried a new restaurant. All of us assumed that I'd likely eaten some spoiled food and had a case of food poisoning. My parents took me to my doctor, and he quickly agreed that it must be food poisoning.

He sent me home to wait it out, without any comprehensive exam or blood work. All of us were quite certain that the diagnosis was correct.

Rather than time making the situation better, it got worse and worse. I spent a couple days in bed, in the fetal position, with unrelenting abdominal pain. I was vomiting small amounts of slimy green-tinged liquid every hour or so. I recall overhearing my parents talking to each other in an adjacent room. "It doesn't seem right. I don't think this is food poisoning anymore. He looks gray now! We have to take him to the hospital!"

After taking a quick glance at me and hearing my symptoms, the emergency room physician suspected appendicitis. He stated, "There is one way to know for sure." He explained that he would have to place one lubricated gloved finger in my rectum to palpate the appendix. The moment his fingertip touched the region of my appendix, I went airborne off the exam table. The pain was indescribable.

"Get this kid to the operating room, right now. I believe he has a ruptured appendix."

I was informed in the recovery room that most appendectomy surgeries took forty-five to sixty minutes to complete. However, mine took four hours. The reason was that my appendix had apparently swollen to the size of a grapefruit and then ruptured. Dead tissue, called gangrene, had permeated throughout my entire abdominal cavity. In graphic detail, the doctor told me and my parents that he had to pick thousands of fragments of infected tissues from my abdomen and slowly suction the gangrene from around my organs. He also told us that if we had waited any longer, I likely would have died that day.

We, of course, were all thankful that I was alive. I stayed in the hospital for a week. They had to leave my incision open for several days after the operation so that more gangrene could be removed from my body. They packed my insides with gauze, and every day, they pulled the infection-soaked gauze from my abdomen. It felt like my guts were being ripped out of my body while I was watching. Then they stuck a foot-long Q-tip into my abdomen to scour for more dead tissue. This, clearly, was far from pleasant and highly memorable.

When I was first allowed to get out of bed and start to walk, I remember that my body was folded forward at a ninety degree angle. I could not stand up straight – my body would not allow me to. They had just stitched up my incision. As I sadly shuffled down the hall, grasping my IV pole for support, I heard a familiar voice coming from the distance. Always the comedian, my Dad was bellowing, in a quasi-Russian accent, "Igor, walk this way!"

I started to laugh. I recalled being told to not sneeze, cough, or strain in the bathroom, but no one had told us that I shouldn't laugh. When I laughed, my stitches ripped and fluid started streaming out of my abdomen. My dad got a nice lecture from the surgeon. I'd never seen my dad lectured to before so I laughed…silently.

I was finally discharged after a week and told that I had to rest at home for another week before returning to school. I looked like a skeleton because I'd lost so much weight. By the time I returned to school I was able to walk upright again, had no more abdominal pain, and figured everything was good and back to normal.

When I resumed soccer, however, I soon realized that things were not normal. I didn't correlate it to the abdominal surgery at the time, but I could no longer run for more than a few minutes, like I always had, without getting crippling abdominal and right hip cramps.

From about the ages of six to thirteen, I was a very competitive soccer player and always played on offense. So I ran and ran and ran for full games without any issue whatsoever. After the appendectomy, due to the pain brought on by running, I played defense for the rest of the season. My passion, however, was in offense. Since prolonged running became associated with intense pain, I stopped running. Since running was out, my soccer days ended. There was sadness and loss, but life went on. It wasn't part of my plan to become a professional soccer player, so I got over it.

Whereas the first and deepest layers of restriction in my fascial web from early childhood were mostly psycho-emotional in nature, the second layers were predominantly physical. What were the after-effects of all that infected tissue swirling around in my guts? What about the surgical instruments and gauze and suction tubes that invaded that sensitive region? Does my body now see that whole region as a post-war zone? Is that long scar just on the skin, or does the scar run deep into my body and wrap around parts of my insides?

Let me clarify that when I speak of layers of restriction within the fascial system, it's not neatly separated layers like you'd find in a lasagna. I'm giving a fairly linear description, for ease of understanding and in order to formulate a meaningful mental picture. However, these restrictions do not form linearly or stack up neatly.

I love how John Barnes compares the intermingling of fascial restrictions to "Splat Art." John shows a slide on the screen of paint that has been hurled at a canvas and splats multi-directionally over the canvas. Then the next slide shows a different color of paint that was thrown onto the canvas over the first color. The second color doesn't just cover the first color; it also intermingles with the first color in some places, and extends in different patterns as compared to the first color. Then another color superimposes the first two.

This is a great visual example of how the traumas and insults to our fascial system mix, mingle, and morph over time.

One of Phil's clients shares...

David

I have been an active athletic person for most of my life. I was working out with weights five times a week and running twice a week. I also enjoyed many outdoor activities such as hiking and biking. I had been pretty much pain and injury free for most of my life.

Two years ago I fell onto my back and ended up with a herniated disc. I was in intense pain for about a month. I was unable to go to the gym or do any kind of exercise for four months after the fall due to persistent pain. Before finding MFR, I was having episodes of intense back pain and numbness in my foot. It would be unpredictable when it would occur. I would go to the doctor and get shots in my spine to help the pain. I was about to give up and schedule to have the disc removed when a friend suggested I go to see Phil before taking that step.

It was the best decision I have ever made. After the first one hour session of MFR I walked out of Phil's clinic without lower back pain and without the numbness and tingling in my foot! I had come to find out that there were other issues within my body that were contributing to my problems. Phil taught me that even though I had a herniated disc, it was not the only pain-producing structure or tissue involved. As I came to understand my fascia more, it made sense why I was feeling increasingly better after each MFR session.

I was able to slowly get back into many activities that I was doing before the injury that I never expected to be able to do again. Through MFR I have learned a lot about the connections between my internal and external worlds. Once my back pain resolved, I also learned about other areas of restriction in my body that were present, but "below the surface." I continue to go on a regular, but less frequent, basis and have never experienced the pain again that I had before MFR.

I have gone back to see my back doctor twice since I started MFR and have been told that he cannot believe how well I am doing and what I am able to do physically given the nature of my injury and how I have been without serious pain. Through MFR, I also learned how connected absolutely everything is within the body. When one part is being worked on I feel the connection it has to other parts of the body. It really does feel like a big web is being stretched deep within my body.

Although I started MFR because of an injury and pain I have learned that MFR is vital to maintaining a happy and healthy body!

Chapter 4

ICE PICK IN THE BACK

D r. Jean Claude Guimberteau is a French plastic surgeon who has captured astonishing videos of the fascial system during surgeries. Dr. Guimberteau has been researching how body tissues move on and in relation to each other. If you would like to see what fascia looks like in a living human being, then purchase one of Dr. Guimberteau's fascinating DVDs: *Strolling Under the Skin, Muscle Attitudes, Interior Architectures,* and/or *The Skin Excursion.* Short clips are also accessible on YouTube.

I am a very visual person. When John Barnes showed us a clip of Dr. Guimberteau's DVD, *Strolling Under the Skin,* in a seminar in 2009 I was transfixed by what I was seeing on the screen. All of a sudden, everything I was feeling, both as a therapist and as a patient, visually made sense! By using a limb as a lever, or by gently sinking both palms into a client, or by slowly allowing three adjacent fingertips to sink into a body region, I was directly engaging or "anchoring into" the fascial system. Up until this point I knew this intellectually, of course. I knew it in a very left-brained, analytical, this-makes-sense kind of way. But when I saw the fascia in this video and then partnered that observation with what I do as a therapist, it became crystal clear why MFR is so effective!

When a John Barnes trained MFR therapist engages your fascial system, he or she engages your full three-dimensional, head-to-toe, uninterrupted connective tissue system. It doesn't matter if the therapist is gently pulling your arm; it will reach into and affect the entire fascial web, head to toe. If the therapist does what we call a cross-hand release on a region of the body, let's say a thigh, it will reach into and affect the entire fascial web, head to toe. If the therapist places one hand under the body on the lower back and the other hand on top of the belly, what we call a diaphragm release, it will reach into and affect the entire fascial web, head to toe.

Myofascial Release is so effective because it doesn't partition off the body into isolated subsections. It is based on the knowingness that every single part of the body is intimately connected to every other part of the body. This connection occurs via the fascial web.

I started doing gymnastics when I was in the fifth grade. By the time I was in the seventh grade, I was invited to be part of the Lakeland High School men's gymnastics team. My friend, Mike, and I were both "bussed" to the high school from our middle school every day for practice for two years until we were actually in high school.

I loved being a gymnast. It was so freeing to flip and twist and soar! Although I learned how to work on all six events (high bar, parallel bars, pommel horse, still rings, vault, and floor), my favorites and best were vault and floor. For me, the acrobatics of floor and vault was the most exhilarating. I absolutely hated the rings and I was horrible on the horse. I had fun on the high bar and parallel bars but, if given the option, I would practice and compete only on floor and vault.

By the time I reached the eleventh grade, I reached my peak height: six feet. You don't see too many competitive six foot tall gymnasts for good reason – it's a whole lot of body to fling around! When I started tumbling into the bleachers I pretty much surmised that my gymnastic days were numbered.

Although I can't recall the date, I'll never forget the moment when I knew my time as a gymnast was over. I was practicing what are called "giant swings" on the high bar. This is when gymnasts complete full revolutions around the bar, holding the bar with both hands and pivoting the hands as needed over the surface of the bar. Because I was six feet tall, the bar was set about six feet, five inches above and parallel to the floor.

On that particular day I was practicing doing three consecutive giant swings and then my new dismount – a double back flip. I was finally getting the swing of it, pun intended, and was ready to try the dismount. I built up the necessary speed and momentum via my giant swings, released the bar, tucked my body into a compact ball, flipped two times, and solidly landed on my two bare feet!

But, when I say I "solidly landed", I really solidly landed. It turned out that the mats weren't pushed together like they should have been, so I landed **between** the mats versus **on** the mats. Yes, I solidly landed, barefoot, on the gymnasium's hard wood floor! Immediately upon impact I felt a lightning bolt rip up my legs and into my right lower back. I was in shock but I didn't crumple to the floor. I'll just try to "walk it off", I thought.

Well, walking was kind of hard since I fractured both heels upon impact. They were hairline (very small) fractures, thankfully, but they were enough to cause the doctor to prescribe heel cups in my shoes and two canes to walk with. Yes, get the visual in your mind. For a couple weeks I had to walk on the balls of my feet and coordinate not one, but two canes. I guess since my high school was two levels and didn't have an elevator, a wheelchair was not a viable option.

Since the x-rays of my lower back didn't show any fractures or dislocations, it was deemed that my back was "fine." Well, then why does it feel that I suddenly have an ice pick lodged into my right lower back? The doctor couldn't quite explain that, so he pretty much dismissed it.

What I came to understand later in life, as a physical therapist, but not at that point, was that I sheared my right sacroiliac (SI) joint. Sitting for more than five minutes at a time brought on that ice-pick-in-the-back pain. Slowly, over time, my right hip got stiffer and stiffer until eventually it became a "frozen hip," like you hear of people who develop "frozen shoulders."

And thus, my chronic spinal pain began at the ripe old age of sixteen.

Two of Phil's clients share...

Sue

As I was having MFR this morning, laying on a treatment table with eyes closed and tuned in to my body, I was marveling at so many things. The immediate issue was a flare up in my left knee. This was an old injury that decided to speak to me after an overly energetic week in my garden.

At first it seemed as though Phil was doing nothing more than applying light pressure to stabilize my knee, but then I began to feel the pain in the knee relax its hold and begin to melt. Then I could feel that there was a correspondence between the left knee and other parts of my body. I had observed earlier that day that my left shoulder blade was tight but had not made a direct connection between the left knee and the left shoulder blade. Somehow, without me saying a word, the next thing Phil knew to do was to use his other hand to probe along the left shoulder blade area until he found the tightness that I then could feel going down in a line to my knee. I always am astounded that Phil knows instinctively how to find just where to touch and probe, often right on the first try with no direction from me. It's as if my body is directing the action.

With these two spots connected, my body starts to move and unwind on its own without conscious direction on my part. By unwinding I mean that before long, another part of my body, often even on the other side, will begin to move and flex and direct its own action as if it is sorting itself out. That's when I begin to be aware that it's not just a platitude that "everything is connected." I think sometimes that I am a microcosm of the vast universe itself, the far flung lower limbs as far away from my head or arms as the other galaxies are from the milky way, but all part of some great whole so that a movement or disturbance in one part is linked to the rest, as indeed, the parts of the body are enclosed by the fabric of the fascia.

Sometimes, as this morning, Phil uses a technique called rebounding, whereby he uses gentle shaking and pulling motions with my limbs and core to activate what I feel is the buzzing vibration of all the cells in my body so that the energy can course through the whole. It's as if all the cells come alive and there is free flow everywhere.

What starts out as a physical manipulation of the body morphs into something profound. I leave my sessions with a fluidity in the way I move and an easing of painful and achy joints and muscles, but I also carry with me a subtle transformation in my mind, or really in my consciousness. As the session progresses, I feel I move into a state where my consciousness is expanded beyond my physical body. It is a still and soothing place. I seem to lose my consciousness often in the hurly-burly of living but when I find it again in my MFR sessions, I am grateful.

Florence ("Flo")

I have reached the venerable age of ninety-three. During this lengthy period of time, I have been host to a number of varied and sundry maladies. The last six years had three particular challenges:

I fractured a vertebra while tucking in the bed sheet.

I was heir to a fractured sternum as a result of a fall.

After a bout of colon cancer, I was lucky enough to have dodged the bullet without the need of chemotherapy or radiation.

Despite their diversity, what they all have in common is how they responded and improved via MFR sessions administered under the capable and well-trained hands of Phillip Tavolacci.

I find it truly amazing that MFR, under the proper hands, can be so incredibly healing!

Chapter 5

SWORD TO THE NECK

So now you have a concept of what fascia is. If you have viewed one of Dr. Guimberteau's videos, you have actually seen living, moving, glistening fascia. The cover art of this book is a very simplified graphic representation of the continuous fascial web within a human. I suggest you take a minute to simply gaze at the graphic on the cover of this book. Look at it as if you're looking at a being you have never seen before- as if you are seeing an extraterrestrial, perhaps. Soak in the truth that every living being has this spider web-like network running uninterrupted throughout their entire body. Go ahead, visualize and imagine for a moment.

So now, how do John F. Barnes-trained MFR therapists access and influence this big web? As is true with many seemingly complex things, it's actually quite simple, if one lets it be simple!

Firstly, before placing a hand on a client, we observe the client's entire body, in standing, from a short distance. Knowing that under the skin, and deep to the core, is the web-like fascial system, we look to see where that web may be tightened or shortened, therefore pulling the body out of optimal alignment.

For example, if viewing a client from the front and their head is pulled off-center to the right, we might speculate that the muscles and fascia ("myofascia") in the right shoulder, neck, and chest regions are possibly shortened and pulling the head to the right of midline. We speculate, but we don't assume "correctness," for using observation and logic alone only provides a small portion of the necessary information!

The bulk of our information comes from placing our hands on the client and "connecting with" or "tuning in" to their fascial system. When a trained therapist sets their intention that their hands will gently sink into the fascial web to assess it, then that is what, in fact, occurs. The therapist is then able to leverage, or mobilize, the fascia via the skin or via the bones of the body.

Let us stick with the same hypothetical client that was observed in standing a moment ago. The therapist can now place a hand on that client's left shoulder blade (with the client laying face-down), sink their hand into that region of the body, as if their hand were sinking slowly into moist clay, and then, without sliding or gliding over the skin, assess whether the shoulder blade moves easily and freely in all directions. Let's say the left shoulder blade moves freely and easily in all directions over the client's ribcage, but the right shoulder blade, when similarly tested, doesn't move as freely in a couple of the tested directions. In this case, the fascia has informed us that it is restricted in the region of the right shoulder blade.

Let us now say that, with this same client, we place them face-up on the treatment table and cradle their head in our two relaxed hands. We gently and slowly side-bend the head to the right, bringing the right ear towards the right shoulder. It moves easily and through a full range of motion. However, we then side-bend the head to the left, bringing the left ear towards the left shoulder, and the quality of the movement is different and the range of motion is limited compared to how it was on the other side. So now, in this specific hypothetical case, we have assessed that the muscles and fascia in the right neck and shoulder blade are restricted. Recall, we observed in standing that this person's head was being pulled to the right of midline. Now we have palpable evidence that the tissues in the right neck and shoulder are restricted and tight. They are likely contributors to this client's altered head position.

So, now how would an MFR therapist actually target and treat those tight and restricted tissues in the right neck and shoulder? There are a multitude of options, AND, if ten different MFR therapists found the same restrictions, they may choose to treat the restrictions in ten completely different ways! And, they would all likely have successful outcomes, as long as they followed the basic principles of JFB-MFR.

Stay with me and visualize here. Let's say the therapist in this scenario chooses a basic, but highly effective, MFR technique called a cross-hand release. With the client in a face-up position on a treatment table, the therapist places her right hand underneath the client's right upper back, directly over the right shoulder blade. She then places her left hand under the back of the client's head. She then simply allows her two hands to sink into the tissues in those regions. She is basically "anchoring" into the fascial system, so she can then use those two hand-holds to gently stretch the fascia between her two hands. Once her hands are firmly anchored into the tissues, so her hands won't slide or glide over the skin, the therapist gently moves her hands in opposing directions to place the tight tissues on a slight stretch.

Then, she simply waits. She waits for a butter-melting and taffy-stretching sensation under and between her hands. This is evidence that the tissues are beginning to respond to the low-load sustained stretch by softening and lengthening. It takes roughly ninety seconds to two minutes for fascia to even begin to release and elongate. This therapist feels for that subtle release and then adjusts her hands, still sunken and anchored into the tissues, slightly further apart from each other – again, without sliding or gliding over the skin.

This subtle increased stretch is done repeatedly for five minutes, on average, so that taut right sided neck and shoulder fascia is now physiologically altered! That fascia is now both softer and longer than it was before.

Now, let me clarify that a simplified hypothetic is just that – a simplified hypothetical. I'm offering this stripped-down example so you can have a basic visual of what an MFR therapist does to assess and treat a restricted region of the body.

We'll get into further explanation in future chapters.

When I could no longer compete in gymnastics, after I injured my lower spine, I turned to bodybuilding. Firstly, I did not want to lose the hard-earned muscle I had gained from doing gymnastics for several hours every day. I worked hard for that muscle! Secondly, I made the assumption that an injured back is now a weak back that must be strengthened. I would have to pack muscle around the back to stabilize it, I thought. It certainly made logical sense. It also seemed to be the basic ideology of physical therapists. The "knowing" seemed to be: It hurts? It must be weak. You must strengthen it. Once it's strong, it won't hurt anymore. Problem solved.

So, off to the gym I went every day. At this point my lower right-sided back pain was fairly constant and it didn't seem to be affected by what I was doing in the gym. You would think, after some time, that I'd tune in and believe what my gut started telling me: "Hey, Phil, you are getting really strong, but your back pain isn't changing. Do you think, maybe, it isn't going to resolve by getting stronger?! Might you be barking up the wrong tree?"

By the time I graduated high school I was able to leg press one thousand pounds. I was pretty darn strong and, I must say, had a rock-solid physique. I was a teenager, so I was, of course, happy to accept the accolades of "damn, boy…how'd you get that body?!"

But, the great physique and ultra-strong frame were not changing the fact that it still felt like there was an ice pick sticking out of my lower right back. It also wasn't changing the fact that my right hip was getting stiffer and stiffer. I could no longer, at this point, sit cross-legged on the floor and I even had difficulty putting a sock on my right foot. I had to contort my body because the right hip simply wouldn't rotate out like it did before the gymnastic injury. I was beginning to feel old, and I was only seventeen.

I tried a short course of physical therapy around this time. The very nice and certainly smart therapist used ultrasound, moist heat, and electrical stimulation on my low back and right hip. They were comforting, but didn't really produce any change in my symptoms once I got off the table. She also had me do a few strengthening exercises. After probably eight or ten sessions, I didn't feel any difference so I stopped. I remember thinking that if one thousand pound leg presses weren't effectively strengthening my back and hip, how in the world was hooking a yellow stretch-band around my ankle and kicking my leg out to the side going to help my situation?

I didn't complain or bring any attention to what I was dealing with though. I was still living in the belief system that I should be able to take care of everything myself. My internal rationale was still that my brother needed full attention and assistance with his much more significant issues. I was sure that with more time I would figure out and fix my lower back myself. No need to bother anyone.

I graduated from high school in the summer of 1990 and began college that fall. I was accepted to Ithaca College's Masters of Science in Physical Therapy program. The five-year program was structured in a way that you would finish your Bachelor's degree after three years, and be awarded your Master's degree after five years. I was excited to study physical therapy for two reasons: (1) it seemed to be a perfect blend of things I loved-- science, health, medicine, fitness and helping people; and (2) maybe I would learn how to get the damn ice pick out of my back!

The first year of college, in beautiful Ithaca, NY, was both awesome and difficult for me. It was awesome in that I loved what I was studying, I made great friends, I was having fun, and I was doing extremely well academically. It was difficult partly because my perfectionism became quite disabling. I had convinced myself that I had to be the perfect student and get straight A's. I had to maintain the physique I'd worked so hard to gain prior to college. I had to be funny and likeable. Basically, I had to maintain an identity of Perfect Phil.

I ended up with a bleeding stomach ulcer and my first bout of depression. I begrudgingly went to see a psychotherapist on campus. At the end of the first visit, he gave me a book to read and when I looked at the title, I got really pissed off! The title of the book was *Little Miss Perfect*.

The book didn't just piss me off because he immediately pegged and diagnosed my perfectionism. It triggered in me what I had been subconsciously suppressing for years – the possibility that I might be gay. As irrational as it sounds that a simple book title could trigger this fear, that is exactly what it did. Was this therapist able to see that I might be gay, just as easily as he saw that I was a raging perfectionist?

I didn't go back to the therapist. That was not something I could deal with at the time. It was time to get back to being Perfect Phil. So, I delved back into my studies, and working out, and being with friends. I had become a master avoider of the whole "gay possibility" by this time. So, deep into the earth it went again. Bury, bury, bury.

The title of this chapter is Sword to the Neck, so let me get to that finally!

I had completed my first year of college. My parents had moved from New York to Virginia during my first semester of school. It was a business move for my Dad. I had never lived outside of New York so I wasn't too excited about now calling Blue Ridge, Virginia "home." I spent that summer with my parents in Blue Ridge, not too far from Roanoke.

Roanoke did have a great fitness center, The Roanoke Athletic Club, "The RAC." I was still a workout fanatic at this point so I spent about two hours at the gym every day in the summer of 1991.

I was lifting weights one day at The RAC that summer when another significant trauma occurred. I was doing standing bicep curls with a 100 pound barbell. I had my headphones in my ears, and the music was cranked up. I was totally "in the zone" – in my own world and totally oblivious to anything and everything happening around me.

Towards the end of my eight to ten repetitions of bicep curls, with the music holding my full attention, I suddenly felt a tap on my left shoulder. By pure reflex, I quickly turned my head to the left, in response to the tap. Because I was straining every muscle in my upper body to complete that bicep curl, including my neck muscles, the quick head turn caused a muscle to tear in my neck!

It was as if someone slashed through the right side of my neck with a sword or battle axe. It was searing, hot, ripping pain. I dropped the weight and grabbed my right neck and shoulder. My right shoulder shot up towards my right ear, into immediate spasm. I felt nauseated and thought I might vomit. My music was still blaring but I looked around to see that everyone had stopped working out and were staring at me with wide eyes and open mouths.

I was certain that they were staring because I'd just dropped a heavy weight. Had I also blurted out a curse word? I soon realized, however, that they stopped and looked before I dropped the weight, when they actually heard my neck muscles rip. People reported to me that it sounded like someone had torn a phone book in half or lightening had ripped through the building.

And, thus was the beginning of a whole new region of body pain and dysfunction.

It turned out that the shoulder tap came from a woman who wanted to get in front of where I was standing so she could grab a light weight. You just never know when a simple tap can change your life.

One of Phil's clients shares...

Deena

My journey into the world of fascia began several years back when I was desperately trying to find something other than drugs to relieve my constant pain. I stumbled upon a weekend seminar about Myofascial Release. As a massage therapist, I am always looking for new modalities to help my clients and myself. This seminar seemed very different than all the rest and I have been to many seminars and continuing education classes over the past twelve years.

The first thing I thought after being in class for a while was "Wow, this is really interesting!" My second thought was "Oh my God, what is happening?" Some people were crying, yelling and having emotional outbursts. Then, there was this "calm after the storm" - a sense of peace I would say.

After having my first treatment during the class I felt a little calmer, more fluid, and even a bit longer. I was really surprised by how the simplest techniques and movements could be so effective. This was the missing link! In all the classes I had taken, no one had ever mentioned the word fascia before. It should have been the first thing I was taught about, considering that everything in your body is covered in it. At the end of the seminar I was so excited, I couldn't wait to learn more and start treating my clients.

I learned while at the seminar that not only can myofascial release treatments help pain and dysfunction, but it can also help with infertility. Unfortunately I was having trouble getting pregnant. My husband and I had been trying to conceive for eight years with no luck. I was a little apprehensive about receiving myofascial release treatments internally, but I was willing to try anything. I had one treatment and was hopeful for the first time in a long time. Then I got into a car accident.

I never would have thought that getting into a car accident would turn out to be a blessing, but it was definitely a blessing because it forced me to take a closer look at my body and my life. What I found was not only physical restrictions, but emotional restrictions as well and they were preventing me from living and functioning at my full capacity. These restrictions, most importantly, were likely preventing me from conceiving another child.

What I didn't realize at the time was that my cesarean section with my first child caused so much scarring and led to the beginning of my fascial destruction. Everything in my body started to twist because of the restrictions in my fascial web. My reproductive organs were caught in this twisted web and couldn't function properly. Once freed from the incredible force of twisted fascia they began working to their full capacity.

By the grace of God I was introduced to a few remarkable MFR therapists who helped me more than they'll ever know. With the help of Phil Tavolacci and Ann Udofia and the incredible power of MFR, I was able to have two more beautiful and healthy children! I was also able to finally live free from pain and resume the active lifestyle that I loved.

When I came to see Phil and Ann at TAVO Total Health I was in constant pain in my hips, groin, neck and shoulders. I saw them twice a week for six weeks. I received both external and internal MFR treatments. As the fascial restrictions in my body started to release, so did the emotional restrictions that I thought were dead and buried. Phil and Ann made me feel so incredibly comfortable even when I had several emotional outbursts, and should have felt like a blubbering idiot. They said it was all a part of the healing process. Well I did a lot of healing and feel so grateful that I met these amazing people who helped me so much.

Having Myofascial Release consistently for six weeks was literally such a freeing experience, both emotionally and physically rejuvenating. Before my last session, I found out I was pregnant! All the fertility drugs were unsuccessful, but the myofascial release treatments did the trick! I will be eternally grateful for this amazing work and to Phil and Ann for all their skill, guidance, love and support throughout my healing process. Thank you from the bottom of my heart!

Chapter 6

DEPRESSION

In the beginning of the last chapter, I explained how an MFR therapist might release a tissue restriction in the right neck and shoulder area. This is an example of a structural release. There are many types of structural release techniques but three main types are: (1) Cross-Hand Releases; (2) Diaphragm Releases; and (3) Traction (Pull) Releases.

With the cross-hand release, the therapist allows his two relaxed "tuned-in" hands to sink into two (typically somewhat close-together) regions of the body until he reaches what we call the Depth Barrier. This is where the therapist feels as if the body is saying, "Ok, that's as far as we're letting you in for now, buddy." Then, without sliding or gliding through the skin, the therapist slowly places the tissues between his two hands on a gentle sustained stretch. The tissue is never forced. John Barnes trained MFR therapists are trained to feel for and honor these fascial barriers. The therapist then waits patiently for the tissues to melt, like butter, and stretch, like taffy. As these releases occur, the therapist is adjusting his angles and pressures, in order to follow the releasing tissue three dimensionally, while maintaining stretch through the fascia. We typically hold cross-hand releases for five minutes, on average, because that's how long it takes for multiple layers of taut fascia to effectively lengthen and soften.

Another structural release technique is called a diaphragm release. This is not to be confused, however, with the actual respiratory diaphragm muscle. There is a dome-shaped muscle at the base of the lungs, called the respiratory diaphragm muscle, which is responsible for assisting the lungs in expanding and contracting.

"Diaphragms" within the fascial system, however, are regions where many of the fascial fibers are directed front ⟷ back in the body. If you, again, glance at the picture on the cover of the book, you'll see that the artist oriented the fascia mostly up and down the body. The majority of the fascia **is** generally oriented up and down the body, except at the diaphragms. Think of diaphragms, basically, as separators of regions. There is a diaphragm where the top of the neck meets the base of the skull. There is a diaphragm in the upper chest area. There is a diaphragm in the lower chest area. There is one at the level of the belly. And there is another major diaphragm at the pelvis.

Let's take, for example, what we call the Thoracic Inlet Diaphragm, which runs from the top of the chest, through the body, to the upper back. When a therapist does a "Thoracic Inlet Diaphragm release," she places one hand on the front of the diaphragm (upper chest) and the other hand on the back of the diaphragm (upper back). She gently allows her hands to sink towards each other, as if her hands are the bread of a chest/back sandwich. She tunes into the region via her highly skilled sense of touch and feels for softening and shifting of the fascia between her hands. For five minutes, on average, she facilitates the releasing of all the restricted connective tissue within that diaphragm.

The last structural release technique that is very commonly utilized is a Traction/Pull Release. Therapists can use limbs (arms and/or legs) or other body parts (ears, hair, fingers, toes, etc.) to serve as levers that can reach into the fascial system. As an example, a therapist can gently lift a client's arm, have them relax the arm, softly grasp the wrist, and then gently lean back to lightly traction/pull the arm. That arm then serves as a lever into the fascial web. For clients who are sensitive enough to feel subtle sensations throughout their bodies, a five-minute arm pull might result in perceived releases throughout varied regions of the whole body! If you look again at the woman on the book cover and imagine gently pulling her right arm for five minutes, you can visualize how that pulling force would eventually travel through the entirety of her body's fascial web.

All of the above general techniques are used by John F. Barnes-trained MFR therapists to structurally release and physiologically change restricted fascia. But, there are two additional and very important MFR components: Rebounding and Unwinding. We will delve into these exciting components at the beginning of the next chapter.

When I was in the Physical Therapy program at Ithaca College, it was structured such that the students completed Gross Anatomy (dissection of human cadavers) in the summer after the sophomore year at Rochester University in Rochester, NY. I was excelling in my coursework, ranked towards the top of my class, and really enjoying what I was learning. My lower back and my right-sided neck and shoulder pain were escalating, but I was pretty good at ignoring the pain.

I was extremely excited to take Gross Anatomy. I am a very tactile and visual learner so I was eager to get directly into a human body and see exactly where everything was, and what connected to what! The perfectionist in me was stressed, of course, that there was a lot to absorb and memorize, but I knew that all would be good.

While in Rochester, I was fine during the days while I was engrossed in learning, but it was the nights that were beginning to unravel me. You see, this was the first time I was living with multiple people (five or six classmates/friends) in a small living space, and there was no avoiding the simple reality that I was different than them.

As conversations occurred about sex, and I would hear sex taking place in our suite and adjacent suites, the in-my-face reality was that I wasn't like my friends. I didn't have the same wiring. Why, at twenty years of age, was I still not sexually attracted to females? What was wrong with me?!

Up it bubbled. I couldn't keep the lid on the boiling pot anymore. I couldn't avoid the topic by going to the gym, or taking an extra class, or working. There was nowhere to run, nowhere to hide. It was right there staring me in the eyes and forcing me to DEAL.

After a few weeks of increasingly sleepless nights, anxiety-ridden days, and spiraling depression, I had a complete nervous breakdown. I just had to get out of there. I felt like an atom bomb about to detonate.

I called my parents and pleaded to be picked up and brought home. My explanation for needing to leave was a total lie. I explained that the coursework was too intense, and I'd simply come to the conclusion that physical therapy wasn't really what I wanted to do. I told the same thing to my friends and classmates that I adored and would desperately miss.

My dad came and picked me up, and we drove from Rochester, NY to Blue Ridge, VA. God bless my parents – they should be sainted. They didn't understand what was going on but they supported me unconditionally and held space for me to heal. And, for the first time in my life, I actually allowed my parents to focus attention on me.

I was completely devastated. I sunk into a deep dark depression. What was I going to do? I had dropped out of the PT program that

I loved. Would I go back to Ithaca College at all? I only chose Ithaca because it was one of the best PT programs in the whole country. Would I take a year away from college and sort things out for myself? My head spun with scenarios and projected realities.

Depression is not just "sadness", as many people often think it is. It is not something that you can just happy-yourself-out-of. Depression is a complex and multi-layered beast that defies simple definition.

My own experience with depression was that it was nearly impossible to get out of bed. I wanted to sleep for twelve hours minimum per day. I couldn't attend to or remember anything. I loved to read but while depressed, I would read the same paragraph over and over and over again and the information wouldn't stay in my head. I had no appetite. Even though I logically knew that exercise was helpful to combat depression, I couldn't bear to exercise at all. I was hypersensitive to the ringing of a telephone. It wasn't so much that the noise startled me, it was that there was a human being on the other end of the line who was going to ask the dreaded question: "How are you doing?"

When depressed, answering the "How are you doing" question was agonizing for me. I was forced into choosing one of only two options: (1) lie and say that I was ok and things were getting better; or (2) explain what I was experiencing and cause the caller to become concerned. It was a damned-if-you-do/ damned-if-you-don't scenario every time the phone rang.

The summer was quickly coming to an end and I needed to figure out my future. I simply didn't have time to be depressed anymore! At this point I had told the "I decided PT wasn't for me" lie to so many people that I too started to believe the lie. So, I decided I would go back to Ithaca College in the fall but I would change my major to Exercise Science. I would continue to study the things I was interested in, and it would be like a pre-med track. Maybe I was meant to be a doctor instead of a physical therapist, I rationalized.

I got so caught up in this logical what-to-do-next plan that I completely forgot the TRUE ISSUE! So again, I chose to bury the real issue that was likely driving my depression.

One of Phil's clients shares...

Lynne

By the time I reached Phil's office in April, 2008, I was convinced that I would never be rid of the severe headaches that were a defining feature of my life for almost ten years. I had run the usual gamut of practitioners. Anyone with intractable migraines knows the drill: first you try conventional Western medicine, with its armamentarium of pharmaceuticals. For some, that works. For others, not so much; I was in the latter category for whom these treatments are only band-aids that can cause a rebound reaction and exacerbate the problem. So I turned to a variety of other specialists who promised relief: acupuncturists, massage therapists, chiropractors, even a guy who stuck needles directly into my sore shoulders and neck, causing me to invoke words unacceptable in polite company. Acupuncture was nice and relaxing, but did nothing for my headaches. Massage therapists sometimes made me feel worse. I feared the spine-cracking techniques of chiropractors—physical violence didn't seem the right path for me. And the needles guy—well, it was fun to cuss, but it didn't really help.

I even tried modifying my diet, as recommended by one of the foremost headache experts in the country. The regimen was so restrictive that I began to subsist on what might be called the "P" plan—plain pasta and pancakes. I was rapidly losing weight—this was a bad thing, as I am already thin-- and was still suffering from disabling headaches at least 15 days out of every month. The pain made it very difficult to plan activities, to work, to live. And to make matters worse, now I was hungry.

Finally, my internist, who, unlike some, is open to alternative approaches, recommended that I see Phil for myofascial release therapy. The difference was immediately evident; here was a healer who didn't see me as a "headache." Instead, to Phil, the headaches were a symptom of something else that was deeply rooted in the stuff of my body, amenable to lasting change.

Thus began a partnership between Phil and me that continues today—a partnership in healing and wellness. Through myofascial therapy, Phil identified the stuck, stiff, foreshortened and unyielding soft tissue that throws my body out of alignment and creates pressures on nerves that can lead to headaches. Slowly and patiently, with talented hands, Phil has performed his myofascial magic on me. Of course, I have some responsibility too. When I do the simple home exercises that he prescribes, the results are more than one would expect from such gentle movement.

Soon after I started seeing Phil, I was off all medication. My headaches were reduced by at least eighty percent. Now, five years later, I am no longer defined by my pain. Instead, thanks to Phil and our ongoing work together, I live much more easily in my body. Myofascial release, as practiced by a gifted healer like Phil, has allowed me to enjoy life again.

Chapter 7

DÉJÀ VU

In the last chapter, I stated that I would explain more about Rebounding and Unwinding in this chapter. As a refresher, there are three main elements of MFR: (1) Structural Release; (2) Rebounding; and (3) Unwinding. I gave various examples and visuals of structural release techniques in the last chapter. Structural release work is necessary to facilitate physiological change (lengthening, softening, detoxifying, and rehydrating) in the fascial system.

Rebounding is the introduction, maintenance, and expansion of wave-like movements into the fluid aspect of the myofascial system. Roughly eighty percent of the body is made up of water, and by oscillating, or rocking, the body in a skilled and tuned-in manner, the therapist is able to mobilize and utilize that vast amount of fluid. John Barnes, in his nearly fifty years of practicing and perfecting this healing technique, has discovered that rebounding is an incredible pathway to resolving subconscious holding, or bracing, patterns. What makes sense to me is that Rebounding is such a foreign sensation to the body that it serves as a means of resetting the nervous system, which may have been stuck in a persistent unhealthy pattern or program for a lengthy time.

Unwinding is spontaneous, involuntary, self-corrective movement of the body. When someone is receiving MFR, it is not uncommon that parts of their body, or their entire body, begin to move without the client instructing the body to move. A therapist doing authentic John F. Barnes MFR work cannot "unwind you." However, if a client begins to unwind, an MFR practitioner is trained to facilitate this natural and highly healing process. The therapist might add compression, or traction, or resistance, depending on what the body appears to be asking for in the moment. If the whole body becomes involved, and if emotions begin to release, then the therapist ensures that the client is kept safe, facilitates the process, and encourages the client to simply LET GO.

There is a phenomenon that tends to occur during unwinding called the Still Point. This is a stopping point within a motion pattern and the point, or pause, holds significance. Sometimes this still point is a position in space/time where an injury occurred or it is a body position that triggers cellular memory.

For example, let us say that I have a client who goes into a spontaneous unwinding during a treatment session. Her body is moving on the table in various positions and patterns for a few minutes and then, abruptly, she sits up and thrusts both arms out in front of her and screams. She stays in that position, or still point, for, let's say ten seconds, and then she starts moving again. That posture and pause was likely relevant to that specific client in some way! The client may or may not have a conscious awareness of what happened in that moment, but they'll oftentimes report a noticeable shift after such an experience. In this scenario, let's say the client did have a strong awareness of what was happening within the still point. She might say something like, "You know, I had a car accident in 1985 where I had to slam on the brakes to try to avoid hitting a motorcycle that cut in front of me, and that just brought me right back in time to that experience! That was so wild! And, you know what's really weird? I feel lighter than I've felt in years and feel like I'm breathing easier. Is that possible?"

I went back to Ithaca College in the fall of 1992 with a new major and a fine-crafted tale. My new major was Exercise Science, with a minor in Cardiac Rehabilitation. My fine-crafted tale was that I had decided I would prefer to be a medical doctor eventually, versus a physical therapist, so I switched into a more pre-med type tract of study. There was no way I could tell my friends that I had a complete nervous breakdown, followed by a summer of depression! I would most definitely lose my Perfect Phil status.

It wasn't long before I fell right back into my practiced patterns of perfectionism and overachieving. Because my major had changed, and I felt an absolute need to graduate in 1994 with my friends, I had to take extra courses. Instead of the already full and rigorous (eighteen credit) semesters I had become accustomed to as a PT major, I now had to take twenty-one or twenty-two credits per semester. Of course, I also had to get A's in all of these courses. On top of this ridiculously strenuous class schedule, I accepted a position as a Special Events Manager with the college's campus center. And, to top it off, I had to make time for the gym because not only did I have to maintain a perfect physique, I also had two damaged spinal regions that needed to be strengthened.

There was one last item on my must-accomplish list: prove to myself that I was not gay! I finally started pushing myself to have more sexual experiences with women. I kept telling myself it was just a matter of time and experience before I'd know that I was, in fact, a "normal heterosexual man."

I decided to stay in Ithaca for the summer between my junior and senior years. I enjoyed my job with the campus center and it was nice to experience Ithaca when it wasn't five degrees and covered with snow, which it was for the majority of the academic year. The joke about Ithaca was that it had two seasons: Winter and Fourth of July.

During that summer, in 1993, I began dating a girl that I had been good friends with up until that point, Carol. Carol was funny, smart, attractive, and athletic. I really enjoyed spending time with Carol. When we'd shift into an intimate situation, however, I would feel my body start to throw grenades. A stomachache grenade here. A headache grenade there. A back spasm grenade thrown in for good measure. My subconscious seemed to have a fully stocked arsenal of sex-sabotaging grenades!

Just give it more time, Phil. You just need more time!

Carol and I continued dating into our senior year and were excited to graduate together in May of 1994. I was asked to be one of two students from the School of Health Sciences and Human Performance to carry the school's flag at graduation. The two of us were chosen because we had the highest GPA's in the entire school. I was flattered and appreciated the recognition for all my hard work. I accepted the task and looked forward to graduation day.

But then IT happened again. Within the course of two or three weeks, I spiraled into a deep and dark depression. This time, however, was worse than the first episode. This time I began having suicidal ideations. I recall driving my car and having moments where I'd wish my tire would blow out and I'd crash into a tree. Or I'd have other fleeting visualizations of my life ending abruptly.

I couldn't believe that this could happen again. Why was it that at really pivotal points of my life, I was becoming severely depressed? This time I did see a psychotherapist and agreed to try an antidepressant drug.

The talk therapy might have helped me to relax a bit and the medicine seemed to eliminate the suicidal thoughts. Nothing, however, could remedy the fact that I was too ill to complete my courses and, thus, could not walk in graduation with my classmates. I was devastated. I felt like the most "successful" failure in the world.

I completed my final exams and papers in the beginning of the summer of 1994 and received my diploma, unceremoniously, in the mail in August.

It was time for a break. I had been pushing myself academically since elementary school and felt a strong need to step away from studying for a year. Carol and I moved into my parent's house in Blue Ridge, VA in the fall of 1994. I got a job as a personal trainer and also waited tables some nights. Carol taught aerobics classes at the gym.

Without the distraction of a jam-packed school schedule, it should have been the case that Carol and I were having more sex. However, the contrary was the case, and I'm certain it was because I was not initiating. Or, if she initiated, out came my grenades. Still, however, I was unwilling to accept that the core reason was my sexual orientation.

Being gay just wasn't an option. How could I possibly be Catholic, Italian, perfect AND gay?! It just did not compute! No, No, NO!!!

Eventually Carol and I broke up, Carol moved back up to New York, and I decided it was time to get back to school. I did briefly consider going to medical school. But when I really projected into the future and visualized myself working with patients, I still saw myself more as a PT than an MD.

I was accepted into several graduate schools for a Master's degree in physical therapy and chose the Medical College of Virginia (MCV), the medical branch of Virginia Commonwealth University (VCU) in Richmond, VA. Not only was it a highly ranked graduate school for PT, it was also cost-effective since I was an in-state resident. And, since my parents were no longer footing the academic bills, off I went to Richmond, VA.

I absolutely loved MCV. I was the president of my class the first year. The coursework was rigorous, but I loved everything I was learning. My classmates were incredible people. I did extremely well academically. Dare I say it – Perfect Phil was back!

I dated three different incredible women over the three years I was in graduate school. Although the women changed, by mind/body reaction to sex didn't change. I started to fear that this was one arena where focus, dedication, and persistence might not be sufficient to overcome this "problem." But, this was not the time, again, to burden myself with such enormous concerns! I had to keep focused on my grades and graduate. There was no way I would allow myself to miss another graduation.

And then, IT happened yet again. During my last clinical rotation, roughly three or four months prior to graduation from PT school, I sank into another abyss. It became clear to me and my clinical instructor that I could not complete my clinical rotation. I spiraled down, down, down until one morning, weeks after leaving the clinical rotation, and without any conscious thought or plan, I walked into the bathroom and took an entire bottle of sleeping pills and a nearly full bottle of antidepressants. I walked back to my bedroom and wrote on a small piece of paper, "To all those who love me, I'm sorry." I crawled back into bed to die.

I was awakened by a muffled knocking sound. What is that sound? It took minutes for it to register that someone was frantically knocking on the front door of my house. I felt strange and had zero recollection of taking all that medicine and writing that short note. I started to rise out of bed and noticed I felt like I was moving through molasses. It was like the air was thick, and my body was straining to move through the stickiness and heaviness of the air. When I got to the top of the staircase, I felt unsteady on my feet and dizzy. My vision seemed to be really off too. Why is everything so bizarre, I thought? Am I dreaming?

I somehow made it down the full flight of stairs with the assistance of the banisters and fumbled with the locks to open the door. The moment I opened the door and made eye contact with my girlfriend, Leann, she gasped and sunk to the ground. It was like she had seen a ghost. Still, nothing clicked. And then, memory flooded back as Leann kicked into medical examiner mode.

My resting heart rate was well over 120 beats per minute. My skin was whitish grey. My pupils were dilated to nearly the size of my irises. Leann sprang into action and called 911 and my parents. An ambulance arrived within minutes and before I knew it, I was in the Emergency Room at MCV Hospital. The medical team rushed to pump my stomach and administer a medicine meant to rapidly flush out the liver. I overheard that if I was one hour later, I would have lost my liver. If I was any later than that, well, I wouldn't be here now writing what I'm writing.

Leann saved my life. She is now happily married and the mother of a beautiful baby boy. I will love and remain indebted to Leann until the end of time.

I was saved from death, but the hospital couldn't just discharge me, of course. Clearly, anyone who has tried to end their life isn't fit to just go home as if nothing happened. I was admitted to the hospital's psychiatric unit for a week of care and counseling. At first I was extremely embarrassed. MCV, in the heart of Richmond, VA, was a teaching hospital, so trailing every doctor that saw me was a group of medical students. Many of these students were familiar faces since I was in the physical therapy program affiliated with this exact hospital.

These were people who knew me as Perfect Phil! Suddenly, there was no possibility of hiding.

A monumental shift occurred over those days in the hospital. It took hitting rock bottom to wake me up from the distorted reality I had created for myself over the span of my life. As I often tell my patients, "Sometimes you have to break down, in order to break through!" When I relay this, it's not just another quote or cliché; I know it to be true because I experienced it firsthand.

In the spring of 1998, Perfect Phil passed away and Authentic Phil was born! When I walked out the doors of the hospital I had a deep knowingness that an agonizing chapter of my life had ended. I had a sense of utter spiritual freedom. I didn't know how things would unfold, but I knew that life was about to become what it was meant to be – Joyful!

One of Phil's clients shares...

Gillian

In the late fall of 2011, I had the misfortune to be in an automobile accident and the good fortune to meet Phil Tavolacci. The accident caused significant trauma to my upper body and left me in a state of shock. My internist told me that I needed physical therapy. He gave me the numbers of several therapists for me to investigate before settling on one. Most of his suggestions were "traditional" physical therapists; however, he also included myofascial release (MFR) therapist Phil Tavolacci on the list and added, "Oh, Phil, he's terrific." As my doctor had never steered me wrong, I chose to call Phil at his clinic, TAVO Total Health. And, owing to a cancellation that just occurred, I was fortunate enough to get an appointment on the very next day.

Although I knew nothing about MFR, within a few minutes of being with Phil, I knew with certainty that I was in the right place and with the right therapist. Furthermore, I realized that in time I would be healed, both physically and emotionally.

By early spring 2012, I was rehabilitated from the car accident trauma. Still, I decided to continue on with monthly visits to Phil. I am a professional pianist and vocal coach and play the piano for several hours a day with focused attention on the singers I accompany and coach. Not only does this work require my upper body - arms, shoulders, fingers, neck - to work in a concentrated and intricate manner, but my mind is often more dedicated to those I am working with than on the connections between my muscles and state of mind. Needless to say, bad habits can creep in over time and eliminating them and creating healthier practices is difficult to do without help. After a lifetime of helping singers eliminate their own bad habits, I feel I can speak to this with a certain amount of insight. Simply said, it is hard to do alone and it helps to have expert guidance.

Shortly after recovering from the car accident, I was at an event and fell. I broke my right arm just where it meets the shoulder. My orthopedic doctor informed me that my arm must be completely immobilized in a sling for two months. As I am right-handed, this proved to be a truly devastating accident for me because it resulted in a total loss of independence and control over my professional and daily life.

My orthopedic doctor explained that I should start traditional physical therapy soon for my hand, wrist, and elbow. Further treatment, including MFR treatments, would have to wait for my upper arm and shoulder to recover from the surgery. Phil concurred with the doctor's assessment and plan. Once the sling was discontinued, I saw Phil weekly for MFR in conjunction with two sessions of traditional therapy per week.

And so I began a long period, much longer than the first go around, of recovery and rehabilitation with both an excellent traditional physical therapist and my own trusted myofascial release expert, Phil Tavolacci. Having two such capable, fun, experienced professionals made the whole process of healing so much more enjoyable and comprehensive than it might have been otherwise.

Perhaps it is foolish of me to compare the two methods of treatment that I experienced. I feel each approach enhanced the other. Still, I believe there are differences on which I should elaborate. I feel traditional physical therapy is a passive experience for the patient when compared to that of MFR treatment. With MFR, I feel I take a more active role in my rehabilitation. The meditative atmosphere the treatment creates encourages me to be mindful and allows me to receive restorative energy from the therapist, which ultimately, resonates with me long after the session. Traditional physical therapy concentrates on the specific area of the trauma, whereas, MFR deals with the effects of the trauma on the whole body and on its relationship to the faculties of the mind. Fundamentally, it increases one's own awareness of the connection between the mind and the body.

I am compelled to mention how thankful I am to have had Phil come into my life. This past year has been one of the most challenging years for me both physically and emotionally but, without him, it would have been so much worse. Having successfully battled cancer twice, I found this experience was more difficult than any other I have had to endure. Fortunately, even on the bad days, Phil could always make me laugh. And perhaps that is the best medicine. But with Phil I think it is that and so much more - he is intuitive, sensitive, gentle, encouraging, and so very skilled in his work. Not only has Phil been the major factor in my recovery, my experience with him and with MFR has been illuminative. During this long period of mending myself body and soul, I learned it was imperative to take "one day at a time." Admittedly, I had my share of meltdowns, but I cannot imagine what this year would have been like without Phil and his healing presence.

MFR helped me reach and remain in a focused state of acceptance and determination to heal in whatever time it took. Having had two accidents, I was in a state of anxiety - worried that at any moment I could be injured again - and needed reassuring that everything would be okay. Phil reminded me to listen to my body. He gently guided my mind into a place from which my body could heal itself. His positivism and the practices of MFR calmly returned me to health.

It has been one year since my second trauma occurred. I am functioning very well now and am almost back to working at my full capacity. More than ever, I am reminded of my resilience and of my ability to persevere. It is clear to me now that the inner strength I gained has been, and continues to be, crucial to restoring my physical strength.

Chapter 8

SHOULDER THIS STORM

So how does fascia change from a taut, twisted, dense, and restricted state to an elongated, fluid, free, and mobile state via John F. Barnes' MFR? One of the phenomena at play is piezoelectricity. The word piezoelectricity means electricity resulting from pressure. The following is an excerpt taken, with permission, from John F. Barnes' article titled "Therapeutic Insight: The Myofascial Release Perspective- Piezoelectric Transformation." The full article can be found on Massagemag.com.

> The fascia is a piezoelectric tissue; therefore, a therapist utilizing the gentle sustained pressure of myofascial release through compression, stretching, or twisting of the myofascial system generates a flow of bioenergy (information) throughout the mind-body complex by the piezoelectric phenomenon.
>
> Fascia behaves as an electrically conductive medium, which allows this viscoelastic tissue to rehydrate under the sustained pressures of the therapist's hands. This rehydration also allows for an elongation

of the myofascial system, relieving pressure on pain-sensitive structures for alleviation of the symptoms of pain, headaches and restoration of motion

After finishing PT school, I accepted a position as a staff physical therapist in an inpatient rehabilitation unit of a hospital in Salem, Virginia. I loved the hospital and my coworkers were great. I was learning a lot while working with a diverse patient population: individuals with amputations, strokes, traumas, joint replacements, spinal cord injuries, burns, etc. It was evident to me that I had, in fact, chosen the correct profession. I loved the "work" and it was becoming clear that I was actually a really good therapist.

There was one issue, however, that was becoming an escalating problem. I was the only male physical therapist for a large portion of my time there, and since I was strong and fit, I got all of the physically challenging patients. The 300 pound partially paralyzed man who needed to learn how to ascend and descend stairs – put him with Phil. The 250 pound stroke patient who required maximal assistance with all transfers – give him to Phil. The 450 pound woman with cellulitis in both legs – Phil can tackle that case.

Now don't get me wrong, I loved working with each patient I was assigned to work with. Each and every patient taught me valuable lessons, and it was an honor to be a part of their healing journeys. But, the fact of the matter was that my past injuries had caught up with me finally and I was really starting to have problems with my body.

After most work days, I would have to lie flat on the floor, for at least an hour, to allow my mid-back muscles to come out of spasm and for my ribs and vertebrae to pop back into place. On some days my neck would seize up, and I could barely move my head. On other days my lower back would "go out," and I would have to force myself to walk normally when entering a new patient's room so he didn't think I was worse off than him on that day! Just like you don't want to go to a dentist with jacked up teeth, you don't really want to go to a PT with a jacked up body, right?

Around this time I tried chiropractic manipulations, deep tissue massage, and shifted from primarily all weight-training to almost all cardiovascular exercise. I got temporary relief at times, but for the most part, the situation with my body was worsening.

After having several debilitating neck spasms in a short period of time, I decided it was time to see a neurosurgeon for a medical/surgical opinion. The neurosurgeon, after viewing my MRI and X-rays, told me that my problems would only continue to get worse if I didn't have my neck surgically fused. Apparently, at this time, I had two herniated discs, stenosis (narrowing of the canal through which the spinal cord travels), and multiple bone spurs. It was these damaged structures that he deemed fully responsible for my frequent neck spasms and pain into my right shoulder blade or right arm. I was only twenty-eight years old and couldn't imagine having my neck sliced open and screws and plates installed! Nope – not yet.

I had begun working at the hospital in August of 1998. In September of 1998 I walked into my new bank, a few miles from the hospital, to deposit my paycheck. There was a long line and four or five bank tellers working. One of the tellers was a shockingly attractive olive-skinned man with short curly hair and piercing green eyes. I recall thinking, at the moment I saw him from the back of the bank, "Phil, if you truly **are** gay and you're finally accepting **that** reality, then this is who you should be with!"

I began counting people in the line and statistically analyzing my chances of being assisted by this guy. My heart was racing and I could hardly breathe. As the line inched further and further, and I could see this guy better, I was praying for a divine pairing of Attractive Teller to Jittery Bank Customer. And then it happened. "Welcome to First Union. My name is Jeff Coles. How may I assist you today?" Our banking transaction was maybe two minutes long but there was an undeniable energetic connection made. Two days later I was in a clothing store in a mall all the way across town when I heard someone say, "Hello Phillip." Before I turned, I thought "Phillip? No one calls me Phillip." I turned, and it was Jeff. We chatted for a couple minutes and he left. I continued shopping throughout the mall and ended up looking at shoes in a department store. "Hi Phillip." Jeff hadn't told me that he had a second job in the shoe department of this department store, but the Universe guided me there.

Jeff and I have been together for fifteen years now. In September of 1998, I finally accepted who I was and started living an amazing life with an amazing partner. All the years of depression and angst about being gay began to slowly melt away.

Jeff and I were enjoying living in Roanoke, but knew we weren't likely to make it our home for the long haul. It was a quaint little city and the surrounding Blue Ridge Mountains were absolutely gorgeous, but it wasn't the most welcoming city for gay people.

On Friday, September 22, 2000, just a week after Jeff and I celebrated our two-year anniversary, a gunman opened fire in a Roanoke gay bar, killing one man and injuring six others. This gunman had asked for directions to a gay bar so he could "shoot some gay people." According to the police report, the gunman walked casually into the bar, ordered a beer, then pulled a nine mm pistol from his trench coat and began shooting in the crowded bar. The heterosexual gunman's last name was "Gay," and he was apparently taunted his entire life about his name.

Jeff and I had never been to that particular bar, but that was irrelevant. This event gained national attention and brought the topic of homosexuality to the forefront in Roanoke. At this time I was "out" to my parents and close childhood friends, but I was not out yet to my coworkers or others I interacted with.

For the weeks after the shooting I would bear witness to incredibly ignorant and misinformed opinions being declared with righteous pride by the people around me. They weren't holding back on voicing their beliefs in my presence because they undoubtedly thought I was straight, just like them. Because I was always a muscular guy and "masculine", I think most people simply assumed I was straight.

Jeff came home one day and was clearly distraught. When I inquired what was wrong, he shared with me the experience he had in a local sandwich shop that day. He was seated next to a table of men who were saying that all gay people should be corralled and shot. They joked and laughed and made no efforts to hush their voices, likely figuring that they were voicing the majority opinion. I had never seen Jeff so shaken. He said he wanted to stand up and make a statement to these men, but he was too angered and anxious to speak.

I chose to take action in a way that I felt could possibly make some small difference. I chose to write a letter to all of my immediate colleagues at the hospital, roughly fifteen people. This letter not only "outed" me, but brought light to the entire situation that was unfolding in Roanoke which, I felt, was a microcosmic example of what was happening in the whole country. I didn't write a blaming, angry, retaliatory letter. I wrote a letter that simply educated and informed.

Writing and delivering the letters alone was liberating. And then having meaningful discussions with my colleagues who "got it" was very healing. I did have one colleague, however, who thought the best thing to do was to give me a fifty page document from a conservative religious group which discussed reparative therapy to "cure" homosexuality. This was not a mean-spirited gesture, mind you. I believe she truly felt she was being helpful in a "let me show you the path to happiness" kind of way. To me it was a small example of how millions of well-intentioned people believe strongly that GAY is a problem that needs to be fixed. They believe it is a choice. With my years of episodic depression and a near-suicide, I knew within every molecule of my being that my sexual orientation had nothing to do with choice.

With the combination of my body being beaten down daily with the challenges of my job and the whole "being gay in Roanoke" thing, it was time for a change. Jeff and I started researching a move. We both liked the Washington DC area, and Jeff's two best childhood friends lived in the DC area, so DC is where we set our sights. I applied to a busy outpatient orthopedics clinic in Arlington, Virginia and was excited to be offered the position. Jeff was able to transfer to the bank in DC, so off we went to DC!

My new job was significantly different than my first PT job out of graduate school. Instead of seeing four or five patients per day and spending lots of one-on-one time with them, I was now treating fifteen to twenty patients per day in fifteen-minute time slots. In my new job, I was juggling three or four patients every hour.

I had traded the physicality of hoisting patients around in a rehab gym for doing "speed-therapy", as I'd coined it. Every day was like an eight-hour endurance event: ultrasound a shoulder, run down the hall to mobilize someone's knee, run back up the hall to put heat and electrical stimulation on someone's back, run to the gym to add a few exercises to a patient's workout plan, run up the hall to do a fifteen minute evaluation on a new patient, run, run, run.

I was no longer dealing with body stress and strain from lifting and transferring patients. Now I was dealing with stress and strain from running around like an over-caffeinated body mechanic. I was also dealing with the stress of knowing that I could not deliver excellent, skilled, effective therapy in this particular factory-like setting.

One day towards the end of 2001, I reached into the clothes dryer at home with my right hand to retrieve a pair of jeans. When I started pulling the jeans I could see that they were entangled with other jeans. Being in a rush, and, at the time, being an incredibly impatient human being, I gave a hard yank to try to force the jeans out of the tangled mess. Well, the only thing that came loose was my shoulder. I didn't hear or feel anything tear. I also didn't feel any significant pain. But I simply knew that some sort of damage had just taken place.

Over the course of the next several months my right arm got weaker and weaker. My shoulder didn't have the endurance to do simple tasks like hang a shower curtain, or change the stations on the radio, or move an ultrasound device over a patient's sore forearm for five minutes. My shoulder wasn't painful; it was just becoming more and more useless.

I was working at a renowned physical therapy clinic, co-owned by one of the most highly regarded upper extremity orthopedic surgeons in the country. I figured it was time for him to examine my shoulder and give me his opinion. He ordered an MRI of the shoulder and upon review of the MRI, deemed that the problem was most-likely the large bone spur that was pressing into my rotator cuff muscles. Nothing else in the MRI appeared to be linkable to my weakening shoulder. Even though I relayed the clothes dryer incident, he seemed quite sure that the bone spur was the culprit. The surgeon felt that a simple arthroscopic removal of the bone spur, a forty-five minute procedure, would do the trick.

This seemed feasible to me so I consented to the simple operation. I would have the procedure done on a Friday, take off the following week to rest and heal, and then return to work with a reduced patient load for a couple weeks while I gained back my strength. That was the plan. There's a phrase that I've come to know recently that is relevant here, "If you want to hear God laugh, tell him your plan!"

I went into the operating room for a scheduled forty-five minute arthroscopic removal of a bone spur and I was awakened four hours later by a resident surgeon telling me that they chose to fully open my shoulder to address widespread damage within the shoulder. I was in shock. I hadn't consented to an open-shoulder repair. As a physical therapist I treated open-shoulder repairs and knew exactly what the recovery time was. How dare they assume that I'd implicitly consent to having my shoulder filleted open and massively altered!

My shock was cut short by vomiting, however. Since the surgery went from a planned forty-five minute procedure to a four-hour long production, I was given a great deal of anesthesia. I vomited repeatedly for days after the surgery and could taste the chemicals coming up and out. Because I'm not dainty when vomiting, I inflamed all of my spinal muscles and was now in full-blown back and neck spasms. And...I'm allergic to pain medication. With the post-operative shoulder pain, the spinal spasms, and the violent vomiting, I was beyond miserable.

Normally when a patient at this clinic had open-shoulder surgery, they were prescribed shoulder immobility for a week and then at least three weeks of passive range of motion coupled with modalities before beginning to resume more functional and physical tasks. I, however, was told that I was healing so quickly that I should return to work after one week. So, back to work I went as an in-pain, one-armed, angry physical therapist.

It took me eighteen months before I could press a one-pound dumbbell over my head for ten repetitions. For the sake of comparison, when I was bodybuilding I would routinely use fifty-pound dumbbells for overhead shoulder presses.

One of Phil's clients shares...

Denise

My name is Denise, and I am forty-nine years old. My back pain started in 1996 when I was thirty-four years old. While driving to work on a rainy morning I was rear-ended at high speed by another driver. When I awoke, I was in the hospital. I had pain in my neck and back. After X-rays, CT scans, and a host of other tests, I was placed on bed rest for about two weeks, followed by three months with no physical activities. This was anathema to my job as a soldier in the military. My lower back pain was the worst, and I was numb in my left buttock and left leg.

For over fifteen years, I had been to ten or more doctors as I moved around the world whilst serving in the military. This routine continued after military retirement. Several doctors told me I was just going to have pain, and I would simply have to live with it. I was on a lot of medication and went for periodic injections. I think I was taking the medication initially because I was in so much pain, and it seemed to help. Upon reflection, I was masking the pain with medication.

As time passed, I saw traditional physical therapists, chiropractic doctors and acupuncturists. I taught high school for three years and have since moved on to a new career where I give presentations. In both positions, I was standing for substantial periods during the day. The constant standing exacerbated my pain to such an extent that I would end up confined to my bed and barely able to put my shoes on.

The traditional physical therapy I was used to was just not working. One of my colleagues mentioned TAVO Total Health and how much I had to go see the "Body Whisperer." I made an appointment with the "Body Whisperer," aka Phil Tavolacci. Phil explained the MFR approach he specializes in. After seeing Phil for about six weeks, I noticed a substantial decrease in my pain. I quickly realized it might be possible to resolve, versus manage and control, my pain!

For years, I was limited in what I could and could not do because I'd fear the recurrence of my back pain. It was never far from my thoughts. I cannot thank Phil enough for introducing me to MFR. It has changed my life and my view on my relationship with my spine. Now, rather than simply accepting a certain level of pain or drowning the pain with medication, I can actually relieve my back pain and stay in the game of life.

I am no longer dreading turning fifty, because I'm feeling and doing better now than I was at forty! I am feeling more and more fascially free!

Chapter 9

Pain, Pain, Go Away

"Healing is messy."

"Healing is not linear; it is a zig-zag journey."

"Sometimes you will take one step forward and then two steps backwards."

John Barnes teaches MFR therapists these truths in all of his seminars. Early in life some of us somehow formulate the belief that healing "should" look like a straight up-sloping line on an X/Y axis. Day by day you'll get better and better, we assume. The reality is that authentic healing is oftentimes a roller-coaster ride, complete with twists, turns, and nausea-inducing loops.

There is an inevitable phenomenon encountered by many clients who embark on a healing journey via MFR. It is what we call a Healing Crisis, or Healing Response. Although I prefer to call it the latter, the truth of the matter is that when you are knee-deep in one it most certainly does feel more like a CRISIS than a response!

When one enters a healing crisis, it is as if all of your familiar symptoms, plus some brand new ones, come on like a tsunami. It is scary. It is uncomfortable. It is beyond logical comprehension. It unearths what has been hidden, buried, or forgotten. And, it is **necessary** in the process of authentic healing!

Different therapists describe the healing crisis in many different ways. I will describe it in a way that makes sense to me. Please research how others explain this phenomenon so you can understand it and have no fear surrounding it, should you decide to heal via MFR.

What makes the most sense to me is that clients step into a therapist's treatment room with a mind, body, and spirit jam-packed with an entire life history fossilized into their tissues. The client's body has islands and tracts of ancient solidified matter, entrapping debris and cellular memories of trauma and pain. The client's body, upon entering the room, is vibrating at a frequency that has been determined by their cumulative experiences right up to the point that they walked into the treatment room.

Now, into the client's body comes something new and foreign (MFR in this case) that starts to soften this fossilized tissue. Structures that have been petrified and dehydrated for years, energetically cut off from the healthier parts of the body, start to soften and fill with nourishing fluid. The fluid carries nutrients that have previously been unavailable to the hardened regions for a while. The junk that has been trapped in the tissues finally has a pathway out. The materials are now free to find their ways out of the body, where they no longer serve any positive purpose. While all this is happening, the overall vibration of the body is changing. It has to – it is basic physics! Our density or fluidity will dictate the frequency at which we vibrate.

All of this is happening on the inside. There is a massive reorganization taking place, right down to the cellular level. I like to tell my clients that "When all of this reorganization is taking place on the inside, it's not all rainbows and unicorns happening on the outside!" What

I mean by this is that all the really incredibly good things that are taking place under the skin, don't necessarily translate to *feeling* fantastic. With so much shift and change occurring, the client may feel ill and/or worse than they did before starting MFR.

Initially, the healing crisis can be just as frightening for the therapist as it is for the client! When first starting to treat myofascially, therapists are prone to thinking "Did I do something wrong?" "Did my work overload the client's system?" "Could I have possibly harmed the client in some way?" These are rational questions to ask since the client seems to be having not-so-pleasant responses to the work.

We soon come to trust, however, what John teaches at every seminar: "MFR never injures and it never harms." When the principles of MFR are followed, it cannot injure or harm a client. We come to accept this when we observe, time and time again, that after every healing crisis comes a leap in healing! It's like there has to be a storm before a beautiful day can be birthed into reality.

A client might say something like, "Until that so-called healing crisis I thought I'd never be able to sit through a two-hour movie in a theater again. It's been eight years since I've been able to go to the movies. But, after that healing crisis last week, for some reason I can now sit for two hours without any pain! I went to the movies and I'm so happy! I really wasn't a fan of yours last week and, to be honest, I didn't believe your explanation of the healing crisis. But now it makes sense and going through the healing crisis was certainly worth it!"

I was so angry after my shoulder surgery that I knew I couldn't keep working where I was working. I desperately wanted to start my own private practice, but I had no experience owning and operating a business. It made sense to me that I should find a small PT clinic that was in need of a Director and work there for a year, as a stepping-stone to opening my own clinic.

This is exactly what I did. I interviewed with Laura Probert, who had three PT clinics in the northern Virginia area and was looking for a Director at her new clinic in Herndon, VA. You likely recognize Laura's name by now since I reference her in my Acknowledgements at the beginning of the book, reference her again in Chapter 1, and she wrote chapter 25 in this book!

I signed a one-year contract and was off on a new and exciting adventure. This was a perfect job for me at this time of my life because it allowed me to learn the basics of marketing, operations, budgeting, management, and other business-related elements. I also had the opportunity to become a better manual therapist because I was in a very small clinic with limited exercise machines and modalities.

By roughly seven months into the one-year contract I started getting antsy. I had this very strong pull to start my own practice. Around this seven-month timeframe, I had a very interesting scenario unfold. Within the course of two weeks, three different people, none of whom knew each other, told me about a local healer. They each in their own specific way hinted that I should connect with this woman. "She's a massage therapist but she doesn't do massage." "She does energy work and is like a body psychic." "I can't explain what she does, you should just go!" The moment the third person uttered this woman's name, I knew I needed to meet her. I wasn't interested in hiring her or making her a professional colleague. I wanted her to treat and help ME as soon as possible!

I walked into my session with this therapist and she asked me to lie down, fully clothed, face-up, on the treatment table and close my eyes. She didn't have me fill out any paperwork and didn't ask me anything at all about my health history, or current concerns – nothing. "Just relax for the next half hour." This was very different but, for some reason, I trusted her completely.

For the thirty minutes I was on the table, she gently touched different parts of my body. For example, she might have two fingertips of her right hand on my forehead while two fingertips of her left hand were on my left knee. We were totally silent for thirty minutes. I don't recall feeling anything happen during those thirty minutes. By about fifteen minutes into the session I started thinking "What the hell is she doing? This is pointless!"

After thirty minutes she said, "OK. Slowly sit up and let me tell you what your body told me." Part of me was thinking, "Okay, Crazy Lady, sure…let's do that." The deeper intuitive part of me was saying, "Yes! Please do! Thank you! I can hardly wait another second!"

Over the next fifteen minutes this therapist told me in explicit detail everything that had happened thus far in my life. She knew absolutely everything about me. It blew my mind. She already had my attention from the accurate reports on my past when she said, "So now let me tell you why you're really here."

She proceeded to accurately tell me that I wanted to start my own physical therapy practice, but I was scared. I had financial concerns and worries about getting patients and producing great results. She then told me that I had no choice really, I had to start my own practice. I was no longer meant to work for anyone but myself. She told me that it would, in fact, be challenging at first and a lot of hard work, but my business would become a big success.

Every single word out of her mouth resonated for me. Within a couple months Laura, my then-boss and now-friend, allowed me to terminate my contract early and I started my own small private practice.

After a couple years of being in business for myself I tried to find this massage therapist to thank her. She was nowhere to be found. I couldn't even recall her name. It was strange for me, who was still super-organized at the time, that I didn't have her name or contact info or business card anywhere.

Shortly after my shoulder surgery it felt like my body presented its bill for accumulated damage. The following Alice Miller quote, which I've had up on the wall of my clinic for years, resonated with me on so many levels:

"The truth about our childhood is stored up in our body, and although we can repress it, we can never alter it. Our intellect can be deceived, our feelings manipulated, and confessions confused, and our body tricked with medication. But someday our body will present its bill for it is as incorruptible as a child, who, still whole in spirit, will accept no compromises or excuses and it will not stop tormenting us until we stop evading the truth."

This was a period of my life where I had significant physical pain almost every single day. And as those who live with pain know, the pain begins to alter and steer your life. One day it might be the ice pick in my lower right back preventing me from going to a movie I wanted to see. The next day it might be that my neck is in spasm, preventing me from going out with Jeff and our friends on a Friday or Saturday night. Another day my mid-back would be burning and so tight that I'd opt to lay on the hard floor for two or three hours instead of going out for a bike ride on a beautiful day.

This was a picture of my life leading up to the experience I shared with you in the first chapter of this book, The Lecture on the Floor. Even though part of me was excited that I was about to start my own private practice, another part of me was strongly considering leaving the PT profession and seeking less physically demanding work. It was really time for me to make some pivotal life decisions. Thankfully, the lecture on the floor steered me in the perfect direction!

One of Phil's clients shares...

Ashoka

I suffered a traumatic, near-death injury some years ago. I should have died that evening but nature and the higher consciousness it reports to conspired to keep me alive. I spent several weeks in the hospital and in rehab. When I returned home, I had a tracheostomy and a feeding tube. Months of surgery still lay before me.

The surgeries dealt with the scariest injuries. I was lucky to have extraordinary doctors, who were also wonderfully kind. First the feeding tube and then the tracheostomy were removed. There were setbacks along the way, and, at the time, they were heartbreaking. But there was progress. I gradually returned to my work as an economist, and work was itself therapeutic. My colleagues were most helpful in making that return possible.

I began traditional physiotherapy pretty soon after returning, and the physiotherapy continued even during the months that the surgeries were undertaken. I was gratified by the initial response. But I soon began to plateau. For a while acupuncture helped; maybe I was impatient when that also stopped providing quick relief. Over the months, I began to settle to a functional equilibrium. I was able to do most everything. But it was at a slow pace and sometimes the pain was acute. There seemed no simple diagnosis of the source of the pain. Modern medicine seemed to give up.

At this point, I felt it was necessary to change course. The insight was that doctors treat; the body heals. For most, this is an uncontroversial statement. But let me explain. The body is a mechanism of great subtlety and power, and its abilities vastly exceed that of medical science. Indeed, some of the core secrets of how the body functions are yet to be identified by modern medicine.

All too often, however, the body is afflicted by a disease or trauma that overwhelms and disables its healing functions. At such times, the violence inflicted on the body can be so severe that, in trying to protect itself from the immediate onslaught, the body acts against its own long-term well-being. Modern medicine is invaluable in those situations.

But ultimately, the medical treatment must end and the body's healing power must be harnessed. The best and the most gentle way of harnessing that power is not always obvious. At this point in my recovery I relied on homeopathy and yoga. I also visited, whenever I could, a wonderful chiropractor who practices at the Himalayan Institute at Honesdale, PA, with a focus on soft tissue treatment.

My starting yoga practice was a basic one, with an intense focus on breathing. My many teachers and friends at the Himalayan Institute guided me through several sessions of instruction. Relearning how to breathe may seem an odd goal; after all, we have always been able to breathe. But even when we are in the best of health, our breathing habits can be very poor. The breath may be short, shallow, and forced. In sickness and in injury, we often react by imposing further restrictions on our breathing.

My breathing practice includes pranayama (especially, alternate nostril breathing), stretches to expand and strengthen the diaphragm, the main breathing muscle, and a more conscious effort to nourish the whole body with breath. It is easy to relapse into inefficient ways of breathing, but soon you realize how wonderful it is to breathe properly, and that reinforces the practice.

But despite a dedicated practice, once again, I found that temporary gains tended to evaporate. My primary physician did not give up and sent me Phil's way, where he sends his patients when all else has not worked. This is where Myofascial Release (MFR) came into my life. It is a system that actively encourages the body to release its defensive posture against disease and injury and thereby, helps open up the possibilities of healing.

What have I learned from MFR? First, let the body speak to you. In the very first moments of our first session, Phil asked me if I had any reactions to report. I had noticed a slight twitching in my left temple (head) area, quite far from where Phil was working, at one of my ankles. A bit embarrassed, I told him that I was probably only imagining it. He reassured me that I was not. Over time, I have learned how to tune into that sensation myself. It has also intensified, and Phil has explained that some of the deeper restrictions in the body lie there.

I have also come to understand and appreciate the MFR philosophy that the body's fascia is an interconnected whole. During my yoga practice, certain postures connect long tracts of restrictions. There is a general sensation of stretching, as if a plastic wrap were sticking to the body but struggling to obtain release. It is an odd sensation at first but one that is more welcome with the passage of time. An intellectual understanding that the body is connected is enriched by the more conscious physical sense of the connections that are most relevant for the body's healing.

When these connections become more salient, the body has begun speaking to you. Or, as the title of this book would suggest, you have made contact with the body's web. This takes us to the second stage of MFR. Phil will often suggest that we breathe into the connections— those that are still in the form of restrictions—and allow them to "stretch like taffy and melt like butter." This is the point at which breathing becomes central. The stretching and melting will be easier and more fun as a gentle breath flows into those areas. The body will seem to expand, protest a little, and retain a mild glow.

This experience need not be—should not be—limited to the physiotherapist's table. It should certainly be continued in daily yoga or myofascial stretching practice. With time, it will be in the consciousness even when not in active practice. That should be the goal.

Finally, a third aspect of the treatment is patience. This may seem an odd theme to highlight. But it is critical. Healing requires patience, and as we practice patience it becomes more a part of us.

Why is patience so important? For good reasons, no doubt, the body takes its time in restoring health. The most superficial injuries do heal quickly. But the deeper the trauma, the greater is the healing time. This is, in part, because the trauma may actually lead the body into a posture that inhibits recovery. The fight-or-flight response suppresses the immune system, sometimes chronically. So, the first task is to undo that collateral damage. The body needs to be coaxed back into believing that the threat has disappeared. It is only when the negative response is undone that the positive healing can begin.

And the point is that none of this can be rushed. With each step on this journey, new avenues open up. Nature, acting through the body, takes the most intelligent path, but it is a path that evolves as circumstances demand. No doctor or therapist can foresee the full progression of the body's response to treatment. Hence, small steps reveal new opportunities. As the wise man counseled him whose eyesight was weak: walk ten steps and you will see the next ten steps, and soon you would have travelled a long distance.

Our pain continues through this unfolding. But rushing things does not help—indeed, rushing will likely hurt.

Just as patience helps deal with the trauma, the trauma teaches us to be patient. Sickness is therefore an opportunity to learn the value of patience and, with luck, begin a deeper lifelong practice that extends into all aspects of our relationships.

In summary, to gain the most from MFR, listen to the body, breathe in a natural, relaxed manner into the restrictions that need to be opened up, and be patient as the healing unfolds. And the promise is that in doing so, you will gain more than relief from your trauma. You will learn to step back from an obsessive engagement with life's daily transactions and, as an observer of life's twists and turns, come to more sensitively appreciate your role and place in nature's great drama.

Chapter 10

AHA! MFR!

So, what are some basic "rules" of authentic, John Barnes, Myofascial Release? The following are in no particular order or hierarchy but all are applicable if one is delivering true John Barnes based MFR. This list is also not all-inclusive.

(1) It takes a minimum of ninety seconds for fascia to even BEGIN to release/lengthen. For this reason therapists will hold positions of stretch for five minutes on average. If a release is proving to be particularly effective, a therapist might continue the same technique for double or even triple that time. Restrictions are multi-layered, like onions. The longer one holds a release, the more layers of the onion are able to peel or melt away.

(2) There is no sliding or gliding through the skin. MFR is not synonymous with massage. There is no lotion or oil used because this would cause the therapist to slide/glide. The therapist needs to be able to gently "anchor" into the fascia and utilize

leverage to facilitate release. This does not mean, however, that some therapists won't integrate some massage techniques into a predominantly MFR session. There are times where a therapist might add some soft tissue mobilization (a massage technique) to break up regions of particularly dense tissue or utilize some other type of massage to supplement the MFR. Each therapist has unique skills, talents, and intuitive capabilities that fit each client's specific needs, in that specific moment.

(3) MFR is best delivered via skin-to-skin contact versus through articles of clothing. In order to optimally connect and anchor into the fascia the therapist's skin (palm of hand, forearm, finger pads, elbow, etc.) needs to directly connect with the client's skin. Clients will receive the greatest benefit if they are wearing appropriate attire. A pair of loose shorts only for males is ideal. A jog bra plus loose shorts; or two-piece bathing suit; or bra plus underwear are ideal options for females.

(4) There are no protocols for MFR. In other words, there is no such thing as "For sciatic nerve pain, do techniques A, B, and C at session one and then proceed to techniques D, E, and F at session two." Clients are not treated as diagnoses or isolated body parts. An MFR therapist looks at the entire being and then treats what she sees, feels, and intuits. One of John Barnes' frequent teachings in seminars is, "If you know what you're going to do before you walk into the room, then you don't know what you're doing." You see, every single "sciatica" client is going to be completely different. They are

going to be different from each other because they have completely different fascial histories! What worked for fifty-seven year old, non-athletic, four spinal surgeries Mrs. Jones last April won't work for twenty-eight year old, athletic, high-stress lawyer Mrs. Smith on the schedule for tomorrow. These are two completely different human beings with completely varied life experiences. We treat the whole body, because everything is connected and everyone is unique.

(5) It is imperative to assist clients in attaining and maintaining a level and balanced pelvis and equal leg lengths. The majority of clients that find their way to John Barnes MFR therapists present with uneven pelvic bones. This imbalance in the foundation of the body leads to leg length discrepancies (one long leg and one short leg) below the pelvis and a twisted spine above the pelvis. When the pelvis is out of alignment, the leg length differences are "functional" vs. "structural." In other words, if a client with an imbalanced pelvis were to have X-rays taken of both legs and then have the X-rays measured, the two legs wouldn't measure differently. However, because the pelvic bones act like wheels at the level of our hips, if a pelvic bone rolls forward, it pushes the leg, making it "functionally" longer. If a pelvic bone rolls backwards, it pulls the leg, making it "functionally" shorter. Now, it should be noted that a small percentage of the population (roughly 10%) do have true structural leg length differences. It is likely that roughly ninety percent of people with leg length differences, however, have functional (correctible via MFR) leg length discrepancies.

(6) MFR therapists honor "fascial barriers." When a therapist sinks their hands into a region of the body, they will sink until they feel resistance from the tissue-what we call a fascial barrier. We never force through these barriers; we honor them and wait patiently for the body/tissues to invite us in further. One of the primary reasons why MFR "never injures and never harms" is because we honor the barriers that we feel. The barriers let us know how far into the body the body/client is ready and willing to let us in.

(7) The client is always in control. If something feels too intense, we educate our clients to say "ease up" or "Halt." Most MFR therapists also adhere to using a basic zero-ten (0-10) pain scale during treatment. "Therapeutic Pain", in general, is in the one-seven (1-7) range; whereas "Non-therapeutic Pain" is in the eight-ten (8-10) range. When someone's pain escalates to an eight or above, the body will typically go into a bracing or protective response. It does little good for therapists to work in this range, because the body is fighting the treatment versus working with it. There is an exception, however, to note here. If a client is unwinding and is recalling a past painful event (like a car accident, or a surgical procedure, or a difficult labor/delivery, for example) then it might be highly therapeutic to BE in the greater than eight to ten pain range until that experience clears from the client. In this case, the therapist would ensure, via clear communication, that the client deems the pain to be therapeutic in nature.

(8) There is a big difference between "talking or chatting" and "dialoguing" during a treatment session.

Dialoguing is a highly valuable enhancement to MFR. The therapist uses simple verbal cues or asks non-leading questions to bring greater awareness to the moment. For example, an MFR therapist might say something like, "If that deep ache in your shoulder could talk, what might it say?" Or the therapist might say, "If you feel ready and it resonates for you, repeat to yourself 'I let go'." This dialoguing is different from talking or chit-chatting during a treatment, which typically draws attention away from the moment and disconnects the client from their mind-body connection. It also tends to lessen the therapist's ability to ground himself and fully connect with the client.

In April of 2005 I got my busted body and ailing spirit to my first John Barnes MFR course in Miami, Florida. The introductory course was aptly titled MFR 1. The course outline conveyed that the first day would be mostly lecture-based and the remaining two days would be predominantly "hands-on."

Like many of the therapists in the room waiting for the seminar to commence, I sat with my arms crossed and a head full of skepticism. If there was really something to this modality, then why wasn't every therapist doing it everywhere by now? Why hadn't I been exposed to MFR in the eight years I'd been practicing physical therapy already? And why in the world, someone please tell me, is the "guru" of this stuff a stocky, bearded, white pony-tailed, leather-vest wearing man?

By roughly the one-hour point of the lecture I uncrossed my arms and softened my brow. My skepticism began to shift towards guarded optimism. Everything this barrel-chested man was saying was making perfect sense to me. But, I still needed tactile proof. I desperately wanted the hands-on portion of the class to start so I could feel what he was talking about. I couldn't imagine that my spine of cement could possibly "melt like butter and stretch like taffy." I would need proof!

We finally made it to the hands-on portion of the seminar. For these portions of John's seminars he first demonstrates a technique in the front of the room and then the students pair off at treatment tables to practice the new techniques on each other. We get to experience the work as both therapist and client.

For the first several techniques I didn't feel much, if anything, when I was the client on the table. I do recall, however, that my brain was racing 100 miles per minute! In looking back I'm sure I couldn't feel because I was too busy thinking. I was in analysis paralysis.

What I noticed most when I was the therapist was that holding a stretch or position for five minutes felt like an eternity. "If it feels like you are working too hard, then you are working too hard," John would repeat often to remind us that MFR wasn't like other modalities where more force is better.

Even though I wasn't yet feeling my body melt into a gooey glob of relaxed wonder, I was feeling subtle shifts when off the table. I started to notice that the lecture chair wasn't as uncomfortable as it initially was. I felt like I was standing taller and walking more smoothly. I felt like when I assumed the therapist role I was feeling less of my own pain and tightness, and more of what was present in the client's body on the treatment table. Huh! Keep it coming – I'm officially intrigued!

On the third and final day of MFR 1 I had an experience that "sealed the deal" for me. I was the client on the table for a neck release technique. We were probably about two minutes into the technique when my right arm began to feel very strange. It felt as though my right arm was becoming lighter and lighter. Also, with my eyes closed, when I scanned my body it felt as though the left side of me was atrophied and shriveled, whereas my right side felt enormous and Hulk-like. Then some muscles began to twitch in my right shoulder and arm. What in the world? Then, as if a puppeteer had attached fine wires to my right arm, my arm floated off the side of the table and up to my right ear! I opened my eyes in disbelief, certain that an instructor came by and stealthily lifted my arm. But, no – no one was there except the therapist who was still using both hands to gently traction my neck.

After I became aware of the involuntary physical motion of my arm, I became aware of some other things. All of a sudden I was very angry. I wasn't angry at the therapist who was working on me or angry for any other particular reason. I was simply angry. Was this anger trapped in my neck and right shoulder- regions that have been sources of pain and trauma for years? As my arm moved ("unwound") spontaneously and increasingly more wildly, it felt as though a trapped creature wanted to burst out of my right shoulder. It was simultaneously bizarre and awesome. As my logical mind was trying to "figure it out," my abstract mind pushed ahead and took the lead, allowing me to simply "Let Go!"

It is impossible to describe in words the shift I felt after that one brief experience. The best I can do is say that it felt like prison bars were lifted from around me! In that moment I knew that I could eventually be free of pain and that MFR was going to be a primary pathway for my healing. Once that new and unexpected experience hit my consciousness, there was an absolute **knowing** that the key to resolving my pain and dysfunction was to release my restricted fascia. The issue was in this whole-body tissue!

As I'd stated in Chapter 1 of this book, I experienced more pain relief in this three-day seminar than I had experienced over the course of fifteen years of varied healing modalities. I knew that I would find a way to take all of John Barnes' courses, and I knew that I had to receive a substantial amount of MFR to resolve my pain, restore my motion, and bring back my light.

When I returned to my new (seven-month old) clinic after MFR 1 I immediately began treating all my patients with what I had learned in that one seminar. I figured that even though I had only learned about fifteen "techniques" I understood all the principles and concepts and that was all I needed. With the basic knowledge that everything is connected via the fascial web, I stopped treating diagnoses and started treating whole human beings. The results were astounding and immediate. Happy clients spread the word, and before I knew it I was booked solid and doing work that brought me joy.

I knew that I needed a great deal of MFR to untangle my mucked-up web. I desperately wanted to go to John Barnes' healing center in Sedona, Arizona – Therapy on the Rocks. I wanted to do what is called "Therapy for the Therapist", an intensive three-hour per day treatment plan where you are immersed in receiving and learning MFR for one or two weeks. The perceived barriers, however, were the barriers that most people face: not enough time and/or money. My schedule was booked fairly far out with patients eager to feel better, and I had no money since I was growing a new small business.

At this time I brought myself back to those important lessons I received during "The Lecture on the Floor":

"You help so many people, Phil, when are you going to help yourself?"

"Are you not important?"

"Do you not deserve to have a better life?"

"Do you even love yourself, Phil?"

The time had come.

PHIL TAVOLACCI, MSPT, PT

I was important!

I deserved a better life!

I did, in fact, love myself!

I pulled out a credit card and signed up for a one-week intensive at Therapy on the Rocks in Sedona, Arizona! It was the best money I have ever spent.

One of Phil's clients shares...

Linda

In 2013, a child's appendectomy is a somewhat traumatic, but routine procedure. In 1959, however, my appendectomy was anything but routine and very traumatic. I had been sick for about a year before the operation, doctoring myself with Alka-Seltzer every night, but not telling my parents until the pain was unbearable. Just before my appendix was about to burst, I was sent to the small hospital in my hometown, which had neither a pediatrician nor a very skilled surgeon. He left me with a huge scar at the age of ten.

The scar was a physical manifestation of a difficult childhood. My emotional trauma from the operation was buried along with anger over things at home I could not control. I had an alcoholic father and a passive-aggressive, verbally abusive mother. There was some sexual inappropriateness from my father, which I totally repressed. I never really understood the depth of my difficulties or that I was a "needy" child. I don't think one ever really does during childhood. My life with my parents was the only one I knew, and it wasn't until many years later that I began to understand my issues.

I developed many coping strategies. A perfectionist, I became an excellent student and an outstanding musician. It was as if I had to tell the world that a "golden girl" like me could not possibly come from an unhappy family. I suppressed my feelings and became a very good actress, while taking on much responsibility for raising my two younger brothers. I can recall babysitting as early as age six. I mothered my two brothers for many years. My shoulders ached from the time I was a teenager.

I first knew there was something really wrong when I was in my early thirties. I had two sons of my own by then, and I realized on a very deep level that I, myself, had not been mothered the way I was trying to mother them. The result was a pain in my upper right back that would not go away.

After going to a medical doctor and not finding relief, I decided to try massage therapy. There was something about being touched that was wonderfully soothing, but not lasting. My massage therapist suggested I try talk therapy. I saw a psychiatric social worker who understood massage therapy. I can truthfully say that the talk therapy I received helped a great deal, and it is one reason I can write this story today. However, it took time and a willingness to look inside. I was taught to trust others, something I hadn't done up to that point. I was understandably, fiercely independent. Nevertheless, the pain remained.

There were trips to a chiropractor, two physical therapists, an acupuncturist, and more medical doctors. The pain would lessen slightly, but never fully go away. I learned to live with it.

I came to MFR through another massage therapist. It was the first and only science that looked at my problems a little differently, by addressing the appendix scar, something no one had considered a problem. It was explained to me that scar tissue could be three-dimensional and affect not only my abdomen, but also my hip and upper body. Could the pain I had felt in my back for years, actually be caused by my appendix scar? In my web was a childhood operation that had affected my growth and my physical and emotional body. Miraculously, as the restrictions in the area of my scar began to be released through MFR, my back and both shoulders felt better. I can't begin to explain how wonderful the pain relief felt!

Releasing restrictions in the physical scar brought up the emotional scars, too. I learned that they are one and the same. Through MFR my body could remember the pain of the knife, and I could remember the pain of parents who weren't really there for me. At first, this was rather disconcerting, but as treatment continued, it became somewhat easier to let go of these obvious scars and others as well. As my shoulders released, my over-developed sense of responsibility lightened. I could even begin to forgive my deceased parents more fully and try to reconnect with my brothers who shared some of the same pain.

My younger brothers, however, are not as willing to look at their problems as I have been. Writing about their pain and my pain is the hardest part of this story, but probably the most important. MFR treatments have opened me up to the feelings that I long ago learned to suppress. I am aware of these new feelings of anger, loss of control, and even elation, in my waking life, but my dreaming life is even more creative. I will share a couple of dreams to give the reader an idea of what I mean.

Dream 1: My brothers

My oldest brother appears as a younger version of himself. I hug him and tell him how much I love him over and over again.

My younger brother also appears as his younger self, but he then "morphs" into his current self, and I know that I can't solve his personal or financial problems.

All three of us have masks on and we are going somewhere, but it is hard to see where we are going because of the masks.

Dream 2: An abusive, passive-aggressive boss

As a teacher, I have left a badly managed school for a new one. It was hard to leave because I loved the children and the parents, but I am making the adjustment. I get a package from my former principal that is full of medicine he says I might need and some nice notes about my leaving his school. I am touched until I see that one of the medications is "asshole cream."

I've continued the MFR treatments primarily because of dreams like this, which represent the emotional issues still locked in my web. My responses to situations, like everyone's, are unique to my experiences. However, the general ups and downs of life, which we all experience, also affect my body. Getting MFR treatments keep me healthy. A difficult childhood is not a prerequisite. Simply reacting to the pain in our world can be burdensome. Our bodies store these reactions and experiences and leave scars or restrictions that can cause pain, or even illness.

When I see Phil, I'm sometimes confused about whether we are treating a physical issue or an emotional issue. I've come to understand that it really doesn't matter. I simply feel fortunate that I've had the self-awareness to seek help, and I wish MFR had been around when I was younger. I also have been given many tools to self-treat. I can do as much or as little as I want with this new amazing science.

I encourage all of you to begin this MFR journey of self-discovery.

Chapter 11

THE PATH UNFOLDS

Authentic healing is not a passive event. Sometimes clients arrive for an initial MFR session and verbally state, "I need you to fix me." Other times the words are not verbalized but the energy and expectation are palpable.

MFR does not "fix," and MFR, in itself, does not heal. The human (or animal) being treated self-heals with the *facilitation* of the MFR practitioner. MFR assists the body in unlocking its inherent self-healing capabilities. As restrictions melt away and trapped emotions finally process, the client regains more of his or her innate capacity for regeneration and vibrant living.

Those who are truly ready to heal come to understand that they must do their work outside of the treatment room and play an active role in their healing journey. Myofascial home stretches done daily are a necessary component for healing to unfold. Clients who grasp this concept early on in their healing journeys tend to make the greatest strides.

I have a very simplified way of making sense of how healing takes place with the facilitation of MFR. Nothing is, in fact, this basic and nothing truly takes place in purely linear fashion but for the sake of clarity please follow along. Also note: I am NOT a physicist. If you are a physicist reading this, please send me technical corrections for the second edition!

+ Jane, like all human beings, is a pressure system

+ What dictates the overall pressure in a system is the amount of force within a fixed space (Pressure = Force/Area)

+ Fascial restrictions ADD pressure to our systems because they create more force within the body

+ Let us say, hypothetically, that for Jane five thousand pounds of pressure is optimal and healthy

+ Let us say, hypothetically, that once Jane reaches eight thousand pounds of pressure, her alarm systems start to relay warnings in the form of symptoms

+ Now, let's say that those warnings/symptoms are ignored by Jane, or she simply doesn't know how to interpret them and goes on with life as normal

+ After more time marches on and more restrictions form (another car accident, a death of a loved one, working at a computer ten hours per day, etc.) Jane now holds ten thousand pounds of pressure within her body

+ At ten thousand pounds of pressure, double the "healthy" five thousand pounds of pressure in her system, Jane is likely dealing with a multitude of symptoms and challenges

+ Jane finally makes her way to an MFR therapist

+ After the first session Jane reports to a friend that she somehow feels a bit lighter – hypothetically she went from

10,000 pounds of pressure to 9,500 pounds because the fascial releases allowed excessive force, and therefore pressure, out of her system

+ Jane doesn't have her second session with the therapist for two weeks but she commits to doing the assigned home stretches daily; and by the time that two weeks passes she is down to nine thousand pounds of pressure in her system

+ At nine thousand pounds of pressure, her pain is less intense and less frequent; something is shifting

+ Over the course of the next two months she receives another six MFR sessions with her therapist and continues with her daily home stretches and MFR exercises and the pressure in her system drops to 6,500 pounds

+ She is feeling better and on her way back to optimal health and function!

One of the things I like about this simplistic explanation is that, once it is grasped, clients understand the importance of consistently releasing pressure from their systems. When they become bored with initially assigned stretches, I suggest they purchase a Myofascial Stretching book (please see the section titled Myofascial Release Resources at the back of the book) and start varying their home stretches. When asked what stretches they should do I simply say, "Work the web." The beauty is that it doesn't matter where you access the fascial web because every release will take pressure out of the entire connected system!

Roughly six months after I attended my first MFR seminar I began my one-week "intensive" (called Therapy for the Therapist) at John Barnes' MFR center in Sedona, Arizona- Therapy on the Rocks. I was set to have three hours of MFR every day for five consecutive days. I was both eager and terrified! I knew that it was exactly what I needed but I also knew that it wasn't going to be a luxurious week at a spa. This was going to be like body boot camp!

I don't believe it is for the highest good to relay a day by day account of my healing week at Therapy on the Rocks. And, honestly, since I didn't journal throughout the week, I could not accurately convey everything that happened each day anyway. I also wouldn't want people to think that their journey "should" look anything like my journey. Everyone's journey should and does unfold as it is meant to unfold. No one's journey should be compared to anyone else's journey.

What I will discuss are some highlights, insights, and outcomes.

I woke up on the morning of day number two feeling as though I had been hit by a train. And it felt as though the train conductor must have stopped, threw the train in reverse, and ran me over again for good measure! Every part of my body that I had previously injured or had issue with were screaming in pain. My sacrum was especially painful. It felt like a mass of molten lava that wanted to burn its way out of my skin. I was bent forward at the waist, with my torso stuck at a roughly forty-five degree angle from vertical. "Hmm," I recalled thinking, "this is like the position I was temporarily stuck in after my ruptured appendix surgery at age thirteen." Interesting.

It was interesting but I was also mad. Like any person in pain seeking "help" I wanted to feel better, not worse! "You will sometimes feel worse before you feel better." Okay, I get it, but...damn!

Throughout the week I had multiple violent coughing episodes during treatments. I noticed that during these coughing fits I could taste something chemical-like and almost metallic. It came to my awareness that I was likely coughing up the anesthesia from my two surgeries! Recall, in both my appendix surgery and my shoulder surgery I was under general anesthesia for four hours. Had that anesthesia been trapped in my lungs for all these years? Could it be that I had felt like I wasn't living fully and joyfully because I had been walking around anesthetized for years? Did this play any part in my depression? Fascinating!

Many of my treatment sessions were "multiple-therapist" sessions. Because John Barnes' two MFR Centers are teaching centers as well as treatment centers, there are typically MFR students completing what are called "Skill Enhancement Seminars." Clients can opt to have sessions be one-on-one with their assigned MFR therapist or they can opt to have one or several of the available students join the assigned therapist. I opted to have multiple therapists about seventy-five percent of the time I was at Therapy on the Rocks that week. With a seven-year history of gymnastics, I had a lot of tissue memory in the form of acrobatics that seemed to be coming up and out during unwinding. At six feet tall and 200 pounds, I figured the more hands, the better when I was airborne and flipping all over the place!

The unwinding never ceased to amaze me. Here I was at thirty-three years of age, tight as the Tin Man, and hadn't done anything remotely acrobatic in decades, and yet my body was capable of maneuvering in Cirque du Soleil-worthy fashion. And the JOY it unlocked! Unwinding, for me, seemed to be a master key that unlocked my buried and forgotten joy.

I learned to trust, without a shadow of a doubt, that absolutely everything in the body is connected via the fascial web during one of my mid-week sessions. My therapist, Tina, in this particular session was working on releasing a bone in my head called the Sphenoid. This is a bone that is located behind the eyes and it touches most of the main bones of the skull. After a couple minutes of perceived nothingness, I could feel this area begin to regionally unwind and

I began to get a visual in my mind's eye that this bone was like a mighty bird, swooping and flying gracefully through my head. All of a sudden the bone made a sudden jerking motion and, simultaneously, the ice pick in my right lower back sensation that I'd lived with for sixteen years went away. In that instant I knew that my right lower back (sacroiliac joint region, specifically) had corrected! My logical brain was utterly perplexed. How in the world did the movement of a small bone in my head cause huge bones in my pelvis and low back to shift and correct? "The fascial system is continuous from the top of the head to the bottom of the feet. EVERYTHING is connected." Yes – it made sense before that, but now I fully believed it.

From day one of my intensive almost every single therapist told me I would greatly benefit from internal work. Recall, I discussed earlier how the fascial system can be accessed from the inside out if the therapist works in the mouth or in the pelvic cavity via the rectum or, for females, via the vagina. Given the trauma and pain I had for years in my right hip, sacroiliac joint, sacrum, and lower back, I knew that I must be riddled with deep internal fascial restrictions. I also knew that the appendix scar and the gangrene that occupied my abdomen after my appendix ruptured would be more directly accessed if the therapists did some MFR work internally. But, day after day I refused the internal work. Fears and beliefs were blocking me.

Finally at the end of the fourth day I consented to have my first pelvic internal work session. Within a minute or two, I could feel connections throughout my entire body. The internal work reproduced the burning I often got in my mid-back muscles. It reproduced the upper neck pain I'd lived with for years. I could feel the intrapelvic work all the way up into my head!

I had another intrapelvic MFR session the fifth and final day of my intensive. I could feel subtle shifts occurring in my hips, pelvis, and lower back mostly during this session. What I vividly recall is that after this session I was able to sit cross-legged on the floor for the first time in sixteen years! I also noticed, as I was walking from the clinic back to my hotel, that I didn't feel like the Tin Man anymore. There was fluidity within the motion of my hips, sacrum, and pelvis! I didn't have to be guarded or cautious with my walking – there was a newfound bounce in my step and a sense of sureness that all was safe, good, and healthy.

Now, did I wrap up my five-day intensive feeling like I was 100 percent "fixed" and ready to sing from the rooftops? No, not exactly. But I would say that within three weeks of this five-day MFR experience I felt at least seventy percent better than I had felt in over fifteen years! I was, of course, excited about the progress I had made but I knew the journey was to be continued. If this work was capable of helping me feel seventy percent better after fifteen sessions, I knew I was capable of feeling even better by peeling away more layers.

Because there weren't any conveniently-located Barnes trained MFR therapists (yet) in the Washington, DC area for me to see for consistent treatment, I chose to get my treatment via a combination of self-treatment and MFR seminar completion. Over the course of the next few years, I took all of John Barnes' courses and began repeating courses. The fantastic thing about John's classes is that you are learning and getting incredible treatment at the same time! Repeating courses is so valuable because you learn at deeper and deeper levels each time you take a class. Also, you are not quite the same person, when you really think about it, the second or third time you take the "same" class.

Throughout the classes I had incredible healing experiences. Again, I don't think it's beneficial to highlight every detail of my specific healing journey. I will, however, highlight two experiences that were completely life changing for me.

During John's seminars there is often quite a bit of emotional release occurring in the therapists receiving treatment. Those who are ready and willing to "let go" can very freely allow any trapped emotional energy to leave their bodies. This emotion may release via tears, screaming, fits of rage, laughter, or any expression of emotion that exists.

Like many beginning MFR therapists, I felt blocked and unable (unwilling?) to allow any emotions to release early on in my MFR healing journey. I was happy for those around me who looked so much lighter and freer after they'd screamed or sobbed their guts out. It just wasn't happening for me. Until finally…it did.

I can't recall the exact seminar title or what city the course took place in, but it was shortly after my Therapy for the Therapist experience in Sedona. We were wrapping up the day with a floor-based self-unwinding and guided visualization exercise. The room was dark and packed with the accumulated energy of the day's happenings. I had just completed a great self-unwinding and was enjoying lying in a secluded corner of the seminar room, gently catching my breath. My eyes were closed.

Suddenly I felt a presence close to me. Throughout the seminars it had become typical for me to sense a strong presence close to me while being treated with my eyes closed, open my eyes, and John would be standing within a couple feet of me. So, this time I again assumed that John had ambled by.

However, that wasn't the case this time. I slowly opened my eyes and I saw…ME! I thought I must have been dreaming. Standing in front of me was a roughly eight-year old Phil, complete with the soccer outfit I used to wear and the Phil Fro- my thick, curly, frizzy hair that I used to part to the side when I was young. Okay, I thought, you're either dreaming or you've gone crazy, Phil.

This young Phil stepped up to me, put his hand on my shoulder, locked eyes with me and said, "It's okay now, it's time to let go. It's okay." He then hugged my head into his chest and instantly a torrent of tears flooded from me. I sobbed uncontrollably for what felt like an eternity. It felt as though I was releasing not just my own stored and buried grief, but the grief of thousands of people, present and past.

After this experience I felt lighter and happier than I could ever recall feeling! I could not logically explain what occurred but it was as "real" as real could be. And, ultimately, I could not care less if anyone believed me or thought I was crazy, because that one blip in time completely changed my life.

Another experience I will highlight took place during the Myofascial Rebounding class I took in Minneapolis, Minnesota. Regardless of whom I partnered with, when I was the client on the table I simply could not relax and let go. I was tensing, bracing, guarding, locked into my head. I would hear John say something like, "Rebounding is like a Stealth Bomber; it sneaks under your defense mechanisms and allows you to reset." In my head the conversation would be, "Oh yeah, well that Stealth Bomber must be in need of some upgrades because nothing seems to be cracking this defense system!" Don't get me wrong, I wanted to let go and give in to the Rebounding. It wasn't that I didn't believe in it. I simply couldn't receive it.

Then it dawned on me. This was a reflection of how I was living my life. I was still attempting to control everything. I hadn't yet learned how to fully let down my guard and be vulnerable. With the unwinding I was able to let go and give my body permission to self-correct. Why couldn't I allow the rebounding to do what I knew it could do? Did I not trust every single person that put their hands on me?

"With awareness there is choice." This is one of my favorite John-isms. The moment all of this came into my consciousness, I chose to drop all the control and trust issues and just receive the work. Within a minute of this conscious shift my body loosened, my breathing shifted, and I allowed the work to WORK. This soon led to an uninterrupted, five-minute long, hysterical laughing bout. I laughed so hard that my abdominal muscles and my neck cramped. I didn't care though. I hadn't laughed that much since I was a small child!

Just like after the adult-Phil meets young-Phil experience, this experience fundamentally shifted me. I allowed what happened on the table to carry over to my life off the table. Life became even more joyful and light.

"What if it could be easy," John often says when dialoguing during treatments.

Yeah, Phil, what if it could be easy? I was finally ready to ask and answer that question. I was ready to choose to truly live.

One of Phil's clients shares...

Jean

I learned about my fascia in three ways: resolving my pain and trauma issues, being treated by my MFR physical therapist, and moving/unwinding. With my myofascial treatment, I have become aware of, explored, and begun understanding the fascia itself. As a philosophy major, I read extensively on mind and body relationships, the existence of reality, and the philosophy of science. A major intellectual focus for much of my life has been sensing the here and now, the mind/body as one, and seeking connectedness with people. This is how I explored my fascia.

Part I: Before MFR

Prior to experiencing MFR, I learned that I packed emotion into my body which created physical symptoms, requiring my attention. Pain let me know that something was wrong. I read whatever I could find about the topic. Two of my favorite books are Jay Haley's *Uncommon Therapy* and John Sarno's *Healing Back Pain*.

To release emotions as a teenager, I selected music and danced the emotions into perspective. For example, Tchaikovsky's Symphony No. 6 in B minor, Op. 74, Pathétique was one of my favorites for angst. I felt the cathartic release of emotion during and following dance. Throughout my life, whenever I can, I dance my feelings. While dancing, I often close my eyes. Colors swirl. I have discovered that this is a form of MFR unwinding. Without this unwinding, I fear my fascia would have been severely scrunched and bruised. I am pleased that I did this as a youth, knowing now what I have learned about the body and trauma.

I was raped twice in a five month period in my twenties. The residual effects stored in my fascia showed up periodically over twelve years.

I got professional psychological help through rape crisis outreach and psychotherapy. I continued to work on my issues by providing rape crisis outreach services to others. Shortly following the second rape, I suffered severe headaches for the first time in my life. After going through testing, a neurologist prescribed pain medications and recommended working with a therapist. In therapy, I learned to control and redirect my pain and to confront issues that were contributing to my tension headaches. My mind body connections were clear to me.

Several years later I had hyper-alert reactions which turned out to be related to the rapes. If someone startled me by approaching from behind, I jumped, shook, and cried. While watching the movie "Thelma and Louise," I felt very shaky and had flashbacks. Once again psychotherapy helped stop my startle response. This time I sought the assistance of a psychiatrist with a specialty in Ericksonian hypnosis. He helped me to release my pain and redefine my experience, so I no longer had flashbacks to my trauma.

Following an accident in my early thirties, I developed persistent pain in my left hand. When strong pain medicine did not touch my symptoms, carpel tunnel surgery was recommended. Fortunately, I found a physiatrist who was able to reproduce my pain by pushing on trigger points in my shoulder, neck and back. I spent a year and a half in physical therapy before my pain disappeared. During that time, I changed jobs and eliminated some of the stressors in my life. As time passed, I noticed that a reduced form of that pain returned whenever I felt severe stress. I read John Sarno, M.D.'s book which explained how back pain can be caused by stress and psychological issues. I noticed that if I did not address the stress generated pain, the pain increased or moved to other spots in my body.

While working for an extremely difficult person, I developed gastric reflux for the first time. Each occurrence was connected to the presence of this difficult person. Having read extensively and watching my father suffer from this for years, I understood that reflux can be an emotional response to something in one's life and environment. Instead of medical intervention, I found my first Ericksonian hypnotherapist. He helped me identify my issue and learn different ways to respond to the difficult person. I never again experienced reflux in the presence of that difficult person. Twenty years later, I have experienced reflux only a few times. Each time I identified the issue and changed my behavior before the reflux response became worse or generalized.

Part 2: MFR treatment experience

MFR gives me a way to experience my mind-body connection: an awareness of fascia's physical connections and the revelation of stored emotional issues. I felt my first fascial release while being treated for a frozen shoulder. At the time, I thought I had a physical injury which would be healed through rest and prescribed exercises. As my arm was gently pulled up and away from my shoulder, my eyes closed. I shifted my focus inward, scanning my arm and shoulder. I felt a small linear section slowly shifting, stretching, and yielding. While this was happening, I saw colors pulsating and swirling. I remember sighing and feeling like my arm was much longer than it had been. During my frozen shoulder treatment, I was introduced to MFR unwinding. The therapist facilitated the unwinding by gently pressing or pulling on my body, then kept me safe as my movements became faster and larger, in a relatively small space. I noticed how I kept moving into parts of my body where I felt unease or discomfort. As I did this the movement became more comfortable and fluid. I was amazed as I moved in ways I had not moved in a long time and beyond my expectations. My eyes were closed the entire time. I saw colors that pulsed, swirled, and changed. Now I unwind whenever I feel a need or just want to move.

MFR gives me a way to unlock and heal trauma which I have carried in my body for years. I have found grief and loss. I have remembered times forgotten. I have shed tears of joy and sadness. I have worked on recent and past traumas. I have worked alone by unwinding and monitoring my changes in feelings and behaviors. I have written in a journal about my positive and negative feelings, experiences, wants, and desires. I shared this information with my MFR physical therapist and my Ericksonian hypnotherapist to assist in clarifying, experiencing, and healing my issues.

The majority of my traumas come from my distant past. After having a dental implant, I experienced excessive, unexplained pain in my jaw. I connected it to a violent bicycle accident when I was young. I knocked out six permanent teeth which were pushed back in place, had a concussion, and dislocated my jaw. Three teeth involved in the accident simultaneously abscessed at the age of sixteen. I had to wait to have all three root canals performed while taking only aspirin for the pain. At that time, doctors would not prescribe anything stronger than aspirin to someone my age. I learned to dissociate-- to not fully experience the pain. All of these experiences were buried in my fascia. Working with my Ericksonian hypnotist and MFR therapist, I was able to gradually recall and release the trauma that had been buried in my body over all those years.

Not every MFR experience is from my distant past. I had an hour long, outpatient hand surgery with local anesthesia a few months ago. I was instructed to stay still, to make no sudden moves, and to tell the surgeon if I needed to scratch my nose or make any other movement. I was warned by the surgeon that he was working in very small, tight places, slight movements could be harmful. Although I was told to freeze, I found it was much less painful and restrictive than a root canal, crown, or dental implant. I have had a slow recovery with tingling, pain, numbness, and limited range of motion. While being treated with MFR months after the surgery, I started shaking. The shaking became intense and lasted for more than an hour. I have experienced this sensation a few times in my life. It followed trauma where I had no chance to escape or fight, and froze instead. I am relieved that this procedure's surgical trauma has been released.

My understanding of these issues has developed over the years. I have read and attended lectures by Peter Levine (*Waking the Tiger, Healing Trauma*), Robert Scaer (*The Trauma Spectrum: Hidden Wounds and Human Resiliency*), and psychotherapists who specialize in trauma. Currently I am in the process of working on my remaining physical restrictions and symptoms from surgery, while being open to finding possible underlying issues and trauma. I am confident that my current symptoms will disappear as any related physical restrictions, issues, or trauma are addressed using MFR and Ericksonian hypnosis.

Chapter 12

AND THE JOURNEY CONTINUES

I have now been practicing and receiving MFR for eight years. Because of MFR, I am no longer living a life of pain and suffering. I feel better at forty than I felt at twenty. Am I completely "pain free"? No, not completely. Since I am human I have occasional aches and pains. When I do certain foolish things, like move a heavy piece of furniture on my own or hold an iPad up for two hours to watch a movie in bed, I pay a price. When I agree to treat nine or ten patients per day for sixty-minute sessions, I pay a price. However, I now quickly resolve these little episodes via MFR.

Another thing I love about MFR is that it has opened me up to embark on additional life adventures. It has served as a key to unlocking more and more doors that were previously seen as impenetrable to me.

For example, without MFR I wouldn't likely have completed a Vision Quest two years ago. With John's frequent repetition of "You can't grow in your comfort zone" etched into my consciousness, I chose to complete a one-week Vision Quest, led by a Shaman, in the woods of upstate NY. This particular quest was structured to include three consecutive days of isolation, fasting (no food at all), and journaling.

Each of us nine participants set ourselves up in an isolated spot on the 300 acre property and were instructed to simply "be" for three full days. The only time we could leave our little spot was to, once a day, walk down to the fire and pond to physically (but non-verbally) check in.

Now, let me tell you, I am much more of a Hilton Hotel kind of guy than a Tent-in-the-Dirt kind of guy! And, no food for three days? I typically "needed" to eat every three hours. When I first told my partner, Jeff, about my plans to do the Vision Quest, he chuckled and said "How are you going to survive without hair gel?"

But, deep within me, I knew it was time to really bust out of my comfort zone. It was time to shed even deeper layers of limiting beliefs and fears. It was time to experience the totally unknown and foreign.

I was gifted with so many lessons during that experience! I will share one very powerful life-altering one.

On morning number two of the three days of isolation and fasting I walked down to the pond and fire. I had on a hooded jacket so I could partially cover my face. No eye contact was allowed during this phase of the Quest. Silence was also mandatory.

There were two staff members at the fire- Victoria, our fabulous cook who prepared meals before and after the three days of solitude, and Rose, the Shaman who was leading the quest. I saw them while I walked down the hill to get to the pond so I was aware that they were there but I was not allowed to interact with them in any way. None of the other "Questers" were there.

I sat in a little folding chair directly in front of the raging fire and the serene little pond. All was quiet and calm on this gorgeous summer morning in August of 2011. It was quite early and it seemed as though the creatures of nature decided to sleep-in that particular day.

The fire was mesmerizing. I stared into the fire for a few minutes, completely lost in its flickering beauty. Something in the periphery caught my eye and caused me to deflect my gaze to the pond. Over the last few minutes several dragonflies and a few swallows came to fly over the pond. I watched them for maybe five seconds and then brought my attention back to the fire.

Again, I allowed myself to get lost in the fire. Since my perception of time was so altered during these three days I'm not sure if this segment of trance was two or twenty minutes in duration. When I again brought my gaze over the pond it was interesting to see that a sizeable layer of dragonflies had formed a short distance above the water and, roughly eight to ten feet above the dragonflies, were a layer of darting and diving swallows. The sun was now at an angle where its rays were reflecting and refracting off and through the dragonfly wings, creating a myriad of vibrant colors over the pond. It was really captivating but for some reason my full attention was drawn back to the crackling fire.

Yet again, I got fully engrossed by the fire. It was completely hypnotizing. **"Look up!"** It was as if someone shouted inside my skull. When I looked up over the pond I saw something I will never forget.

At this time there were likely hundreds of dragonflies circling in one unified direction above the water, all in one layer. Above them were now at least fifty swallows, circling in their own distinct layer, but in the opposite direction of the dragonflies. It was like two counter-rotating vortexes! Rainbows of light were everywhere because of the multicolored dragonfly wings. I felt like I had been transported into another dimension, another realm. Words cannot capture how magnificent this was!

"This is miraculous," I thought. I desperately wanted to look at Victoria and Rose and see if they were observing what I was observing but I knew I needed to honor the agreements I had made going into the solitude. I would just have to wait and ask them about that morning once we all reconvened and broke our silence.

Once the three days of solitude ended, and the full group was reassembled by the fire, Victoria came up to me and said, "I've got to tell you, Phil, that morning at the pond was miraculous!" I simply replied, "What do you mean?" Victoria then stated, "Phil, you came and all of that came. The moment you left, all of that left. That was all YOU, Phil!" While Victoria was relaying this to me, Rose was standing a few feet away smiling and nodding, with teary eyes.

As Victoria said this to me, I got goose bumps (truth bumps) from head to toe and my whole body began to buzz. That one experience caused something deep within my soul to activate (reactivate?). It was like I was being reminded **who** I really am and the true power I possess. This was not an ego-driven awareness. This was a soul-level epiphany! I was made aware that **everyone** holds within them this vastness and power.

I share this experience because I firmly believe that MFR played a key role in the unfolding of this event. Firstly, as noted above, it was John's repetition of "you cannot grow in your comfort zone" that opened me up to embarking on a Vision Quest. Secondly, I believe that the six years of MFR I had experienced up to that point got my fascial system into a more fluid, open, and receptive state so my vibration could resonate with and attract such an event.

In addition to the Vision Quest, I have done many other workshops and seminars over the past several years to stretch the confines of my comfort zone. I have gained great insights and grown via my work with Inner Journey Seminars (www.innerjourneydc.org), Landmark Education (www.landmarkeducation.com), I Am Light (www. IAmLightMeditation.com), and work with Amun Brown (www. amunbrown.com), to name a few. I also continue to repeat all of John

Barnes' seminars and will continue to repeat them indefinitely. For me, learning and healing is a life-long journey and commitment.

In this upcoming phase of my life I am taking steps to work less and play more! I am in the process of converting the large detached garage at my new house into TAVO Total Health clinical space. By eliminating my commute and drastically slashing my overhead expenses, I will be able to maximize my work time and create better work-life balance. This will also allow me to achieve another life goal – become a father. After 15 years together, Jeff and I are eager to become parents via either adoption or surrogacy. Working from home will afford me the ability to be a stay-at-home dad.

It's also a goal in this upcoming phase to optimize my physical and fascial fitness! The last several years have been remarkably busy and in that busyness I've allowed my commitment to my best health to slide. I, like you, am only human. Once my new home clinic is complete I will be dedicating at least one hour per day to self-treatment of my fascial system and to maximizing my physical fitness. Since I no longer have chronic daily pain, thanks to MFR, there is no reason why I cannot be healthier in my forties and beyond than I was in my twenties! As noted earlier, I already FEEL better at forty than I did at twenty.

It is my hope that reading my story has benefitted you in some way. I'm also confident that the stories shared in Section 2 of this book will touch, move, and inspire you! Once you complete reading this book, you will have a better understanding of your fascial system and how attention paid to it may positively impact your life.

As John Barnes stated in his Foreword to this book, "The 'inner journey' is not the most important journey, it is the only journey!"

One of Phil's clients share...

Juliette

At the heart of my web is a small miracle, a baby we thought would never come. Our first child was born in 2001, and we had very much hoped for a second. My husband and I had tried to conceive for five years or so and, thinking it would never happen, had moved it to the back of our minds. My uterine lining was too thin for implantation. This was where I found myself in January 2011. In the previous year I had visited Phil to work on lower back pain. He would be working on my leg, and it would feel as though an electrical charge was running down my arm, or that he would be able to sink right through my body to the table below. Phil discovered that my pelvic girdle was being pulled out of alignment on an almost continual basis by my C-section scar. This explained why, when I rode my horse, I could not get my knees to align on the saddle, and also explained my lower back pain. Each time I left my MFR sessions feeling taller and lighter. I felt as if I could glow. I was finally starting to fix a problem that a chiropractor had worked on for years and been unable to change.

So back to the day in January 2011: snow was falling, schools were closed and my daughter was desperate to go sledding. A couple of the neighborhood kids were already out on the slopes. A young tree had fallen across the path, creating a major hazard. I went to get the saw, and removed the tree. By that evening I was in considerable pain and could barely walk. The next day I hobbled in to see Phil. This time I had really twisted my pelvic girdle. For the first few days the pain was excruciating, even with the painkillers and muscle relaxants my internist prescribed and which I took reluctantly. However after each visit I stood a little taller and the pain receded for longer. Phil gave me exercises to do at home, and I made a surprisingly fast recovery. I continued to work on my C-section scar and the tightness in my abdomen over the next few weeks and months.

At the end of July 2011, to my joyful surprise, I discovered I was ten weeks pregnant! I am sure that there were many contributing factors; however the biggest change I made was to pay my body attention. I tried so hard to listen to the tightness around my uterus, to soften the hard tissues around my scar, to tell the muscles holding my pelvis to relax. I am sure that all the MFR work Phil did, and the home exercise program he gave me, increased the energy flow to my uterus, increasing its health and vitality.

Now we have a very active 12 month old girl, who is the apple of her sister's eye, and very much the center of our family. Every so often my body complains about everything I've put it through, but Phil's assigned home exercise program generally resolves the issues. I think I'm stronger and more in balance than I have ever been!

Section Two:
MFR Therapists' Stories

Ann Devlin-Low, BA, MAT, LMT

Montgomery County, Maryland
annflahive@comcast.net

Reverence for Life

My inevitable journey to John F. Barnes Myofascial Release began in high school biology. It was a tough class, but I became more and more engaged as the intricacy and complexity of the web of life began to emerge in epic proportions. Peering into a microscope for the first time and seeing one-celled amoebas and paramecia swimming around under the slide, I was transfixed. Dissecting a frog, I had my first glimpse into the delicate internal order of nature. The enthusiasm of my teacher about her subject heightened my learning experience, and her clear blue eyes added to my wonder and made a permanent impression in my psyche.

Stage two of my education was a liberal arts degree with a major in literature and minor in music. I wanted to feel deep into the meaning of human life — who are we, where do we come from, and where are we going— and the humanities delved into human nature in more complex and subtle ways than science with its preoccupation on measurement and theory.

I followed up my BA with an MAT in English and a teaching career: 11th grade American Literature and Composition; ESOL in Switzerland, and GED English back home in the US. After teaching for several years, however, I noticed that I felt like something was missing. I had grown tired of being an authority figure, and I had become less interested in imparting knowledge to my students and more interested in understanding them.

Then a huge shift occurred in my life. I went to Esalen in Big Sur California for a week of transformational body/mind workshops that catapulted me out of teaching and into bodywork. The first class I took was "Introduction to Body Awareness" which included an introduction to quality of touch. The other class was Emotional Release. Everyone in that class had recently been through or were in the process of going through emotional trauma which they were currently working on in talk therapy, and they had signed up for this class to accelerate their therapeutic process in a physical instead of an intellectual modality. After four years of immersion in John F. Barnes Myofascial Release, I am convinced that the analytical therapies inhibit our feeling and intuitive senses so that we tend to get stuck in maze-like repetitive patterns of "trying to figure it out." Body therapies open up unresolved feelings stored in our fascia so that we can release them.

The format of the class was that the group leader, a former Jesuit priest, would ask each of us to tell the group about an emotion that we were holding inside and wanted to release. He would then create a setting that would facilitate that release.

On the first day, I volunteered to do some anger work. The scenario was me at one end of the room and, at the other end of the room, two vertical cot mattresses one behind the other held up by two very strong looking men. I was to run across the room as fast as I could, shouting and waving my arms around if I wanted, and charge full force into the mattresses with all the gusto I could muster. I went for it big time and I knocked the mattresses over! I am 5'8 and weigh 130 pounds. Wow, that was exhilarating!

After class that day I went down to the ocean side massage deck for a therapeutic massage, I told the massage therapist about my anger release, and she soothed and balanced me. Throughout the session I kept wondering how she had learned to do that.

Towards the end of the Emotional Release class I did some grief and closure work centered around my loss of a child from a tubal pregnancy. The setting created by the group leader was me lying on the floor on my back with my knees bent and my feet flat on the floor imagining that I was holding that baby in my arms . I was to sing a goodbye lullaby to my baby. I still tear up as I recall that experience. Somebody was finally getting to the depth of my sorrow. The group sat on the floor in a circle, surrounding me, and sang the lullaby with me. I struggled to sing because my throat kept tightening. The group kept singing. I tried to hold back my emotions by tightening my diaphragm. The group kept singing and the group leader gently put his hand on my diaphragm and told me to breathe. When I breathed, my emotions came pouring out and I sobbed and sobbed.

After class that day I again went down to the ocean side massage deck for a session of bodywork. I told the therapist that I had just experienced a very intense emotional release of grief and that I felt exhausted and empty. I lay down on his table feeling like Humpty Dumpty who had just had a great fall; I felt broken. The therapist used a gentle rocking technique and focused on my neck, rib cage and respiratory diaphragm which had been strained from sobbing and gasping for breath. After the session I felt all put back together again. "How had he done that?" I wondered.

I had been astonished and mystified by my bodywork experiences at Esalen. I had to learn how they did that. So when I returned home to the D.C. area, I looked around for massage schools, and a month later I began my training at Potomac Myotherapy Institute.

Twenty years later (and 624 hours of various continuing education later), I finally signed up for my first John Barnes Myofascial Release class. As I felt into the fascia of my practice partner's back, waited at the barrier, and felt it open, soften and flow, I was engulfed by that same sense of deep reverence for life that I had felt in high school biology.

Pelvic Alignment

A year after I took my first John F. Barnes MFR class, I decided to look for an Advanced John F. Barnes MFR Therapist who was also a Physical Therapist so that I could be treated and mentored. My intention was fourfold: (1) to receive MFR from an experienced therapist so that I could feel the work and refine my touch; (2) to learn how the Barnes approach would treat the remaining symptoms from my past injuries and surgeries; (3) to have access to physical therapy consultation as needed for myself and my clients; (4) to optimize my health.

My first appointment began with the therapist assessing my alignment as I stood in front of a body-length posture grid mounted on the wall. He took front, back and side view photos that I could look at, and much to my surprise, the right side of my pelvis was tilted forward and down about 20 degrees!

I had a medical history of right knee and right foot injuries and pain and had been previously prescribed a heel lift to wear in my left shoe because, I was told, my right leg was longer than my left. This assessment had been made by comparing length measurements of my right and left legs with a tape measure. I had been told that my right femur (the large long bone in the upper leg) was 3/8 of an inch longer than my left femur, and I had been walking around for 5 years with a heel lift in my left shoe.

My MFR therapist asked me if the leg length discrepancy had been measured with a radiogram because that would have been the only way to get an accurate reading. The placements of the tape measure on the boney landmarks of both legs, he explained, would have been too random to get an accurate reading. There had been no radiogram, I said, only a tape measure.

It was time for my first John Barnes MFR treatment. I was asked to lie down on the table on my back with my right leg dangling off the right side of the table. Standing on my right, my therapist placed his right hand on my lower right abdomen just above the pelvic ridge with his fingers pointing towards my head. He placed his left hand on my upper right leg, with his fingers pointing in the opposite direction from the other hand. In this cross hands position he waited at the barrier until my fascia began to open up and release, and then his hands sank in until they reached the next barrier. As my right leg elongated and my foot dropped slowly towards the floor, he elevated the table to make more room for my foot to drop. I felt the entire right side of my body open up and release.

After the treatment, my therapist suggested that I very slowly stand up and very slowly walk several times around the treatment table. I felt unsteady as my inner ear tried to acclimate to my new pelvic alignment. He took another alignment photo in front of the wall grid and my pelvis was even – horizontal to the floor! It was time to throw away my heel lift! My legs had not been different lengths; my pelvis had been out of alignment!

That first MFR session had readjusted my alignment and brought me to a place of natural balance. It had also permanently anchored what I had learned in MFR class about checking pelvic alignment before every MFR session.

Restrictions Caused by Scar Tissue

A Structural Integration therapist had once suggested to me that scar tissue from my abdominal surgeries might have branched out to my right hip, pulled it out of alignment, which then pulled my right knee and foot out of alignment. I had been aware of fascial restrictions and imbalance in all three of these areas. I had been in physical therapy for six weeks for knee pain and instability and, before that, I had had two foot surgeries for Morton's neuromas.

Consequently, in my next MFR sessions we began to explore the surgical scarring in my abdomen. My therapist found more than a few areas of excruciating tenderness where I could hardly tolerate any pressure at all. I had had no awareness that they were there; all this pain in my abdomen came as a complete surprise to me.

My first MFR homework assignment was to find one of these spots and to begin to soften and open it by placing a soft yellow MFR treatment ball on it and lying on top of the ball on the floor or on my bed. He said I could support my body with my forearms if I needed to, which I did. And I could let air out of the ball to soften it, which I did. He also suggested that I breathe into the painful area and see if any memories or feelings came up. I went home and began treating the area the next morning. It was very painful, and feelings did come up – feelings of anger, fear, grief and loss.

My two abdominal surgeries had been the result of two ectopic pregnancies. As a result, I had lost two babies, and twice I had almost lost my life. As I lay on that yellow ball and began to feel these feelings, I knew that I did not want to go there. I also realized for the first time that these memories were stored in my fascial web, deep in my subconscious. I had work to do, but I didn't want to do it. I shared this experience and these feelings with my MFR therapist who encouraged me to feel the feelings and do the work in my own time frame, taking as long as I liked and/or needed. He said he would be there if and when I decided I was ready to go deep into these physical and emotional restrictions and release them. I knew he was right, and I remembered from Jungian analysis that repressing the unconscious (as Jungians call it) often leads to illness and pathology.

A year or so after I had started receiving MFR, I went in for my MFR session one day knowing that I was ready to go deep into the myofascial restrictions of my tubal pregnancy scars and release them. I told my therapist that I was ready, and he said that he was ready, too. As I lay on the treatment table, I saw myself in an operating room on the operating table surrounded by several figures in green scrubs with surgical masks covering their noses and their mouths. One of them began to palpate my abdomen and probe around. I lay there quietly, just as I had done thirty years before under general anesthesia. Then the surgeon reached for a scalpel and moved towards me with it in his hand. I felt my whole body go rigid with terror. I began to whimper and beg and plead with him over and over again, "Please don't take my baby...please, please don't take my baby...don't take my baby!" I felt the scalpel begin to cut into my abdomen and I began to cry and cry and cry, and my crying became louder and louder and I was gasping for breath, crying and shouting, "Don't take my baby, I want my baby!!" And my crying became more and more hysterical.

I have a vague memory of time passing and the surgeon quietly saying to me, "I had to take your baby; it was either you or the baby." After slowly taking that in, I began to settle down, and I felt a gradual lifting of a huge burden off me. I had finally been able to relive the traumatic experience of my tubal pregnancy surgery, an experience that had been buried deep in my fascial memory for thirty years. I remembered when I had come home from the hospital, I had sat in front of the window watching all the children walking to school and crying my heart out. An emotional release at Esalen had helped, too, but this reliving of the actual event had gone so deep and had been a huge letting go of all those pent up feelings. I felt exhausted, elated, and much much lighter.

My Childhood Web

I was an introspective only child. My parents were very conventional and highly respected in the community so my childhood web was filled with social expectations of my saying and doing all the right things – being a good little girl. Or as we in the MFR community might say, I grew up in a straightjacket. I had been born on a Sunday and my grandmother said that Sunday's child was full of grace, but my mother said, "there was a little girl who had a little curl right in the middle of her forehead. When she was good, she was very very good, but when she was bad she was horrid." Enter into my childhood web: confusion, frustration and anger inside a straightjacket.

My "honor bead" my first summer at camp was for "Fortitude" – fortitude already at age 10! Armor at age 10? Armor to protect me from a respectable inhibiting upbringing. A lot for a young girl to try to figure out. Lucky for me, however, my mother sent me off to that overnight camp for girls seven summers in a row which gave me a chance to define and develop myself in sports and the arts and social activities. With about 50 girls my age, half that many counselors, and as many younger girls as counselors, I experienced sisterhood. I was okay at sports, but I excelled in swimming, earned my WSA, and taught swimming the last two summers that I was there. I was also recognized for talent in the performing arts in our yearly musical productions. And, I was elected as team captain of the Birches- one of the two teams that competed against each other all summer. That summer my honor bead was for leadership and the counselor who presented me with that bead wrote for me:

> A tree of the fullest blooming
> A leader from her heart
> In every way the birch tree
> And never will from there depart
> Bending never breaking
> Go on!

I was 17 years old, I had survived my childhood, and I would be ready to leave home after one more year of high school. The confusion, frustration and anger from my early childhood had been mollified, but I still felt an uneasy need to be on guard, and at the final council fire of the summer I found out why. After it was announced that the Birches had won and my team had surrounded me with grins and tears and hugs, the eagle feathers of responsibility were awarded. The Pine team captain and I did not get one. I felt humiliated, dizzy, disoriented, and sick to my stomach. "When she was bad, she was horrid." I realized that we were being punished for a prank we had played against a bullying counselor. When she had dropped her canoe paddle in the lake and it had floated away, we had thought we were just fooling around when we picked up her paddle and headed back to shore with it. The lake was calm, we were close to the canoe docks, we knew she was safe, and we all knew how to lie forward on the bow of the canoe and paddle with both hands. But she didn't think it was funny. She got her revenge by making sure we were disgraced in front of the whole camp. I heard from some counselors that they had had a long hard-fought argument about this decision at the Council Meeting, and that Doc Ann, the camp founder and leader, had made the final decision. From that moment on, I hated that camp, I hated Doc Ann. And betrayal, shame and hyper-vigilance moved into the core of my web.

Formative biographical experiences: college and living abroad

My college life and early adult life were journeys away from conventionality towards originality. Curiosity and the conviction that "The unexamined life is not worth living" (Socrates) permeated my web during my college years, and learning became a lifelong passion. I made the first unconventional friend of my life in college; we developed an authentic web enriching friendship based on common interests and spontaneous open conversation on a wide range of topics including religion and philosophy. She, like me, had grown up in New England, but unlike me she had grown up in an open-minded family where creative inquiry and artistic expression were the norm. Her father was an architect, her mother an interior designer, and she and her sister were both voice music majors. She and I were co-presidents of the college choir, we sang in two small vocal ensembles, and we were both picked by Phoenix, our college's version of The Dead Poets' Society. Phoenix was an allegedly secret creative writing group that met by candlelight, published its writing in a small journal, and initiated new members by requiring them to speak for an entire day in rhymed couplets. During the Phoenix meetings and activities, we exchanged bewildering looks when we found the group daunting, but we went along for the ride and, in retrospect, I think its seeming weirdness stretched us. After all, to quote John Barnes, "We don't grow in our comfort zones."

Following college my parents sent me off to Ireland which my mother envisioned as a prestigious year of study abroad that would look good on my resume and in the local newspaper. Maybe it would also increase my chances of Junior League membership or even of "coming out" as a debutante. She was oblivious to my lack of interest, bordering on disdain, for these scenarios, and I have to chuckle about her thinking that a year in Dublin, Ireland would be considered by anyone as even the least bit prestigious. As it turned out when I had my first academic interview there, I learned that I had been registered as an "occasional student" which meant that I had not been assigned a supervisory tutor, that I would not be earning credit for the classes I attended, and that I could audit any classes and participate in any student activities. Auditing Irish Literature classes, singing in the college choir, and socializing in the convivial Irish pubs, I enjoyed my autonomy in Dublin that year. The Dubliners were lively and witty conversationalists and they sang their traditional Irish folk songs with passionate joy or passionate sorrow. Sometimes the men even wept during the historical ballads describing Ireland's long history of political persecution and attempted uprisings -- "the troubles" as they call them. Men weeping? I had never seen or even heard of men weeping openly like that and I was deeply moved. A universe of new possibilities was opening to me, the possibilities of people expressing their feelings openly like that, the possibility of me expressing my feelings openly like that.

When I returned back home to the U.S., my mother told me that she didn't know me anymore. How sad that must have been for her. She had had such specific expectations for the person she hoped I would become during my year abroad, and she no longer knew me. I barely knew myself anymore after that year in Dublin. I was stepping into my true personhood, my passionate Irish personhood.

My Evolving MFR Web

After practicing John F. Barnes Myofascial Release for four years, regularly receiving MFR treatments for three years, and taking nine MFR classes with three repeats, my clients and friends and I have noticed changes in my personality and behavior. I have become more receptive and less reactive, softer and less armored and defensive, more feeling and intuitive and less analytical, more present in the moment and less anxious about the past or the future, and more open and less critical. I feel consistently calmer, softer, more vibrant and more open than I have ever felt in my life. I also feel freer, I feel that I am living fully, and I know that MFR is not only my professional path but also my path for personal growth and enlargement of my soul.

In every MFR session we listen with our soft hands and layer by layer, we gradually sink deeper and deeper into the fascia waiting at the barrier to feel a softening and an opening. When we feel an opening we sink in a little deeper until we feel the next barrier and then we wait again. As the client's fascia opens up more and more and we slowly sink in deeper and deeper, fascial restrictions that have been limiting our client's physical, emotional and spiritual wholeness are being released. Listening with softness, waiting with patience, going deeper, feeling openness. Hours and hours and years and years doing this work can translate into internalization of receptivity, patience, softness, deepening and openness on the part of the MFR therapist. Reactivity, armor, argumentativeness, and analysis can begin to melt away.

Reactivity. One of the first changes I noticed after immersing myself in MFR was that I was becoming less reactive. A verbal or emotional reaction is an involuntary, impulsive, knee-jerk response that spontaneously erupts out of our subconscious. That is why after a reactive outburst, we might reflect, "Oops, I wish I hadn't said that," or, "I feel bad that I said that," or "Wow, where did that come from?"

When we are mindful - grounded and fully present in the moment - we are less likely to react and more likely to be receptive instead of reactive and to respond with awareness and presence of mind. We then might reflect afterwards, "Hmmm, I feel good about the way I handled that situation." How much more satisfying to realize that we have handled a situation well than to feel a pang of embarrassment or guilt because we know we have behaved badly!

Armor. Experiences of suffering and loss can cause us to put up barriers to protect ourselves from ever feeling hurt again. We might shut down emotionally and decide to always be strong and tough so that nothing can harm us. But if we do this, we cut ourselves off from other people and then we feel isolated, lonely and unwanted. If we back ourselves into a corner, our capacity to enjoy life and to live fully diminishes radically. Defensiveness can become a closed circuit of habitual behavior that limits our choices so that we become stuck and even self sabotaging. Conversely, when we open up, we are likely to see all the options and opportunities out there. Then we can move towards positive creative lives.

Argumentativeness. Outside of a court of law argumentativeness is not a highly regarded modus operandi in our culture. Argumentativeness can be excessive and aggressive. We feel frustrated, boxed in and alienated when an incessant barrage of words, ideas, and demands are aimed at us. A person who always has to be right and always has to win comes across as controlling, dominating and maybe even threatening. Improving our own listening skills and our awareness are effective antidotes to argumentativeness in others and in ourselves. As the saying goes, "We have one mouth and two ears for a reason." If we can learn to listen more patiently and more deeply to another person's point of view, we might learn something. And we need to be aware that obsessively and compulsively arguing our own point over and over again is a behavior pattern that leads to nowhere. It is a sign that we are stuck.

Options for neutralizing an argumentative situation aimed at us might be to say something like, "I hear you," "That's one way to look at it," "I get where you're coming from" or, when it is situation appropriate, "Thanks for the suggestion." I have found that the latter stops people in their tracks. They look a bit confused and are temporarily speechless. We can, of course, use the same replies to self dialogue. All of these options are better than remaining stuck in our own or someone else's unproductive alienating patterns of repetitive arguing.

I think therefore I am. In his Principles of Philosophy in 1644, Descartes wrote, 'Cognito, ergo sum." Earlier in 1637 Descartes had first published the same idea in his own French language, "Je pense, donc je suis." The Latin version caught on in the English-speaking world. Before Descartes, Plato had written about the 'knowledge of knowledge,' and Aristotle had also written extensively on the subject. In the 9th century the Hindu philosopher Shankarasharya posited, "No one thinks 'I am not.'" (Therefore, I must exist.) Criticism of Descartes' "I think therefore I am" include the argument that "Cognito ergo sum" is merely a syllogistic inference. Nietzsche criticized Descartes' theory because it presupposed the existence of an "I."

Western culture has had a pervasive tradition of belief that knowledge derived from thinking and reason was the only knowledge, and that all other knowledge was probably only imagination, deception or a mistake.

How encouraging and refreshing, then, when Albert Einstein, one of the greatest minds of our time, (and frequently quoted by John Barnes because their philosophies are so similar) veered off this beaten track of "I think therefore I am" with the following:

"The only valuable thing is intuition."

"Learning is experience. Everything else is just information. Information is not knowledge."

"The true sign of intelligence is not knowledge but imagination, Knowledge is limited, while imagination embraces the entire world and all there ever will be to know and understand."

"Education is what remains after you've forgotten everything you've learned in school."

"We can't solve problems by using the same kind of thinking we used when we created them."

"The measure of intelligence is the ability to change."

The Descartes approach with its emphasis on thinking and knowledge is not helpful on the MFR treatment table. Nevertheless, most new patients and clients initially insist on trying to analyze and label their discomfort or pain as they filter their first MFR experiences through their intellects asking: "What is this supposed to be doing?" "How long will this take?" "Why am I feeling buzzing in my right big toe when you are working on my left leg?" Early on in our lives we are taught that if we can just figure something out, we can take care of any problem, that there is an explanation for everything, and that if there is no proof, there is no truth.

John Barnes teaches us that there is no healing without feeling; feelings are central in MFR. Getting out of our heads and into our hearts and feelings is what Barnes' work is all about. When we have squirrelly new clients, we gently direct their attention to "Feel under my hands," then, maybe later in the session, "Breathe into the spaces under my hands," Or we might suggest that they send an image of a flower bud opening, or butter melting or lava flowing, etc. under my hands. Every client notices a soft opening/release of their fascia when they feel into it with their minds. That experience is a breakthrough for many people who have not felt such a clear mind-body connection before, and they all express their amazement.

"There's no healing without feeling."

I hear my therapist saying to me sometimes, "Stay with that feeling," which indicates to me that he has a clear sense that something is waiting to come up, that an emotional release is probably ready to surface. A release can come in different forms: spontaneous movement which we call 'unwinding'; shaking which we call 'thawing'; emotional release (crying, moaning, shouting, etc.). Afterwards one might feel lighter, freer, gentler, more at ease, enormous relief, etc.

When feelings come up outside the treatment room, we learn that it is always better to find a time and place to feel the feelings, to let them out and move through them rather than to repress them. Repressed feelings are restrictions in the fascia that can over time develop into disease and dysfunction.

Postscript

Although I am a process person more interested in the journey than in the outcome, I do like to consciously update my inner journey now and then looking for growth spurts and important shifts in my awareness.

Resolution of my mother issues. Since my mother's death I have learned a few key things about her that soften my judgment about her difficulty with parenting. One of my cousins recently told me that Grammy beat all three of her girls with abandon when they disobeyed her. Both my parents were very strict with me, and they used physical punishment to discipline me. My mother washed my mouth out with soap if I said anything that displeased her, and when my father was angry with me, he chased me up the stairs whacking my behind with a rolled up newspaper, a method that some people used to discipline their dogs. I have no memory of what I had done to trigger him or what words I had said to trigger my mother. Soon after my mother died, I went to visit one of her sisters to ask for her insights into who my mother was. She told me that my mother was the beauty in the family and the favorite of their father, and that she had had a major disappointment in love having set her sights on the wealthiest and most sought after bachelor in town who did not in the end choose her. My aunt told me that she thought my mother never got over that rejection. On the way home I remembered all the romance novels that my mother constantly read and now I realize the confusion and betrayal that she must have felt when her marriage dream did not come true.

The major breakthrough in my empathy for my mother came during an MFR session after I had told my therapist how terrified my mother was of thunder and how during a loud thunderstorm when I was around 5 years old, I was looking all over the house for her calling out "Mother ! Where are you ?!" and I had finally found her far back in her bedroom closet lying on the floor in fetal position looking terrified. She just stared at me and said nothing and didn't get up. That scared me a whole lot. I closed the closet door and walked away. I never asked her about that and she never brought it up. We didn't speak openly about things.

As I was lying on the treatment table after telling my therapist this story, I began to shake and I curled up really tight in a fetal position on the table. I was shaking and trembling and feeling so afraid, feeling real terror. My therapist told me to hold onto that feeling. I realized later that day that my mother was a very frightened person. Now I realize that she was not a deeply caring parent because she was narcissistic (which my Jungian analyst had one time explained to me), and she never gave up trying to climb the social ladder and had tried to do it vicariously with me. That was the birth of my empathy for my mother. The greatest gift she gave me in addition to the gift of life, was the gift of music. She was a pianist, and had been an organist and choir director, and she played her piano a lot in our house and introduced me to singing in a choir when I was very young and encouraged me to pursue my musical interests. Throughout my life I have sung in 13 choirs, choruses or chorales, and I have played the cello in an amateur orchestra.

Resolution of my tubal pregnancy losses. Several months after my tubal pregnancy surgery, my husband and I began to look into adoption. Eight months later we drove to Baltimore Washington International

Airport to meet the plane carrying our baby boy to us from Korea. I finally had my own baby in my arms. He was nine months old, very active and wiggly and into everything, especially pots and pans. I was overwhelmed with joy! A year and a half later we drove with our son to JFK in New York City to meet another flight that had originated in Korea that was carrying our 3 month old baby girl. Our family was complete. I felt complete. Our daughter is expecting our first grandchild, a baby boy in three weeks, and for the first time I am learning about pregnancy, childbirth, and breast feeding. I am feeling so much more connected now to women because I could never really engage in birthing conversations before because I knew nothing about it. The loss of a child is one of the most traumatic losses there is so I know the feelings of that loss will never totally disappear, but I feel that most of the heavy burden of that loss is gone.

Dear Reader,

Endings do not come easily to a process person like me because the jury is always out. Also, I am finding now that the more open I become, the more extraordinary my life experiences become so that I am reluctant to go about drawing any final conclusions.

It is my hope that what I have written in this chapter has resonated within your web. Maybe it has piqued your curiosity about Barnes' Myofascial Release which will, I assure you, profoundly enrich your life if you open up and think outside the box. It is my belief that we are often potentially on the brink of a miracle if we can just be open enough and aware enough to receive it.

I am excited by Barnes' myofascial paradigm that all the cells in our bodies are both interconnected and permeated by the fascial web, and I feel inspired by recent thinkers such as Bruce Lipton and

Ervin Lazlo who have opened scientific frontiers beyond 'survival of the fittest,' 'genetic determinism' and a 'mechanistic' universe. They all believe that interconnectedness and consciousness are the primary movers and shakers of our existence. Cell membranes have intelligence and consciousness moves the cosmos. Our webs are all energetically interconnected with one another and permeated by the cosmic web that we might envision as 'cosmic consciousness.'

There Was a Child Went Forth

There was a child went forth every day.

And the first object he looked upon and received with wonder, pity, love, or dread, that object he became.

And that object became part of him for the day, or a certain part of the day,

Or for many years, or stretching cycles of years.

And these become part of him or her that peruses them now.

- Walt Whitman, "Leaves of Grass"

A client of Ann Devlin-Low shares...

MFR healing stories often have a miraculous flavor about them: patients with years of pain and anxiety recovering and resuming normal lives; a young woman with a debilitating eating disorder finding inner peace; a middle-aged man with chronic back pain returning to hiking.

My MFR story is about maintenance which is also, I believe, a story worth telling.

I have a shoulder that tightens up every few months due to poor posture in the office environment. A dull pain manifests in my upper left shoulder, and tilting my head left or right is uncomfortable. It's not difficult to know why this condition reoccurs. I sit at my desk in a position similar to August Rodin's The Thinker. The twist in my body strains my shoulder muscles, causing the fascia to restrict. When the pain becomes uncomfortable, I have a session or two of MFR to release the tight spots.

The MFR sessions to release the shoulder restrictions follow a standard procedure. My practitioner first checks for pelvic misalignment which, like poor posture or incorrectly fitting shoes, can be the cause of symptoms anywhere in the body. Next the practitioner checks for spinal alignment: is the spine straight or curved side to side or front to back? She also checks for shoulder alignment looking to see of one side is higher than the other. It is interesting that she does these checks before even examining the shoulder itself! This is because MFR looks for the cause, not the symptoms. A restriction in the MFR web, or cloth, in one part of the body can result in a referred symptom to somewhere else entirely.

This brings me to an observation of my experience with massage therapy. The few times I did have a massage I never came away satisfied. The relief was immediate but short-lived, and because the underlying causes had not been addressed, the presenting symptoms returned. If a shoulder hurts because of referred pain from the pelvis, then treatment should first be applied to the pelvis not the shoulder. This is one of MFR's remarkable advantages: the practitioners look for the cause and explore the patient's body until they find it.

My youngest son has a phenomenal talent for playing the piano. His style reminds me of Billy Joel. I thought to myself, "If my boy can play piano with just a few lessons, then I can learn to accompany him on the drums with just a few lessons myself." Therefore at the age of fifty, I had decided to take up the drums. I signed up for a few lessons at the music store. My mellow teacher with a raspy voice explained to me that I needed to place my left foot on the high-hat pedal and the right foot on the base drum pedal (one was higher than the other, and one was lighter than the other) one heel on the floor and one heel off, while bending the knees at particular angles. It was all very complicated, and I was feeling extreme pressure in my inner thigh. It wasn't long before I was feeling a significant cumulative injury. I was limping and complaining, but I knew that a series of MFR sessions would relieve the condition, as it did. This is why, for me, the Barnes MFR healing doesn't fall under the category of 'miraculous'. I know that it works!

I did have a surprising experience with MFR that highlighted the connection between emotions and the myofascial web. I have a struggle with a stepmother whom several psychologists have described as a narcissist—just like the stepmothers in the fairy tales. I feel fortunate that she came into my life late enough that I could see through her tactics, but the damage she caused to my relationship with my father, which had been solid until then, is very difficult for me. I mentioned the feelings of anger and loss to my MFR practitioner, and she dedicated a session to treat the condition. For the first time, she worked on my face. Almost immediately, I started breathing deeply and felt a draining. I repeated several times, "It's great to be free." The session didn't eliminate the step mom situation, but it clearly did bring me what seemed like almost instant relief. When the session was over I felt that there was no energy left in my body. The release had been so intense that I needed to sit in my practitioner's backyard for ten minutes to recover before I drove home.

Setting is important to me for MFR and all alternative therapies. I feel extremely fortunate that my MFR practitioner works in her own home. The neighborhood is quiet, she doesn't book her clients back-to back, natural light enters through a large window, and her backyard abuts an open space full of trees which give an added dimension to the treatments.

One sensation I feel during almost every MFR treatment is a 'still point.' About fifteen minutes into the session, my breathing is quiet, my thought stream is still, and my muscles feel entirely relaxed. This quiescent state lasts for a few minutes and then my body's rhythms pick up again. This still point cycle is extremely helpful for people like me who suffer from anxiety and who are always pursuing some goal. Just recalling the feeling of the still point during the day helps to calm the nerves.

At age 52, I take no medications, stand on my head, see a traditional physician once a year for hangnails, and drive my beautiful long-suffering wife up the wall with my insistence on a vegetarian diet and pleas to turn the volume down on the television. But I am aware that even this healthy lifestyle is not enough to keep away the blockages that can throw us into illness. I have found that MFR treatments in a calm setting keep me at balanced energy levels and purge the physical and emotional toxins that can build up inside of anyone. For me MFR is a wonderful healing modality to maintain my good health, and to prevent illness.

Derek Metzler, MPT

Richmond, Virginia
RESTORE-PT, Inc.
info@restore-pt.com

In December of 2009 I attended my first John F. Barnes Myofascial Release course in Orlando, Florida. As I think back on the first five minutes of John's Lecture, I can easily recall that experience as a huge "aha" moment that would shift the direction of my life both professionally, as well as personally. I have had a few tipping points in my life where everything afterward seems so dramatically different, that my life beforehand seems unrecognizable to me. This moment was one of those radical shifts that began a wonderful journey that continues for me today. To understand that shift, I must take you back to the beginning of my career as a physical therapist.

I graduated in 2000 from the University of Pittsburgh with a Master's of Physical Therapy degree. Excited to finally begin my career that I worked so hard to achieve, I was hired by a large corporate outpatient physical therapy provider as a staff physical therapist. Like many professionals green around the edges, I remember just trying to stay above water most days. I was seeing patients at 15 minute intervals with ever increasing corporate pressure to be more productive. I remember the early twinges of disillusionment that I quickly set aside as just beginner's frustration that would fade as I gained more confidence and experience. The twinges, however, instead of disappearing, began to get stronger and stronger. This was not what I thought I signed up for, was it?

In an attempt to squash the ever increasing frustration and anxiety that was growing day by day, I moved around from clinic to clinic within the region of my employer thinking that a change in setting would shift how I felt about my career choice. I took as many continuing education courses that were offered by my company in order to gain the confidence that I thought was missing. If I could learn enough, do enough, find the right setting, the pit of anxiety in my stomach would cease to grow and I would settle into my career and life would go as I had always hoped it would. It never happened.

I woke up most mornings in a state of dread. It was like this cloud of heaviness that followed me throughout the day would grow and grow, enveloping me until I fell into bed at night exhausted from the fight of it all. I hated my job. I hated what I had become. I felt like a fraud, a failure. I was stuck. I became obsessed with trying to find a new career. I wanted to feel good about what I was doing. I wanted to feel like I had a purpose. It all just felt so wrong. Understand that I tried hard to help the people who came through my door as best I could with the tools that I had. It just never felt like it was enough, like we were just scratching the surface. We were treating the symptoms, not the cause. The root of the problem always seemed beyond my reach. As if we were treating a mindless machine. If we just turned this screw and twisted that bolt and in the correct order, then all would be well and patients would leave better for the experience. That did happen of course, but it seemed as though it didn't happen as often as it should. The bar, in my opinion, was set way too low and I was a part of it. The disillusionment began to grow toward apathy as I was stuck and saw no way out at that moment in time.

Life continued on, much of it in a mechanistic manner, until I finally said enough was enough. I found my way out. A college friend of mine was involved in another business and had an opportunity for me. I took it, walked away from my career as a physical therapist with no intention of ever returning. That moment was significant for me, taking the action to change my circumstances empowered me in a way that I had not experienced in my life up to that point. It was also at that time that I met my wife who was and has been my biggest supporter. Without her love and support, I would not be where I am today (more on that later).

Looking back on this interim period of my life, I have come to view it as a time of preparation for the next step which just happened to be my journey into MFR. Of course, at the time, I had no idea what lay ahead. After a few years, and a couple of moderately successful business ventures, things began to shift. I could feel the contentment that I had immediately after quitting my career, begin to crack and fade. There was a familiar rumble that I could feel in my gut as the anxiety began to return. Chaos was growing in both my personal and business life. My wife, whom is my partner in every way, began to feel it as well. The business we were running was stressful and draining. It provided us a living but very little meaning or purpose. That old sense of incongruence was building.

Chaos was continuing to grow. Relationships were shifting; both professionally, as well as, personally. It was an incredibly uncomfortable time period in our lives. We knew that change was necessary and that we could not continue in the direction we were going. We had no idea what was next. I spent much of my time trying to figure out how we were going to get out of the business we were in. Nothing seemed right. It was a goal of mine and my wife's to continue to work together, but in what manner we had no idea. She is an RN, but after a successful nurse management career, had also stepped out of healthcare in search for something different. I once again found myself in this place of feeling stuck, not knowing what I wanted and trying very hard to avoid what I did not want.

Once again, life marched on mechanistically. Our business at the time was in renovation and remodeling and, like many others in this field, was not immune to the economic slowdown that began in 2008. The phone just stopped ringing. Fortunately, I had a degree in which I had a viable way to make a living, and I had kept my license to practice active. So, I suddenly found myself immersed back into my profession as a physical therapist. It would have been something that I would have greatly resisted just a year before, but for some reason my resistance had softened and there I was back at it; part-time at first in a setting similar to those in which I practiced earlier (without the corporate pressure).

As my license was coming up for renewal, I needed more CEU's to meet my state requirement. My wife, whom is responsible for most of the good things in my life, found John F. Barnes courses online and suggested that I take one that was in Orlando at the same time that we had a long planned trip with my extended family to Disney World. I recalled the numerous advertisements picturing the white haired, bearded man with a pony tail that I passed over many times, thinking that these were not for me. Too far out on the fringes, I thought! This time, I didn't question it. It sounded like a great idea. After all, we could combine it with our trip we had already planned. So I signed up for MFR 1 with little idea of the changes that would be on the horizon.

I found myself sitting in that first class with a mixture of emotions. Excitement to find something that seemed to resonate in a very deep place within me, as if I had known this new information all along, yet it was inaccessible to me until that moment. I felt anger that my education up to that point had ignored something so important and vital. A sense of surprise that I found myself, at that moment, in a place that I was meant to be and many of the events in my life and career seemed to have been pointing me there all along. A sense of purpose, as if what I was meant to do and be just plopped into my lap so easily and surprisingly it was startling. I had spent so much effort seeking, trying to figure out my purpose, turning over every rock, and here it landed on me seemingly without any of my own interference. Little did I know that this is one of the great lessons that I would learn through my journey into MFR. Without force, and in many cases with very little effort, seemingly miraculous changes can occur in our lives and in the lives of our patients.

With renewed excitement and a new found perspective, I returned home to practice what I had learned. MFR was a completely new way of looking at, treating, and managing the patients who came to see me. I threw myself into it, all but abandoning many of my former tools. With just a few things learned from just one weekend class I began to see results in my patients that I hadn't been able to achieve using the techniques learned from multiple years of manual therapy courses. I was hooked from the beginning.

Over the next year, I took several more courses, each one adding to my understanding of John's work with ever improving outcomes with my patients. It was extraordinary because it works and patients were so grateful for the changes that were occurring for them. Often the changes were dramatic and surprising to both me and the patients.

One of John's intentions, in each of his courses, is that we as therapists receive the treatment, as well as, give them. The purpose of receiving MFR treatment as a therapist goes far beyond merely understanding what the treatment feels like. MFR treatment can change you at a very deep level, both physically and emotionally. I began to understand this during that first year of exploring MFR. I could feel myself shifting my beliefs, my emotions, as well as my relationships. It was mostly like a rumbling that was occurring deep within me. Much of it seemed outside my control. It was what I have come to know now as the chaos before a major shift. It is rather like the opposite of the calm before the storm.

Many old feelings, things that I thought I had resolved were surfacing during and after treatment. The same thing seemed to be occurring in my patients. And when I gave myself permission to truly feel these things deeply, a shift would occur. My belief systems were shifting, and I was gaining more courage and clarity once the clouds of chaos would lift. Sometimes the shift would happen quickly, but often it would take time. Sometimes it seemed as if the chaos would not lift.

About a year after taking my first course, it was becoming clear to me that my wife and I would have to open our own physical therapy practice specializing in MFR. I was finding it more and more difficult to operate in a more traditional physical therapy practice setting. Again, I found myself at a point of intense internal conflict. There was part of me that wanted to take the leap into the unknown, and the other part was screaming in fear that it was not time and financially it made no sense. I was in a state of strong resistance for several months as the chaos once again seemed to be building around me. Finally, one day in a rather seemingly impulsive manner I offered my resignation.

"Leap and the net will appear." Much of MFR is about leaping into that place of the unknown. We are often so stuck in our patterns, both physically and emotionally, that leaping seems an absolute impossibility. Fear keeps us where we are, longing for something different yet unable to make the choice toward real change. This is often true physically, emotionally, and spiritually. I have found that in my life in order for real change to occur, the discomfort of where I am must exceed the fear of what is unknown. I am brought to a moment of choice in which there is no other possibility except to choose a new path or to remain in the old pattern repeating the same mistakes over and over and over.

MFR has brought me to the point of choice in a way like nothing else in my life ever has. Our fascial webs seem to become clogged with untruths about who we are, what we are doing here, and where we are going. It is an accumulation of conditions that we have accepted, roles that we have played, traumas that we have endured, and belief systems that were handed down and unquestioningly adopted. My web was full, inflexible, and weighted down with fear, anxiety, worry, anger, guilt, and frustration. Much of my life was driven by fear and the need to prove something. I was constantly attempting to feel better about myself, to feel worthy and deserving. In short, life was difficult. This was a pattern that drove my entire adult life and most likely much of my adolescence. In fact, I don't remember a time that I wasn't being driven by fear.

Yet, I was not aware of this. Sure, I felt my discomfort and was very good at running from it. I knew exactly how I didn't want to feel and spent great effort in attempts to squash those feelings. I just kept moving, numb, unaware, but moving. If I kept moving away from my fear, distracted and numb, I thought it would eventually tire and fade away. It never happened. Instead, each time, it would rear its ugly head and it seemed to grow larger and stronger. The pattern was repeating itself over and over and over.

As I continued to take MFR courses and receive treatment, I began to notice my patterns. Not just my physical patterns, but my emotional, relational, and spiritual patterns as well. As my fascial system would release, belief systems that were the engines of those repeating patterns would surface leaving me with a choice of whether or not I would challenge them. If the belief system was no longer serving me, I had to choose to let it go or continue to repeat the pattern. If I chose not to challenge the belief system, then the pattern would continue physically, emotionally, and spiritually as there appeared to be no separation to these components of my life. I also became aware that the pattern would often get worse and situations in my life would trigger me continually bringing me back to the point of choice; the stronger the resistance, the stronger the trigger. I was not being let off the hook. I had chosen a path toward change and growth and it was as if some force greater than myself was directing me toward that goal. I could no longer run from my pain. I was being taught to turn and face it instead. This was completely foreign territory. After all, pain is the enemy and we must fight it at all costs, right?

With MFR we are given the choice to stop running from our pain and turn towards it. In a gentle and non-forceful way, a skilled MFR therapist will help a patient to move into their pain in order to experience it, fully allowing the body-mind the opportunity to finally resolve it. The key here is, once again, the concept of choice. It is always our choice, as a patient, whether or not to let go of our resistance and feel into our pain. MFR creates the opportunity. It does not fix. It does not heal. Healing comes from within and can occur when we choose to move toward our discomfort, as well as, our fear. MFR can provide a space which allows this to happen.

I think that early in my experience as an MFR therapist, I did not fully grasp this concept. I thought that the power to heal came from the therapist and the tools he/she were using. If I could just take more classes and achieve greater aptitude, then my patients would be healing all over the place. I am sure you can feel my ego growing here. Yet, this is the beauty of truth. It has a way of revealing itself when you come up against a wall/barrier and after a bout of pushing finally drop your effort and surrender to the moment and "aha", the truth appears. As a therapist, it is not my job to fix, heal, manipulate, or even convince any of my patients that MFR is for them. It is my job to show up, get out of the way, and allow for the opportunity of healing. The rest is up to them.

These are the lessons that my wife and I learn every day in our MFR practice as we encounter many people whose lives are riddled with pain and trauma, much of which is far beyond anything that I have had to endure in my lifetime. MFR has given me back my courage and my compassion, and has allowed me to open myself to gently guiding these people back toward their pain and ultimately toward healing. My wife calls what we do a "scary privilege" as many people who come through our door choose to lay down the most vulnerable parts of themselves in a search for true healing. They allow us to walk with them through the often messy process of finding themselves emerging strong from the rubble. What an amazing thing to watch the light return in their eyes, once again hopeful that life can be more than what they have been living.

Two clients of Derek Metzler share...

I came to learn about MFR serendipitously. For fifteen years I had been experiencing stiffness and spasm in my low back after working in the yard or vacuuming for three hours or so. The stiffness and spasms would resolve in a day or two and I never sought any treatment for it because I really did not think there was anything to do other than exercise to get my back stronger (and I don't like going to the gym!). I work in the health care industry at a fairly high level and worried that if I did seek care I would be told I needed surgery and I did not want to go that route. I was somewhat limited in endurance but I was managing UNTIL... my middle son became a personal trainer and was helping me with a workout program. Yes, he got me going to the gym.

As I was going through the workouts I was finding I was having trouble with some of the back exercises and with more strenuous weight lifting. My son made sure I was using correct technique but this did not seem to make a difference. So off I went to a Sports Medicine Physician who found that I had a sort of frozen area around my left hip and pelvis. He referred me to Physical Therapy (PT). Even though I work in medicine I had little exposure to PT and did not know what to expect. I thought maybe some massage type work, possibly hot packs, and some exercise and that would be about it. I was wrong.

I was very fortunate to land with Derek. At the time he was in a traditional PT practice but he had found MFR and was incorporating this work into his practice. The difference in the two philosophies was evident from the beginning. Instead of fifteen minutes with the therapist, then fifteen with hot packs, and a few more minutes doing exercises, I had one hour of work with his hands stretching; pushing, pulling and moving not only my low back but anywhere else where I was feeling pain or restriction. I was given stretching exercises to do at home also. Within a few weeks I could tell there were changes not only in my back but also in my posture. I was standing taller and straighter.

I was also feeling some emotional tension at the time that I was attributing to menopause and work issues. Every session Derek would ask me how I was feeling and of course for a while the answer was "fine." He then began to explain little by little how MFR can sometimes cause old memories to rise to the surface as the old restrictions are released. So I began to share more of how I was truly feeling with him when he asked. By this time he had started his own practice and his exam room was very private. His wife was now working with him and is a Registered Nurse. She would assist him if the need arose. As several more weeks passed the emotional/spiritual tension was continuing to build. I felt I was going to pop I felt so full of it. I kept thinking it would just get better with time.

At this point Derek had given me a book by John Barnes on MFR that explained the emotional and spiritual connection between the fascia and the mind. It is a wonderful book, short and easy to understand. I soon realized I had some emotional work to do in the form of what MFR practitioners call unwinding. I had two sessions with Derek where I experienced this profound jitteriness after he had finished and this lasted about ten minutes or so. It felt just like I had too much espresso, but kind of scary too. After reading the book and in talking with Derek I found that this jitteriness is called thawing. The weird thing was that I felt better after that shaking stopped... for a little while.

We continued the work on my back and posture. I was getting better physically but I just kept having recurring thoughts of a bad memory from childhood that did not involve abuse but left an emotional scar. It would not go away; it even snuck into my dreams. At this point I knew I had to try unwinding even though I was pretty frightened and anxious about the thought of just letting go. I knew it would be ugly and loud but I had to get the shame, guilt, and pain out. OUT! And with Derek and Becky's help over several sessions it did come out. After the first session of unwinding I was so profoundly exhausted that it was twenty or thirty minutes before I felt I could safely walk down their stairs. It took a few unwinding sessions to get it out but it did come out and I was feeling better inside and out. My body was strong again and so were my emotions. We are not made to carry all our accumulated stress and pain around with us. If we don't get rid of that stress and pain, it will hurt us, in the form of bodily pain, headaches, high blood pressure, indigestion, depression, anxiety, you name it.

Well, since going through MFR and unwinding I can truthfully say that I am not the same person I was before MFR! Not to say that I don't experience stress or pain, I certainly do, just not in the same way. I am much more in tune with my body and I now know when it is appropriate to seek out care. I am much more emotionally tuned in to myself and have made changes in my home and professional life to better manage my stress. I did not change careers or husbands or children either! It has been over two years since I first met Derek and was introduced to MFR. It is difficult to remember how badly I felt before MFR. I struggle to try to find the words to express where I am now compared to my previous state of being. Let me just say that I feel confident, free from old memories that haunted me but no longer have any power to influence my well-being. And that is a good feeling.

In conclusion I would recommend MFR to anyone needing therapy or who might be facing surgery. Certainly not everyone needs to unwind like I did. It just takes longer than fifteen minutes of hands on therapy once or twice a week to effect a change in muscle or fascia. You will get much more than that with MFR. You might just get some peace of mind along the way too.

Chronic pain engenders desperation, changing a person's entire outlook on life. I discovered this in 2007, when a simple act of moving some boxes of books triggered severe lower back pain that would not abate. When the experience began, I feared for the 'worst', as a similar episode some years before had led to a period of six months of chronic pain before the condition eventually settled to manageable levels. Little was I to know that this recovery path was to take more than four years of misery. As I neared the fourth year, I remember quite lucidly stating that if a doctor could propose a treatment that had a 90% chance of successfully stopping the pain and a 10% chance of killing me, I would take the risk in a heartbeat.

There are no words that can meaningfully define pain. At best, it is like describing a color – quickly becoming self-referential and relative. I had known horrible pain before, having experienced a sports injury that left me writhing with a twisted testicle that cut off the blood supply to my abdomen. So I felt that I could withstand the more modest back pain, by comparison, as doctors measure it on an abstract scale of 1 to 10. The problem is the constancy. It is like Chinese water torture: never allowing the victim to be free of the torment, day after day, year after year. I could not sit without significantly flaring up my back, so I took to standing all day at work. I would stand for international flights, sometimes upright from the time the seat belt sign came off until we began to descend eight hours later. Simple pleasures of playing with my children or modest exercise became impossible without triggering increased pain.

I received every manner of diagnoses and misdiagnoses, from bulging discs to arthritic joints. Yet no form of treatment seemed to have a positive impact. I had no less than seven cortisone injections and nerve blocks. I worked with three neurosurgeons, two chiropractors, four physical therapists, two osteopaths, two acupuncturists and countless specialist physicians and alternative medicine practitioners. I ingested or was injected with every kind of anti-inflammatory or pain medication that was available with little or no impact. Only through narcotic pain medications was I able to find some relief, and then only for short periods of time and with awful side effects. Twice I nearly resorted to surgery, only to be told it was a low probability outcome. Before I finally found Myofascial Release, I was exhausted, out of options, on the verge of quitting the workforce and scheduled in a last ditch attempt at relief to undertake a painful procedure to burn off all the nerves serving my lower back.

Ironically, the first signs of the possibility of treatment came not from a physician or physical therapist, but from a non-expert who had experienced a similar injury years before. He had finally found relief through careful stretching regime recommended by an Argentine doctor and modified by the patient. I tried his regime, and though it did not make a significant impact, the fact that there was any change in my pain level was a thought-provoking breakthrough. Despite the failure to get any relief from past work with physical therapists, I reopened the book on non-invasive options, and through the research of a patient advisory service and a very good osteopath who supervised my overall treatment, I eventually found the practice of TAVO Total Health. There I came under the care of Derek Metzler and Phil Tavolacci, practitioners of John Barnes based Myofascial Release.

It would be misleading if I suggested that the journey that followed was easy or that the results were immediately apparent. For the first two weeks I endured treatment that was sometimes very difficult and often resulted in what MFR therapists call 'healing crises', flaring my back worse than when I came in. I again became skeptical, having been through so many failed treatment regimes that promised gain after increased pain. Then shortly after the second week of treatment I woke up one morning without the normal level of pain. Bit by bit, day by day, my back began to relent, releasing more of its propensity to spasm and flare up. Taking primary responsibility for my treatment, Derek came to understand my body intuitively in a way that was almost alien to me. Each layer of restriction brought a different phase of healing – sometimes releasing emotional bursts, sometimes spurring sudden energy or enervation. There is a point of surrender in your MFR treatment when you accept what will come without understanding why it works or needing to make sense of the pain and the healing. Derek once said to me that it's not important that someone believes in everything that is taught by MFR practitioners; you can take what works and leave an open mind for the rest.

I am still feeling my way along this path, but the journey is no longer a struggle of fear and disappointment. I am about 75% better than I was, fully functional in my work, and still making improvements. Sometimes, I have a bad day or even a bad week, with increased pain. At times I feel better and try things I used to be able to do. I went skiing with my children – and survived. I flew 18 hours to Africa without the unendurable pain that was the hallmark of my previous plane flights. Yes, the journey is not yet over, but I now face it with faith that I am and will be well.

KATHY MONKMAN, BSN, LMT

Tempe, Arizona
The Heart Space
theheartspace@yahoo.com

The world of Myofascial Release caught me by surprise. I was a practicing RN in an outpatient head injury rehabilitation facility and a part time massage therapist trading massages for haircuts in a busy salon. My then boss heard John Barnes, PT was coming to town to offer this course and asked me if I'd like to go to scope it out as an option for our neurological rehabilitation program. Little did either of us know this offer would change the entire course of my life and career.

My shameful little secret, at that time in my life, was that I was silently struggling with a severe anxiety disorder. I've typically been viewed as a strong person so most people had no idea about the burden I was hiding inside. I was broken and ashamed of it all at once. It was not a happy life for me.

I had received all kinds of traditional therapy, medication, hospitalization and was, as John Barnes says "rearranging deck chairs on the Titanic." I was 29 years old, and had been living with this debilitating condition for over two years. I was functioning but always guarding myself for the next panic attack, at times having a hard time leaving my home and, most definitely, leaving the city limits. I could not get on an airplane without being highly medicated or intoxicated. I lost hundreds of dollars having aborted many trips, sometimes right at the airport because I suffered extreme claustrophobia on planes. I walked off two planes unable to even stay for takeoff. I once spun out in a panic attack on a vacation because I was walking on a beach and saw too many clouds in the sky and that triggered a feeling of being "trapped".

As a former Psychiatric Nurse I knew the labels of what I was experiencing but had no idea how to deal with it. My Psychologist father, well meaning as he was, kept telling me I was going to have to learn how to manage this. But something greater was operating in me that said "you will not live with this the rest of your life, you need to find a way to heal this." So I went off all the medication and started looking around beyond my traditional scope as a Nurse. I was not even 30 years old! It was right about that time I found myself sitting in the front row in a seminar room listening to John Barnes describe to me a way out of this nightmare. I could feel it in my bones, if anything could truly resolve this, this was it.

So as serendipity would have it, I was so enamored with this work that the head injury facility took me off my nursing duties for the most part and set me up in a treatment room where I began practicing, and I do mean practicing, Myofascial Release with their patients. At the time I began, I had two courses under my belt: MFR 1 and MFR 2. And with that small foundation I treated recovering brain injured patients for an entire year. This was the best initial training ground I could have asked for. The brain injury patients taught me how to treat with MFR and I experienced the miraculous power of this work every day.

I can share one of many examples of learning by success that taught me the value of this distinct form of addressing trauma. We had a patient in our head injury program I will refer to as "John". John was the son of a physician and he had been living in Boston, had gotten engaged, had recently been accepted to a PhD program in another state. While he was walking home one evening, he was randomly and without provocation jumped by a group of street thugs and left for dead in the street. He suffered massive head injuries and had been in a coma for weeks.

By the time John entered our program, it was toward the end of his rehabilitation. Yet he was still severely impaired. He had almost zero short term memory and had lost most of his long term memory as well. He hadn't remembered his fiancée since the accident and sadly, she had moved on with her life.

John was referred by the program to me because he had severe ambulatory issues. If you were to see him on the street, I think the average person would think he had Cerebral Palsy by looking at his gait. So I was to treat him with Myofascial Release to see if there could be any improvement.

The first time he came for treatment, I had to go fetch him in another building as he couldn't remember simple instructions moment to moment. I had to walk him over to my room. I remember standing with him in the room, giving him the instructions about getting disrobed and on the table, waiting a few minutes and knocking on the door only to find him still standing in the center of the room where I left him, having forgotten the instructions the moment I left the room. This is how we began. I was a novice at MFR but I knew to assess him for "hot, hard, or tender" areas. His entire body felt like a mass of concrete. It was more a question of where to begin for me.

Once during a session, as my soft spa style music was playing, John asked if I had any rock and roll music. I did not but my stereo had a radio in it so I found a rock and roll station and played it for him during his session. One day he asked me the number of the station on the radio.

In the first weeks of treating John, I still had to retrieve him from his previous appointment and walk him to my room but gradually I noticed I would walk out of my last treatment and find him sitting in the waiting area all on his own. Then I noticed he was preparing himself for the sessions and getting on the table without need for instruction. I'll never forget the day I walked in the treatment room to find John on the table ready for his session listening to rock and roll music on the stereo. He had changed that station all on his own! His body was softening, his gait was improving and his cognitive function was returning all at the same time. I was astonished!

About two months after John's first session with me, I sat in on his discharge meeting with the entire staff. He was ready to go home to live back with his parents in a nearby city. I asked for the Physician's notes to be passed to me and the words I read were "John has experienced a quantum leap in cognitive improvement in the last month and is ready for discharge". Quantum leap! The one and only thing that had been added to his treatment regime was MFR!

Being a novice still, I kind of bookmarked those words in awe, thinking that could be the reason! Of course after 23 years of practice and seeing a multitude of miracle stories like this one, I know it was the X factor. John had not been touched with loving care throughout his course of rehabilitation. That alone undoubtedly helped his mind release some of the trauma and come back in to focus.

A year after I started my MFR journey with that head injury program, it was sold and many of us were laid off. I was given the opportunity to either go back in to Nursing or continue the MFR work. I took the leap at that time and opened my own MFR practice, fueled with the successes I'd seen over the last year and believing this was my life's work.

But I was still struggling personally with anxiety. I was a true believer, but still struggling.

A couple of years after I started my practice I received a phone call that John Barnes was thinking of opening a clinic in Sedona AZ, right up the highway from me in Tempe. They were just inquiring if I could pass along some basic info about licensing and things like that. I was elated! I had traveled back to Pennsylvania to intern with John Barnes but now he would be right in my backyard!

From that point on, the MFR courses started being offered more and more in Sedona which meant I didn't have to board a plane and could have easier access than most. I started signing up and taking every course I could manage. But still, silently and secretly I was suffering with anxiety. Suffering, but still believing. Many times just leaving the city limits and driving to Sedona was an excruciating journey for me. Many times just staying seated in my chair in the seminar was the biggest accomplishment of the entire weekend. I was in a near constant state of fight or flight to some degree in many areas of my life, particularly when traveling. But I almost never experienced these symptoms in my treatment room. It was my one refuge from that tsunami always waiting to engulf me.

I heard John Barnes once say "you will notice that your symptoms lessen in severity over time and the episodes of pain become less frequent". I did start to notice this. I would clock my anxiety attacks and noticed the space between them was getting broader. I also noticed the severity and lengths of the attacks become lesser. I would get very discouraged when an attack would hit, feeling like I'd not made any progress, but when I stepped outside of it and noticed the changes that had occurred over time, I would feel a sense of optimism. If this thing could change at all, maybe one day it would go away.

I'm not saying I recovered from anxiety in the most accelerated way. It took me about 8 years total. In hindsight I might have done some things differently, like do more intensive individual therapy vs. working out all of my restrictions and issues in seminars. But I did recover 100%! And I know it was Myofascial Release and clearing the trauma out of the matrix of my cellular memory that allowed this recovery to happen.

I used to be able to tell you the last day, exact moment, exact location of my last panic attack but that's been long forgotten now. It's been well over 10 years. I experience fear and apprehension like a "normal person" now. But I'm no longer plagued by the black cloud of panic. I travel everywhere I want now and live one of the most abundantly free lifestyles of anyone I know. I shudder to think of where I would be at age 53 now if not for the miracle of MFR. To this day I don't know what "caused" it and I don't care. I am free!

I was once a person who was crippled, grounded, and unable to board a plane or travel from my home without severe discomfort. Like many people I had severe anxiety speaking in public, even simply introducing myself in a large group. I've now evolved into a person who recently boarded a plane with comfort and ease in order to fly to a distant state to appear on a national talk show! I was invited to discuss past traumatic events in my life in order to help others. There is no longer even a shadow of the disorder that once controlled my entire life.

I now know that I have a road map to help others find their way clear of this debilitating condition. Just the very essence of my being and my recovery is that road map. My clients can feel safe in my confidence that they too can recover. Some people come to me specifically for anxiety conditions. I feel this seals my place of belonging on this planet and gives all that pain a sense of purpose. I believed, I patiently waited, and I kept stepping in to and through that suffering to find that light at the end.

In that spirit, I would like to share a poem that burst into my mind while giving an MFR treatment recently that, to me, describes an aspect of this healing process in a way that reflects my ability to now shine. I hope this sharing helps someone out there to unearth their inner light and embrace their unshakable brilliance as well.

Flawless
by Kathy Monkman

Try not
being
the bigger person.
When life's crushing blows
come,
be small.

Collapse.

Get smaller. Wait.

A perfect diamond won't apologize
for taking all that time.

It patiently pauses for
it's moment to shine on
The World.

The watch glancing, toe tapping
World.

So much pressure,
tick tock tick tock.

Waiting becomes
it's salvation.

Unearthed,

bursts
just one proclamation:

While you were busy being
disappointed
in my disappearance,

I was becoming
Flawless.

Francis 'Chino' Ramirez, DPT, MS, CPT

Springfield, Virginia
MYO Physiotherapy

I am Dr. Chino Ramirez, a physical therapist working in Northern Virginia. I have been in practice for almost 12 years; seven of which using John F. Barnes' Myofascial Release (MFR). Prior to learning MFR, I had worked in several outpatient-based orthopedic/sports medicine facilities; where I was considered to be a young up-and-comer in the area. Many saw me as an "ace" that could easily see 20 patients a day, 3-4 patients per hour, and could perform *skilled manual therapy* on patients to force frozen joints to move again; to make stiff necks and backs go into directions that they could not go to on their own; and to "call out" malingerers and fakers who insisted that they were in pain, in spite of what X-rays, MRI's and their physicians told them. Professionally, my peers told me that the world was my oyster; and the fact that I always had orthopedic practices and clinics knocking on my door (to sway and woo me to join them) reinforced this notion.

Personally, I was a young bachelor who wore his heart on his sleeve. I was paid well, lived a comfortable life, regularly went to the gym to body-build, and practiced various martial arts. As a physical specimen, I was quite imposing and impressive: there were few challenges that I could not overcome. I traveled to many places, and was often out in the town weekend after weekend celebrating life and trying to meet the ideal woman. My friends told me that I had it all, and that they, too, wished that they could have my happy and complete life.

What I grew to discover, however, was quite the opposite: as time passed, work not only bored me, but angered me. Inevitably, it was not unusual for me to hurl stacks of charts in the direction of our receptionists because, innately, I realized that seeing 3-4 patients per hour (day-in and day-out) was not only detrimental to them, but to me, also. Personally, I felt *empty*; as if my very existence had no substance. My personal relationships suffered. The burn out that I was experiencing at work began to seep into and mirror the burn out that I was experiencing in life. I began to quarrel more with family, with friends, and even began to think self-destructive thoughts. Surely, I had the problem here because I, apparently, had it all: a good job, a good life, a good physique. How could I not be happy when I had all of this? I needed big changes in my life quickly, if I were to survive.

As if by divine providence that summer of 2005, Phil Tavolacci asked a common friend of ours to reach out to me for an introduction. I had no idea who Phil was, only that he had worked in the same physical therapy clinic where I was currently working at that time. Co-workers and patients (previously treated by him) described a gentle, personable, intelligent man who had also become disgruntled with the confines that had been built around him and limited his professional and personal growth. He had recently ventured out to build what was then known as TAVO PT

& Fitness, a small clinic in the metro-Washington, DC area that emphasized 1-on-1 treatments with patients; focusing on *skilled manual therapy*.

We met; and I welcomed Phil's invitation to help him develop and grow his practice as a means to start anew. I was eager to see if a slower clinical pace would be better for me and to see if it would rekindle my love for my career. One request he made of me, however, was to be open to learning new clinical techniques and a new treatment philosophy. He told me that he had just started using a manual technique called Myofascial Release and that he wanted me to experience it both as a patient, and then as a therapist.

"Sure," I thought. "Why not?" From what I knew about Myofascial Release, all one needed were thumbs of steel, a gritty determination to overcome the resistance coming from the patient, and the mantra, "Relax, patient. Relax…" Besides, having already been practicing for a few years, I'd already picked up a few joint mobilization techniques that had worked for *me*.

And so I asked him: "Which company would it be: Travell? Great Lakes? Hands-On Seminars?" He answered: John Barnes. "You mean the bearded guy with the ponytail and leather vest?" Yep, that's the one.

I remembered receiving those brochures in the mail and seeing ads in various PT magazines: "Take your treatments to the next level," it said. MFR was supposed to be something that I could *add* to my current skill-set to improve my practice.

That December of 2005, I walked away from MFR 1 in Sacramento, CA with more questions than answers. What was supposed to *help* what I already knew actually *contradicted* what I had learned in PT school and in the clinic. Be *soft* when I touched or used *skilled manual techniques* on my patients? Wait 3 to 5 minutes to *slowly* sink in with just *one* technique? At that point in my career, 5 minutes was already getting close to wrapping up a whole manual technique treatment session! It quickly became apparent that I was not as *skilled* as I had thought when using manual techniques!

Something that really caught my attention during those 3 days of MFR 1, and something that I've actually held on to (and have kept in my dresser since then) is a piece of paper with a tale that was handed out to the class: "The Scared Little Boy & The Warrior" (author unknown).

"The sick, scared little boy, who cringed at night, never really grew up. He just hid inside the armor of the Warrior. When the day was over and the lights went out, he would curl up and pray that no one ever found him. Oh, if they ever found him: they would surely tease and hurt him again. So, he went deeper and deeper; until he found that he could go no further. He built up walls to keep him safely hid, and let the Warrior fight to keep people away from them.

The Warrior was strong and smart; no one could come close to the walls. But, something happened one day, and the Warrior got hurt. Although he had been hurt before, this time he was hurt beyond hope. As he lay on the ground bleeding, he cried for the fate of the scared little boy; he knew that his tormentors would find him, laugh at him, and hurt him again. He cried so loud that the little boy heard and reached out his hand from behind the wall. He pulled the Warrior behind the wall, safe from the world. Then, he wiped the blood from his head.

Softly, the scared little boy said, 'Sleep now, great Warrior. The war is over. You have done all you can. I will be fine.' The boy, frightened and in tears, stepped from behind the wall. Not sure of what to do, he looked frantically around. Then, he heard the Warrior whisper, 'Be yourself and you'll be fine.' Tears rolled down the boy's face, as he watched the Warrior die. But the Warrior smiled as he watched the boy begin to live."

Again, I couldn't explain *why*, but this short story struck a chord within me and I kept it. At that time, I related more with the mighty Warrior because at that point in my life, I had fought so many battles and had rushed head-on to meet so many challenges. But in spite of all the working out in the gym, the bodybuilding, and the jiu-jitsu that I took part in to demonstrate my physical prowess…I felt **broken**… inside and out…and longed for the *peace* that this dying Warrior was about to achieve. I felt that all I needed in my life, at that time, was to find this "young boy," this child whom I could protect, fight for; and, yes, *die* for. *That* would, at least give meaning to, and validate my existence; even if it was fragmented and in many pieces.

I'm actually a bit surprised that I'm having a hard time thinking back to that time of my life when this was all going on; not because my being older has compromised my memory, but more because I truly can't relate to it anymore. *That* Chino Ramirez seems like such a totally different person. So much has since changed for the better in my life because of the influence that MFR has had on me.

As I worked with Phil and helped him transform TAVO PT & Fitness into TAVO Total Health, I was blessed to have been exposed to a loving mentor who nurtured my budding MFR capabilities; and who also helped me reclaim those parts of my professional and personal life I had thought lost to cynicism, hatred and bitterness. We would review and rehash techniques that I learned in the seminars so that I would be more comfortable and correct in performing them. At the same time, as I progressed through the series of MFR seminars, he helped me appreciate the message of love, patience, and acceptance that was taught in class. I learned that just like fascia penetrates, supports, and is interspersed throughout the body, MFR can also penetrate, support, and be integrated within my professional practice and my personal life. I was a completely different therapist and person when I moved on from TAVO Total Health and Phil's daily supervision. I was *whole* once again.

An interest in esoteric, deeper thought was also awakened within me. It made me realize the *interconnectedness* between people: how a person's state of mind and emotion can actually affect everything and everyone around them. Particularly, I realized how a person can be moved, affected, and aided by being around Nature and "good or pure" environments. I learned to look past the outcome, to focus on the **present moment**, to pay attention to my intentions, and to delve deeper within myself and my treatments when I connected with my patients.

Personally, whatever value I had placed on the rigid, hard, judgmental, and inflexible system that is so prevalent in mainstream medicine gave way to the chaos, love, acceptance, surrender, trust and synchronicity of MFR. I began to see that within this chaos, there existed an order: a series of repetitive fractals that exist not just within us, but throughout the wholeness of Creation. And how MFR, when performed gently, lovingly, and patiently taps into this system. It helps us truly see and feel, and helps us grow as human beings.

I've come to recognize the falseness of arbitrary (man-made) demarcations, and to instead embrace the concept of wholeness and interconnectedness. Professionally, I no longer myopically treat a body part, but broaden the expanse to treat the entire person. Personally, with the decisions that I make in life, and paths that I choose to follow, I'm able to recognize that it not only affects me, but also those around me. That love and acts of good, when initiated and propagated, will ripple through and spread out; while conversely: hate, bigotry, suspicion and malice, when initiated and propagated, will also spread out.

Thanks to John Barnes and Myofascial Release, the sleeper within me has awakened. I have come to learn and know that true strength lies in *surrendering*: surrendering the outcome, surrendering to our intuition, and surrendering the need to force another person or situation into becoming something for which it wasn't intended. In coming to discover these basic tenets, I have grown to be happy, to be successful in my practice, successful in my life, and feel more whole.

Treatments with patients have never been easier, too. What I've come to learn is that the more I practice MFR in the clinic and in life, the easier it is to use. When I first introduce myself to a new patient, I send out my energy to the Universe; a message saying that I am open to learning and wish to help my patient. Without failure, I am able to successfully engage and connect with my patient and effectively treat them. Doing this repeatedly has allowed me to grow my practice, make more money, and enjoy my life tremendously.

Living an MFR-based life has also led me to my life partner and best friend: my wife Rachelle. Whereas previously (before being introduced to the use of MFR), I would go out for a night-out on the town in order to meet my ideal woman, I learned to let go of the outcome of meeting someone. And you know what happened? *She found me*! It was only when I learned to stop forcing something to happen or go my way that it happened so easily on its own.

And while people are people, and things won't always go the way that we would want or hope that they would go, living an MFR-based life allows me to see the entirety of a situation; so that I can do what's best for me and everyone around me. Again, guess what eventually happens? Things turn out well.

I have come to a point in my life and career where the technique (MFR) has transcended and gone beyond its perceived boundaries; and has been successfully integrated into me. What I mean by this is that I had originally learned MFR because I wanted *it* to help me treat patients better. In attending the seminars and in using MFR in the clinic, I have also found it to be effective in all life situations. And that, in fact, it dovetails and flows with the life patterns of Creation. It is, truly, based in love and true complete healing.

Myofascial Release has helped me get out of the hole that was my previous life, and has helped me reclaim it. In rereading The Scared Little Boy & The Warrior, I have come to recognize myself as *both* the scared boy *and* the Warrior. I am able to now see how the life pains that I had endured from others and myself led me to body-building: to grow an actual physical *armor* of muscles to protect me and prevent me from connecting with others and my body, because I was scared to hurt more and was scared to trust anyone. I no longer need my armor and no longer body-build. I have found that exiting the "hamster wheel" that is the gym and, instead, being active and enjoying the wonder and beauty of the outdoors is sufficient enough exercise to keep me fit and healthy.

I am really eager to learn what *more* there is to discover with an MFR-based life. I hope to grow further as a person by being able to delve deeper within me and my Being. I wish to further connect with Life and the Creation that surrounds me. I wish to become more comfortable with my own Divinity, spread my wings, and interact with others in this capacity. Lastly, I look forward to be as proficient as I can be with Myofascial Release; for it is said that a person can continue in the proficiency of a task so long as they are willing to learn as much as they can about it. I intend to continue with this great Gift because as I had previously stated: love and acts of good, when initiated and propagated, will ripple through and spread out. With the state of modern healthcare, it is even more imperative that we practitioners inject as much love and acts of good into it so that it continues to ripple through, spread out, and hopefully, help it in its own evolution.

Two of Francis Ramirez's clients share...

Before I begin, I thought I should share a little about me. I am a female in my mid-thirties. I have a graduate degree and work full-time at a desk job. On most days, I enjoy my job (although to be honest, if I won the lottery, I wouldn't stick around!). I am probably an average exerciser – I walk 45 minutes a day and, on occasion (when the weather is nice enough and the feeling hits), I go for a jog.

I have practiced yoga weekly for many years. It was by taking these classes, where I began to experience firsthand the importance of the mind-body connection. While I initially tried yoga for its fitness benefits, I continued to practice simply because of the peace of mind I was able to reach through the use of asanas (positions) and vinyasas (flowing movements). My openness to the benefits of MFR was undoubtedly a result of my positive experiences as a yogi.

I went into my first MFR treatment excited... how great will it be, I thought to myself, to have my back rubbed, face caressed and limbs stretched! To my disappointment (at least initially), I soon found out that this therapy was quite different than your typical relaxation massage.

First, physically the MFR experience isn't always gentle and soothing. I was quite disappointed to find out that this treatment included not just pressure but what, at times, felt unpleasantly like poking, prodding, pinching, squeezing, and crushing! It took some getting used to and many times my therapist would have to tell me to "stay in my body," or "feel the pain all the way through," rather than try to distract my mind with something else.

It was at these times that I would experience overwhelming feelings of hatred and violence. Sometimes the pain was so great, the pressure at a certain point in my body so irritating, I had to hold back with all my might the urge to strike my therapist, curse at him, and run away. It sounds quite crazy, but my therapist somehow had a knack for placing his hand on the exact place on my body to unearth extreme gripping fear! Who knew that a palm pressing down on my upper thigh or a little pressure to my inner hip or coccyx could cause such pure panic in my mind? Honestly, the feelings were so intense that, a few times, I wasn't even sure of whether I was about to vomit or even die! On the flip side, at other times, MFR treatments would have me laughing and giggling uncontrollably. This often happened when my body was being rocked back and forth, a method my therapist calls "rebounding." And other times, the treatment, when combined with beautiful music, would result in powerful feelings of peace, joy, and love.

Another surprise in the MFR learning curve was what MFR therapists call "unwinding." This is basically what your body does when it lets go or releases a restriction in your fascial tissue. When a restriction in your fascia is released, it sometimes looks and feels like your body part is twitching, shivering, or shaking uncontrollably. It's kind of like body tremors at a very micro-level. Once I learned that this shaking was a good thing, I stopped fighting it and just let my body do what it wished. Sometimes I even feel my body unwinding while I'm just lying in bed. Instead of judging the movement, now I just allow it to occur.

Quickly, I found that MFR – a physical manipulation of your physical body – brought up some very deep, often uncomfortable, sometimes downright painful feelings. At times, these feelings were things that made complete sense to me. I'm sure it wouldn't surprise anyone to have feelings of being overwhelmed during a very stressful time in their work life. However, sometimes I would experience feelings that I couldn't explain (at least initially).

For instance, the first time I had MFR done on my abdomen and also internally (intra-pelvic), I literally was overtaken with sadness. I cried and bawled for many minutes during that treatment. It was only during a subsequent treatment that I realized the bad feelings I was experiencing were actually guilt and regret. Let me give you some background: I have suffered for many years from cervical dysplasia (i.e., when the cells in the cervix change and eventually, if untreated, grow into cancerous cells) and have been visiting my gynecologist two or more times a year, receiving abnormal pap smears, having biopsies of my cervix taken for analysis, all in an effort to pinpoint the abnormal cells. It was not a great surprise when I started seeing my MFR therapist – and I learned more about how trauma and injury can form restrictions in the body – that the ongoing trauma to my cervix would eventually impact my physical as well as emotional health.

I realized in that one treatment, I had been living in a state of fear that the choices that I had made many years ago – that is, having contracted HPV from a sexual partner – might result in the ultimate outcome of infertility. My past choices would, like it or not, affect my current partner. It sounds crazy just writing this down, but it was so clear to me, during a moment in MFR treatment, that I had so much bottled up guilt over my past choices. I couldn't understand why the love of my life – the man who is now my husband – would want to be with such a broken woman. It wasn't until I was able to deal with these undercutting thoughts and emotions (and have my fascial restrictions released) that I was able to accept them, accept myself, and move on with my life.

This is but one example of the strong emotions that MFR has unleashed for me. Needless to say, that during those early treatments, I was hesitant to let my feelings show. I mean, how embarrassing is it to cry like a baby in front of your therapist, simply because he is pressing on your stomach! But with some reassurance from my therapist – "let it out" he said, "don't fight it; embrace the feelings" – I began to feel like my treatment time was a safe place where I could let my emotions out. It took me multiple treatments, with my therapist's encouragement, to get to a place where I could truly let go.

After much treatment, months and years later, I have my MFR therapist to thank for my physical and emotional health!

To start off on a journey has many emotions that come along with the actual trip. First and foremost there is excitement of a change, actually making a difference, it's the big picture that seems so wonderful. If only we can hold on to the anticipation of the journey; without letting the other emotions peek in. These emotions of fear, and failure, and all the negativity are which hinder our growth and progress.

When I was younger, showing emotions as a hug, a kiss, or saying I love you, never seemed to need thought, it was second nature. As we grow older these signs of affection are looked at not as signs of love, and respect, but something more to the effect of promiscuity. Somewhere down the line showing emotion was looked at, and labeled as negative.

Time after time in my childhood I was labeled as "sensitive"- things bothered me. I would take on a lot of my family problems and digest them as my own. If people fought in front of me, discussed finances, yelled, it seemed like I would get this pressure in my chest, and stomach pains. If I couldn't fix the situation myself, I felt overwhelmed and felt like I had failed. I was hospitalized with ulcers and other stomach problems at a young age. I was in and out of the doctor's office with digestive issues, with the cause being very elusive.

The structure of my WEB is anchored on emotions, and how I dealt with the negativity in my life: "digesting", pushing it away, but it was consuming me. I became very introverted, quiet and self reflecting. I felt alone in my adolescence.

The layers of restriction in my WEB continued to build, but instead of emotion it was structural. When I was 19 years old

I was driving home from college, ironically going to get my car serviced for an oil leak. The roads were cleared from a recent ice storm. Unfortunately, there were a lot of people out of power. There were a lot of electric companies called from surrounding states working long hours to restore the power. I was happy that day because I ended chemistry lab early so I knew I would be on time for my car appointment (I like to be punctual). I was on my way on a two-lane hilly country road. The song "Come on Eileen" came on the radio and I couldn't help but sing along. Coming down the hill the speed limit was 55 mph, there was a side street to my right, an electric company truck was there waiting to turn on the main road (which I was traveling on).

As I approached the side road, and going the speed limit, the truck pulled out in front of me. I impacted the truck at the driver's side door- a complete "T-bone". The accident happened so quickly, "poof" is the sound I heard as both of my front windows blew out and I saw the driver's side air bag deflate, and dust and smoke filled the car. The car was dead, but I was alive.

There would be a few more smaller "fender benders" in the years following, which also contributed to the layers of my WEB, but this first accident was defining. To this day I believe I had been looked after by angels, from walking away from the accident, and a kind person allowing me to use their phone to call my mom since I was out in the middle of nowhere, but that is another part of my journey that develops later.

I remember being in shock after the accident, waiting for my mom to come and get me, looking at my car crumpled and "bleeding" on the road, the very fluids I was going to get checked were flowing out on the asphalt. I didn't feel my body until several hours later. I was detached and all I wanted to do was sleep. I slowly pieced together what happened to my body during that fast "poof" of an accident, as the pain and bruises developed on my body. Surface injuries were one thing, but I wouldn't realize how deep the impact had gone until several years later.

After several months of pushing myself back to normalcy I became functional again, but I wasn't the same. I couldn't go a day without having an underlying nag or pain in my upper back and neck. Being a college student, and then graduate student, hunched over a computer or book became my life. I learned to deal with my pain, it became part of me. I never had a traditional massage or even physical therapy for my injuries. People who tried to help could never seem to reach my pain, or would just make it worse. My neck would lock up for a few days, with pain and headaches.

As I became a treating practitioner in the field of physical therapy, I never asked for help. I didn't want to bother people or be a needy person as I saw it. I didn't want people to think I was just using them. When I did allow someone to touch me I felt guilty that I wasn't helping them in any way. I wouldn't allow myself to feel. I was detached.

I was first introduced to MFR in PT school but it wasn't exactly taught as a "positive". I remember an instructor briefly defining and explaining MFR. I know now that this description was very wrong, and clearly the person who made these statements was misinformed. This professor demonstrated by placing his hands on the patient and sliding through the student's skin. The instructor asked the student "So do you feel any different?" Of course the student didn't and the class laughed. In Barnes' MFR, I later learned that an MFR therapist doesn't slide or glide through the skin.

However, another time in PT school we did have a TMJ specialist speak to our class, and he did show a myofascial release technique he uses with his patients, and we practiced on each other. To me, the people I practiced on enjoyed the release very much and I used that technique for several years to follow. I didn't know why people thought it felt so great because when it was done to me it was ok, but again I wasn't allowing myself to receive treatment.

Being a new therapist out of school I was still a perfectionist and stickler for time management. For all intensive purposes I was high strung when dealing with my schedule. I wasn't happy with the places I was working and I was still in pain, but I was still functioning. I just started a new relationship, and got a puppy. There was lots of change in my personal life, as well as a change in jobs, which I wasn't sure I was ready for, but was being sort of pushed into by my new boyfriend.

One morning I woke up and the light from the alarm clock was so intense to look at it was extremely painful. I couldn't tolerate any light, it was blinding me with pain. I went to the eye doctor and the exam was torturous! He had to hold my eyelids open because they were reflexively shutting against the exam light. He originally diagnosed me with pink eye in both eyes and gave me some drops to take. The drops seemed to help, but the pain was still there. I could get some relief by shutting my eyes and blocking out the light. I thought the pain I had experienced so far was bad, but I was in for much worse.

The pain in my eyes intensified, nothing I did would relieve the pain. The old standby of shutting out the light wasn't working anymore, nor did cold compresses. Heat and pain poured out of my eyes, I was thrashing in pain without relief, it felt like my eyes were burning and throbbing. I couldn't tolerate any light. I went to see the eye doctor the next day, the exam was beyond torture, when finally he dilated my eyes, FINALLY, relief! The muscles around my irises (the colored part of my eye) were in spasm, it was so bad that I started to develop scar tissue in my eyes, with a smudge left on my left lens from where the colored part of my eye started to scar down and then broke free and left a mark, which I see to this day.

The treatment to calm down the inflammation in my eyes was to keep them dilated constantly, and treat with steroids. So every day for the next couple of months I had a daily routine of dilating my eyes and putting drops of steroids every couple hours, which burned every time I had to put them in. I worked, drove and functioned with dilated eyes. They never figured out the cause of my bilateral iritis, even after it occurred again the following year, and I was sent to a specialist, it was written up as an insidious onset.

Physically I was no longer able to run outdoors like I used to, because of my light sensitivity. My personal life was not healthy. I was not happy with my job; I needed a change. A friend extended an invitation to move back up north, I was nervous and unsure but I did it.

I was a mess when I moved back north, I needed a complete overhaul. My friend who is a therapist offered to work on me. He had been practicing with MFR for several years. I was very stiff that first day, remembering that I didn't want to burden him, and of course like always I was sore afterwards and didn't really feel better. As I see it now after receiving MFR for a couple years, not allowing myself to receive was hindering my healing process. So my emotional scars from my childhood were preventing me to heal my structural scars.

He encouraged me to take John Barnes' MFR seminars. My first classes were MFR 1 and Unwinding. John worked on my eyes and gave me a few hints on how to unwind them. I was finally able to help myself! After those first classes I was exhausted but hopeful. I was finally cracking this hard exterior that I had developed since childhood to protect myself from being hurt, or vulnerable. I was becoming happy again, more like the self that I knew that I am, versus what I allowed people to see.

MFR is such a journey, one that I haven't completed yet. I have become more in tune with my body, using the techniques of MFR to alleviate my pain. Listening to what I need and addressing it. Of course it is better to allow someone to treat you, and in my journey I have opened myself to the experience, to receive and not feel guilt.

I am a physical therapist and I use MFR for self treatment almost on a daily basis. I am still opening new pathways with these techniques, learning how to treat myself, as well as my patients. For me, MFR has allowed me to feel again, and I'm hoping that when I do treat patients with whatever they are dealing with, they can learn from what I have learned over the years. Using MFR is a unique experience, and an ongoing journey to use to explore your body, mind and spirit.

Kathleen Troust, DPT

Silver Spring, Maryland
TAVO Total Health, LLC
Kathleen@tavototalhealth.com

My name is Kathleen Troust and as of Nov 2012 I have been practicing and specializing in JFB MFR for 6 ½ years. I've lived and/or worked in the metropolitan DC area since 1998. In 2005 I received my Doctor of Physical Therapy degree from Marymount University after a 7-year career as a fitness professional.

I began my PT career working alongside several advanced orthopedic therapists and the clinic owner was the PT for the Washington Wizards basketball team. I was with the best of them. During my first year, my desire to grow as a therapist was very strong. I went to several continuing education courses, always leaving with the thought of continuing on some specific path in order to become an "expert" in that school of thought. I also had a desire for more manual therapy training.

It was a brochure I received in the mail for John Barnes' Myofascial Release that drew my attention more than anything. There was something different about this marketing. I could see there was a mind-body component to this work, and this already made sense to me. My colleagues scoffed at the idea…"You would never go to his courses if you were a seasoned PT". This made me want to go even more.

I signed up for MFR 1 in Princeton NJ in 2006. After that course, I signed up for the MFR 2 course the following weekend, cancelling the foot & ankle course I had originally planned to attend. Now it wasn't a strange thing that as soon as I took a course, I felt excitement about continuing the progression of courses within that philosophy. However, prior to attending MFR 1, I had been dealing with 3 years of back pain that would shoot down my left hip if I bent over too fast, or lifted something heavy (like a patient in my acute care rotation), or tried to jog. The slight increase in impact was too much. How many PT's did I have assess and treat me? In school, during my clinical rotations, and even while I was practicing, I had people treating me. Nothing ever worked. The closest thing to providing me any relief happened to be a magnet that I would stick under my shirt against my back. Energy?

After 3 days at MFR 1, I recall lengthening my stride and picking up my pace until I found myself making a running loop through the hotel. For the first time, that pain was gone, completely!

Learning about the cumulative physical and emotional experiences that can create new symptoms or exacerbate old ones was a life changing knowledge. Before I arrived at the next weekend's course, I had already realized that the chronic pain I would feel while driving on the highway was actually a tightening of my body, a fear that lived in my body since I was 16 years old and had a tire blowout on the road, driving me head on into a cement wall on the side of a highway. When I noticed the fear coming on again as I drove back up to NJ from DC, I pressed my fingers firmly into my left psoas (hip) muscle region… and the pain disappeared, never to return. I also used to get pain in my left ribcage while I drove and remembered the car accident I was in where I was in the back seat when the car was hit from my left side.

Had I ever connected the experience of the car accidents and the pain I would get later on? No. Had I ever considered that my emotional state would create a trigger for these symptoms to arise? No. Had I ever thought that having an emotional release, a long cry, would alleviate my symptoms to some degree? Well, yes I knew that, but JFB MFR put the structure into it. Understanding the role and impact of fascial restrictions in the body changed everything about how I treated patients. I always knew there was a mind-body component, but now it was actually structurally explainable.

This time I knew that this was the path I would continue on as a physical therapist. It forced me to make some tough choices. I left the clinic I had embraced in order to work in an environment where this work was not only accepted, but also asked for. I was able to continue the JFB MFR education and work alongside other practitioners outside of PT, such as massage therapists, acupuncturists, etc. It wasn't long until the work led me to open my own office in Washington, DC.

For 3 years I practiced PT as an MFR specialist, seeing patients for women's health issues, pelvic floor issues, chronic pain and typical sports related injuries. I did not take insurance so I wouldn't be forced to spend less time with patients than necessary in order to survive as a business. It was successful from day one. My next challenge was to let go of this accomplishment 3 years later and join my other MFR colleagues at a clinic as an independent contractor. I was about to become a new mom.

My journey into motherhood also benefitted from MFR. During my first pregnancy in 2010, I was treated for some expected aches and pains, but more importantly I received pelvic floor MFR. I have no doubt that delivering an 8.5lb baby with a huge head without the need for stitches was greatly impacted by the MFR I received during pregnancy. Although I escaped the dreaded stitches, I did experience a traumatic tailbone injury during that birth. That injury lead me down the road of being an MFR patient, treated by my colleagues.

My second pregnancy in 2012 was similar in my need for pre and post-natal MFR. My son descended and was born in 10 minutes, leaving my pelvic floor and lumbosacral muscles in spasm. This caused debilitating pain with walking for 5 weeks. I had 5 MFR sessions beginning about 7 weeks after the birth. The layers of emotional and structural releases were numerous. Was I surprised at all what I felt in these sessions? No. The John Barnes approach to MFR explains so much that I had the emotional capacity to experience all the tears and pain that surfaced during treatments.

Every doctor was perplexed about my specific symptoms, and I kept asking myself why I even bothered sharing the information. I guess my awkward gait was hard to hide, but I really knew what the problem was. A part of my body was frozen and slowly thawing from the structural and emotional trauma of childbirth. Three months later I am a strong mom of two, still using MFR to help manage the aches and pains of carrying babies and lifting strollers.

What is in my web now? Nothing I cannot understand via Myofascial Release. Life happens, injuries happen, stress happens…but I have the tools and the power to deal with those things. Keeping my body as healthy as possible by treating myself, and having other therapists treat me means that I recover faster and I suffer less. I let the pressure out of my system before it transforms into something worse.

What if you had such an inner understanding of what is happening in your body that all those moments of panic turned into moments of awareness? Ah, feel what is happening. Soften, feel, breath into it. Slow down and do what your body is asking instead of resisting it. There is so much freedom in that.

What if all those moments aren't spent panicking about the latest ache or pain?

What would be available?

Anything.

Kathleen's client shares...

"Ouch! Right there. That's where it hurts," I told Kathleen, my new physical therapist. It was our first appointment together.

"What emotion do you feel when I press there?" she replied.

"What do you mean? Like, in general?"

"Yes, we hold emotions in our bodies, and they can become 'stuck' in our fascia."

"Oh," I said. "Well, scared I guess. That part of my shoulder still hurts from the car accident."

It had been about six weeks since the accident, and my shoulder was still sore. Only days before visiting with Kathleen, I had seen an ad for integrative physical therapy. This was perfect, I thought. I knew I did not want to go to conventional physical therapy and desired more of a mind-body approach. I called her up and set up our first appointment for the next week.

"Is there anything else that you feel?" she asked, sensing my mind drifting.

I hesitated. The accident was the last in a long string of events over the past few months that had jolted me into a stressful time, both physically and emotionally. Though, after three car accidents, a stressful job, family issues, health concerns and other things, I thought I was holding myself together pretty well.

"I did almost die from choking about five months ago," I said. "But I'm fine."

"Ah, wow" she said. "Did you see a doctor afterward?"

I had seen a doctor, who thankfully did not find any after-effects. Yet, I wasn't sure if I had shaken that event or the others. I had often wondered why all of these things happened at the same time. It was like something was beating me on the head trying to relay an important message, but I did not yet know how to listen.

Myofascial release (MFR) planted a seed for me to learn how to listen. Through my work with Kathleen over the next four months, I grew more confident in trusting my body, being present to physical sensations and becoming more aware of my emotional response. I attended weekly yoga and meditation classes, seeking to fully understand this new awareness, and practiced MFR at home. What I did not know at the time was that transforming my relationship to those physical sensations would lead me on a path of mind-body awareness, strength, creativity, courage, and confidence in knowing who I really am.

"I sense a big change," I said to Kathleen during a session four months later. This was our last MFR session together for a while since she was moving on to begin her own business.

MFR was not always fun, and the manual release of fascia could feel uncomfortable at times. But the energy, flexibility and insights I gained after most MFR sessions were testament to the great benefit I was receiving. What I thought were chronic pains were often emotions I had held inside or physical limits I had put on myself. True, conventional therapy offers great benefit to structurally realigning bones, muscles, and tendons. However, complementing that with MFR can produce even greater results.

A seed was planted that first day I visited with Kathleen. Practicing MFR has helped me grow into a mind-body awareness I never knew was possible.

Debbie Walden, MR, RMT

Clarkesville, Georgia
Naturally Divine Therapy
debbiewalden@windstream.net

All of my life I have lived in a beautiful small town in the foothills of the north Georgia mountains. I grew up in a hardworking middle class, traditional family, with strong conservative, Christian religious beliefs. I was the youngest of five children and painfully shy. So shy, that I had a fear of being looked at, much less being spoken to by others outside my immediate family. When out in the community, I would literally stand behind my parents or older sibling so that others could not look at me. Because of my shyness, school was very difficult for me, as I never felt like I quite fit in.

At the age of thirteen I had my first insight into what it might have meant to be different. This insight had to do with an inner knowledge of the power of light, somehow the power of God within us; the power of being able to heal ourselves. I felt that I might have a tool to help heal others. At age thirteen, as a very shy, awkward teenager, and much to my surprise, I spoke in tongues at a church revival.

Get the picture in your mind: an awkward, pretty teenager, suddenly speaking in a strange language that was loud enough for others in the entire church to hear. Then…dead silence. This was an experience of "Interpretive Tongue". After I had my experience of this strange language speaking through me, an 80 year old man stood up and interpreted what I had said to the congregation. As I write this it still is difficult for me to share because the experience was, and still is, so intimate. How can one explain something beyond the five senses? I'm not sure, but I am giving a try in this chapter.

In keeping with my traditional roots, I married at 17 and had my daughter a year and a half later. However, this was not the best of young marriages, because there was much emotional and verbal abuse. I was still the shy girl that I had always been, married to a bully, who loved me but was only able to demonstrate it through control. The night I left the marriage I literally got lifted from my bed by some powerful force beyond my imagining. My body got lifted from the bed, with a voice telling me to lock him out because he had a gun. At age 28 I found the courage to leave the marriage. This was a major taboo in my family of origin, as divorce, breaking a promise to God, was unheard of.

As a single mother, I was led into social work. I was saving other women, from similar backgrounds, helping them find their courage. As I was dating my future husband, Bobby, I had a horrific automobile accident in 1992. Soon after we were married I had four major surgeries, a near-death experience, and no relief from the pain. I felt as though I was on a medical merry-go-round. A friend that I had met from my years of social work recommended "Natural Therapy" because I was on such heavy doses of medications. At that time, "Natural Therapy" led me to massage and reflexology, which opened many other doors for me. This accident, along with my past experiences, led me to a lifelong commitment to helping others heal themselves.

During my physical healing process I was working with a massage therapist who invited me to a women's weekend. This turned out to be a retreat in North Carolina which focused on Edgar Cayce's work. As ignorant as I was at that time, I had no clue who Edgar Cayce was or any of his healing writings. While there I spent some time in meditation and had another experience of seeing Christ's eyes and heard him speak directly to me. This was a very frightening experience because I was being directed by Christ: "now if you choose to help others to heal you will heal as they heal." I was in a lot of pain and did not know if I was up to the physical challenge, much less the challenge of healing others.

Two days later when I came home, with no reservations, I decided to begin my studies in reflexology. After two schools of reflexology training I began a small practice in my home for several years. During this time several of my clients began to have healing experiences that were beyond the typical detoxification and pain management that reflexology is noted for. Some of these major healings included releasing of emotional trauma, healing tumors that surprised surgeons, and shaking of various body parts. I didn't have words to describe the shaking, and later I found the concept of "unwinding". In my previous training I had classes on touching and directing energy, yet I found myself intuitively being directed to specific areas of the body and focusing pressure and energy for extended periods of time. Myofascial Release (MFR) found me before I even knew what I was doing.

One day, after sharing some of my healing experiences with another massage therapist friend, I found a flyer in my mailbox. It was for a workshop on MFR in South Carolina with John F. Barnes, the founder of MFR. My friend had put it in my mailbox, thinking that some of my experiences were more in line with MFR than reflexology and that I needed to know more about this. From the very first day of the training I knew I was in the right place. Everything made sense.

I had a name for what I was doing. MFR was a tool that I stumbled on intuitively or had been led to use.

When I returned to my clients I felt more confident in helping them heal. Now I had more information and definitions of the processes that were coming naturally to me. The following year I attended more training in MFR in Atlanta. There I met a new friend, Phil Tavolacci, who has been as powerful of a gift as the MFR training. Together we have unwound ourselves from a tangled web in our bodies which has allowed us to help others to heal. We have been able to be each other's sounding boards, to help each other with confusion and feeling of overwhelm, and to keep each other grounded. And to laugh a lot- especially when Phil tries to talk southern with his New York accent!

As I continued to take more advanced trainings, and did Skill Enhancements (apprenticeships) with John Barnes, my clients began to multiply. My abilities were more attuned, and I had trained skills on top of the intuition that had been given to me. I began to feel more confident in my abilities, and now I had words to express and explain to clients what I was doing. I was learning to trust myself more, to be outside my head, and to be the conduit of healing energy.

Using the tools that I was learning, I was able to go deeper with healing. For example, I learned to really work on a client's gut (abdomen) because that is where the majority of the organs exist. As complex human beings we store much of our anger, frustrations, and fear in this region of the body. The heavy energy that prohibits us from moving forward can get stuck in the solar plexus.

While I am working on the client's gut, I connect to their energy. Reading their energy for me is like taking their pulse anywhere in the body. I feel their energy with my left hand. After I connect energetically with my right hand, I place my left hand nearby. I pick up an energy reading- a pulsing vibration that feels in harmony or not. This lets me know where I need to work.

I am doing light compression on the client's body, using the MFR techniques. I begin to heat the connective tissue that surrounds everything in the body, which is a fibrous web. When it begins to warm up, with the continuous gentle pressure applied to the restrictions, the fascia begins to soften and elongate back into a more natural state. The vibration and energy changes, while I am asking for healing energy and light to come through. I need to let the energy through, to get out of the way and let the energy flow naturally. The healing is not from me, but from the Light that is being sent through me. I am being directed where to focus the Light.

As humans we bank our stories into our bodies. We collect positive and negative experiences into each of our cells, tissues, muscles, etc. Everything in the body retains memory. These memories, stored in the body, cause structural restrictions that manifest in less movement, problems with circulation, lymph stagnation, and low energy. Also imbalances in the body can set up the environment for cancer, arthritis, inflammatory problems, neurological disorders, etc.

Some stories become so deeply buried that we become totally unaware of them on a conscious level. Depending on the circumstances, one's age at the time of the experience, and the interpretation of the experience, individuals may have stored the experience on the subconscious level. For example, when we interpret an experience as scary, we may walk around braced for "scary", holding our bodies in a protective manner. Scary can be any sort of fear, whether it is too heavy of a work load, a sorrow, regret, shame, etc. We are afraid that we will be hurt physically or emotionally. This may appear on the outside as an individual who has a body posture of carrying a heavy load, with shoulders rounded, chest caved in, and arms guarding the heart. Physical symptoms that the individual may complain about include shoulder problems, neck issues, TMJ, headaches, chest pains, many digestive problems. In MFR therapy, this is called "bracing patterns".

As I have worked with hundreds of clients over the years, I have learned that everyone has their traumas, whether it is physical or emotional. We all need help at times to heal. My job as a therapist is to be the conduit of healing. My responsibilities include allowing people to speak, to create a trusting relationship so that they can receive healing, and to help them understand the influence that the mind has on the body. My job is to help them re-connect with their past so that healing can occur in the present. My main job is to help them get out of their head to allow for healing. On the subconscious level people disconnect from their body. My job is to help them reconnect, reinterpret the trauma, and receive the help that the body needs to release and free itself. Thereby the body returns to a state of harmony. It is the choice of the client to allow for healing. It is their responsibility. I cannot "zap" them into a place of healing. It is their choice to receive and to continue to do their work. I can teach them self-release and unwinding techniques, but they must practice these at home in order to heal. Clients must participate in healing themselves.

It is never too early or late to do the work. My youngest client was less than a week old. His parents had been clients of mine for a few years. They brought him to me because he wasn't sleeping from birth, and a lot of congestion interfered with his breathing. After a few sessions of unwinding, the child was able to throw up some of the congestion and toxins of being in the womb, and release the stress of the difficult labor. The unwinding helped the child breathe and connect with the healing Light. My oldest client, Sally, was in her early nineties. I worked with her about ten years. Though she had lived a happy life, when she lost her husband in an automobile accident, she had to take on the responsibilities of living alone and this was extremely stressful for her. These stressors manifested into breathing problems. Prior to working with me she had been hospitalized several times a year for bronchitis and pneumonia. Her chest wall would literally lock up and restrict the lung capacity, inhibiting the breaths that she could take. After establishing a trusting relationship, and understanding the stress involved in living in the world alone, Sally began to come for regular "tune ups" as she called them. For me, the "tune up" involved being her life line. I gave her an opportunity to really be vulnerable and to talk without editing. The goal, of course, was to get her out of her head, to not need to talk, and to receive the healing Light. Right before she died I went to her house and gave her a treatment. She thanked me for helping bring joy to her during her last days. It wasn't about healing her at the end, but rather about her receiving touch and joy. As we age we all accumulate fascial restrictions in the body from our past experiences. Sally was no different from any of us.

Some clients receive healing more quickly than others. I think this is because they may be more "ready" to receive. They are truly "out of their own way", totally surrendered, and healing can occur. Health issues can often put us into a place of total surrender, making us ready to receive, even if out of desperation.

One client particularly comes to mind, Ms. Dalton. She was a young woman in her late twenties who sought treatment from her local doctor for depression, anxiety, severe anemia, chronic colds, and lymph node infections. When she came to see me she had a lymph node tumor that was the size of an orange. She had already been scheduled to have it removed by a surgeon. Her grandmother had been doing treatments with me at the time and encouraged her to seek alternative treatments before having surgery. Ms. Dalton was obviously open and ready to receive treatment at that time. To my surprise, after the first treatment her tumor began to drain and shrink to half the size. By the third treatment, which would have been about a week later, the tumor was completely gone. No surgery required. With weekly treatments, and detoxification, the depression and anxiety began to diminish. Over the course of about a year, she was able to come off of the medications and her energy of a young woman returned.

Another client that lost her "soul" after years of physical and sexual abuse as a child was able to receive healing. Moria was in her 50s when she first started seeing me. After many years of talk therapy Moria had not completely released her painful childhood abuse. Though she would have periods in which she thought she had overcome and moved past this pain, it would somehow emerge again and the pain would resurface. Moria needed more intense therapy than a typical client because her pain was buried so deeply. After working with her for several months I began to realize that I would have to offer her more intensive therapy than I could give her in hourly sessions. So I began to offer intensive weeklong treatments, bringing in several therapists to collaborate towards healing. Clients who participate in these programs often need an array of tools to break through the barriers that inhibit their healing. Moria taught me many things during this process. The body may need to go into many different formations, the client may be coached to use their voice as memories surface, the body eventually surrenders through the process and releases, then the client is able to remember the place prior to the trauma. Harmony is restored. Over the course of two full intensive treatment programs, and partial participation with other MFR intensive programs, Moria was able to write a letter and take it to the grave of her abuser. There she read the letter aloud and forgave him. Now Moria has a loving relationship with her family and life. She has found ways to be happy.

Some clients don't heal instantly, but they are able to achieve movement in their day to day lives. I am continuing to learn from one client with Multiple Sclerosis (MS) named Matt. Matt can still drive and walk with a cane. Eleven years ago he was told that he would be in a wheelchair within the next two years; that he needed to prepare for this. While he has been successful at continuing to walk with a cane and run his furniture business, he still has MS. He may not be ready for instant healing. Though he uses the MS to teach everyone he comes into contact with. To see him walk, he teaches about the love of God. The MS and his struggle are part of his ministry because he remains upbeat and positive. For people who assume he is a victim, he is able to use the MS to inspire them to focus with a heart of gratitude. My goal in working with Matt is to keep him out of his head, to keep him grounded and focused on receiving healing. In working with the MS we must focus on keeping the body supple. While this is a challenge for each of us, it is particularly a challenge with MS, as the body is attacking itself and restrictions are continuous. Regular appointments are important for Matt, in order to maintain function.

Beyond human clients, I also have worked on animals. This includes cats, dogs, birds, horses, and a lizard. Just like with children, animals respond well as there is not as much mental resistance that hinders receiving healing. Just like with humans I connect energetically with the animal. I earn their trust—there is an unseen power and I connect with it. Then it again is about touch. I begin to heat the fascial system and the animal lets me in. The animal, just like with children, knows where the issue is. They surrender quicker and receive the healing almost immediately. There are no mental barriers that have to be dealt with. Healing is received and harmony is restored.

I continue to receive MFR on a regular basis through working with several talented therapists that are part of my practice. If I don't take care of myself I get sick which is a reminder that I am not taking care of me. Sickness occurs when I am out of sync with the Divine Light of God. If I don't get my guidance I suffer. As a result of my near death accident many years ago, I have five fusions in my spine. I must take care of myself daily so that I can be an effective therapist. I must be centered so that I can channel this energy to heal others.

Each of us must take care of ourselves first. You must love and take care of yourself first before you can take care of anyone else. Until you know who you are you will be affected by others. You will let others influence you. We cannot change others, but we can only change how we react to them. We can allow our need to control others evaporate. We can only change ourselves.

Before I close I want to thank my dear friend, Phil, for pushing me out of my comfort zone to write this. For my friend Phil, you have a luminous light that is always shining through. This quote is about you:

Your art,
your creativity is really your spirituality,
your prayer speaking to the world.

Three of Debbie Walden's clients share...

From Lynda:

The first time I laid face down on a massage table I sobbed. I could not differentiate between bad touch and good touch. Therapists said my back was like a washboard, lots of knots and hard ridges, I could not relax, or let go of the strong desire to run away. When I met Deb, I had slammed my foot into the edge of a door and I was in a lot of pain. Deb started with my feet and over the years we have built a support system on which I now firmly stand. Deb has helped me open many doors, on many levels. Doors I was trying to either slam shut or open up...doors to my young years and doors to the past lives. Growing into this lifetime on an abusive foundation has had its challenges. I have looked in many places for answers.

After hours of bodywork I have come to realize that my life experiences are deeply rooted in my cellular body. I thought that all I had to do was talk about my emotions. Through bodywork I realized that there is a deeper component to healing the pain we experience, both physically and emotionally, because it is embedded in the deepest layer of the self, the cellular level. Not in our thinking selves but our Being selves. Learning to let those deep layers surface no matter what it feels, looks, or sounds like has brought me deep healing, release, and trust. Bringing a sense of freedom and wholeness as old experiences are brought to the surface and then released. I have learned to connect to self and find my voice.

Deb works on such a deep level, holding the painful places until I came to a place of acceptance and then release. I have a history of physical abuse, my therapist and I observed that I had a hard time staying in my body. Deb pulled me back to those painful places until I could look at them instead of running from them. In that place of acceptance came healing.

One particular session of deep shifting came when I was unwinding and started yelling, "Get out of my bed." I was beating my fists on the table and then went to the floor. Deb stayed with me holding that painful place until I was able to release it. That was the turning point when I was able to confront my life instead of running from it.

Over the years I had participated in individual therapy, group sessions, and workshops. Looking at my inner child, Insight, self esteem workshops, etc. As I moved into my work with MFR, I was not initially able to stay in my body during stressful situations. The past has been accepted and woven into what I am now. My physical being does not hold the knots of my childhood traumas. Deb is an incredible healer. She knows when to and how to access those places that I held onto so tightly. With the release of fear has come the love and acceptance of the beautiful tapestry that I have been weaving in this lifetime, for that I am grateful, as I continue to weave beauty in my world.

From Dr. Gangappa:

Being trained and actively practicing 'evidence based medicine' as a Nephrologist, hearing about benefits of MFR work from my son's school teacher sounded uncanny and difficult to comprehend.

The birth of our only child after 9 years of wedded life was a blessing and the happiest moment of our life. We were devastated when our son, SSG, was diagnosed with PDD, in the autism spectrum disorder. After many visits with behavioral psychologists and child psychiatrists, we went from feelings of guilt from missing early diagnosis, to denial, and finally, to acceptance. With acceptance, we made a commitment to invest our time and resources to help our son without reliance on medications. Working on different behavioral modalities, following recommendations from physical and occupational therapy took an emotional, personal, and professional toll on us but with little improvement.

SSG's pre-school teacher, Ms. L, who had worked with Debbie Walden, was very much aware of benefits from MFR. She recommended MFR work for SSG with sincere faith that it would help him tremendously. Given our promise to try every available avenue to help SSG we proceeded to see Mrs. Walden in spite of my lack of trust in MFR.

SSG was hyper-focused on subjects that fascinated him and had poor social skills. He often spoke in a monotonous voice, lacked emotional connection, and lacked social awareness. With exhaustion or excitement, certain physical manifestations like flapping of hands and running in circles occurred.

With MFR, he has blossomed into a well grounded boy who is able to verbalize and understand his emotions. With emotional well being, he is more assertive and confident, which in turn, has helped him tremendously with social skills and to widen his interests. The physical manifestations are also resolving.

With this experience, I have developed great respect for MFR work. I think it is like the internet – it exists but needs the right platform and timing to unlock its abundance. Now, Mrs. Walden is working on me and I have already seen the impact of mind on body and vice versa. I sincerely thank Debbie and Ms. L. They are both SSG's miracle workers.

From SSG himself (after 2 years of MFR with Debbie):

First session I was a little anxious when I saw Ms. Deb. I was only 5 years old. I did not know her. I got used to her pretty quickly. I met

Sassy (her cat) and Garrett (her grandson). After the first session I was "floppy". I was relaxed and happy. The "pressure" which felt beautiful, it hurt a little, but it made me feel so much better.

Sassy visits me when I am in my sessions. It makes me happy. Cranial sacral would make me sleep. I really like it and it unwinds me. It is restful.

Now I work on my Mom, my Dad, Ms. Lynda, and sometimes Ms. Deb and I help myself. I can give something in return.

No more bad thoughts. No more bad movements.
I like spending time with Ms. Deb.

In peace,
SSG

Garth Whitcombe LMT

Nashville, Tennessee
Nashville Myofascial Release Center
therapymuse@comcast.net

Hutia te rito o te harakeke
Kei hea te komako e ko?
Ki mai ki ahau
He aha te mea nui i te ao?
Maku e ki,
He tangata

If you pluck the heart out of the flax bush
How can the bellbird sing?
You ask me
What is the greatest thing in the Universe
I answer
It is the human person

— New Zealand Maori proverb

The John F. Barnes Myofascial Release approach is the most comprehensive hands on modality that I have found in more than two decades of practice as a massage therapist. Fifteen years ago a visiting therapist from Arizona gave my wife Sandy and I our first MFR treatment. It made such a profound difference in one session (with a therapist who had only taken two classes: MFR 1 and Unwinding), that we immediately bought John's first book, *The Search for Excellence*, and within months had taken our first seminar.

I had lingering chronic back pain from growing up working on a dairy farm in New Zealand. Injuries from rugby, surfing, riding horses, car wrecks, along with postural issues from playing multiple musical instruments had all begun to limit my range of motion. I thought I was condemned to coping with chronic pain that made it difficult to sit for long periods in a car or on a plane. That first MFR treatment gave me more relief than any deep tissue massage, rolfing, chiropractic, or osteopathic manipulation had ever achieved. What is more, the relief had a degree of permanence. While the tightness did return over time, it was never as painful as before that first MFR experience. That one treatment gave me hope. I was no longer defined by my limitations. I was no longer a person with a 'bad back'.

We bought John's book, *The Search for Excellence*, and studied the techniques and theory, but soon realized we needed to experience the training first hand. Fortunately John came to our town, Nashville, in December of 1998 to teach MFR 1. John endured country music Christmas show rehearsals blaring on the soundstage next to the convention room at Opreyland Hotel.

After that first class it was obvious that to really benefit from MFR both personally and professionally we needed the Unwinding class. Ahead of a blizzard we drove to West Palm Beach in January of 1999. It was the Unwinding class that really opened myofascial release up for me. During MFR 1 I had tried to move. I had tried to be still. I had tried to control the energy flowing through me. "Don't try to control it," one of John's instructors told me, "don't try to control it." Unfortunately that is what I had been trying to do all my life- control it. Whatever 'it' was. In that first Unwinding class I finally got a glimpse at the 'it' that was controlling me!

Now, 14 years later I have memories of that experience that are like swimming in surf. Some memories are like big waves and some are troughs and some are still submerged. I remember walking on the beach after class feeling expansive and vulnerable at the same time. It was as if my consciousness had grown way beyond my body but felt tender as a new fern shoot unfolding, unfurling.

My complicated relationship with my past was swirling through me. Growing up in paradise but surrounded by dysfunction and addiction, trying to fit into the macho, rugby, beer swilling mainstream identity that defines what a man is in New Zealand. Rebelling and finding spiritual solace among the native Maori; adopting and being adopted by that culture, itself struggling for survival with the language and culture fading, the people coping with drug and alcohol dependence.

On the last day of the Unwinding class I felt a shift, something at once physical and spiritual, a warm sensation in my chest- almost a burning followed by a wave of joy, mixed with grief. I can only think that my heart fully opened for the first time since I was a child.

As we said thank you and goodbye to John he gently reached out and touched my heart. "You're getting it," he said. What I think he meant was I had ceased trying to control it. That was a turning point but by no means the end of my healing journey. For the first time I had the tools to be authentically helpful to myself and to my clients.

For a boy growing up in New Zealand in the 1960s and 1970s, rugby was a force that tended to define your identity and your social acceptability. Rugby is a brutal game. It is a ritualized form of war and not an ideal pastime for a sensitive soul more inclined to healing pain that dealing it out. Until I learned MFR, I did not realize how much I had internalized struggle. Running oneself ragged on muddy fields in the wet and windy winters bashing into other boys teaches one resilience, but while I was good at it, I lacked the predator spirit and the killer instinct that makes for true excellence in contact sport. The sensitivity that allows one to be fully human involves embracing ones duality, both the tough side and the gentle side. Men can become very restricted and constricted living up to the masculine ideal, keeping a lid on emotion even when the emotion keeps boiling over.

I turned to music in my late teens, joined a rock band and fell into all the pitfalls that come with that life. Ten years of touring and performing passed in a blur. I studied dramatic arts at Auckland University and earned a diploma in audio engineering.

Our band collapsed on the cusp of success after the release of our first single when our lead singer died in a car crash. Within a year, two other members died, one from heart disease, the other in a fire. I was left lost and shell shocked. I began searching for meaning and healing through alternative therapies ranging from body and breath work to sensory deprivation. I spent time with my Maori cousins learning the language and spiritual tradition of the Polynesian ancestors. I worked in theater and dance and found healing in movement and psychodrama. I took certification classes in bodywork and experimented with the use of sound and music as therapeutic modalities.

My journey lead me through Australia where I absorbed the rhythms and pulses of Aboriginal didgeridoo music to the Pine Ridge reservation in South Dakota where I studied sacred Lakota chant and drumming. Among the Lakota I experienced a quantum shift, shattering old patterns of addiction and dissociation through weeks of participation in the Yuwipi healing ceremony and the sweat lodge.

Upon returning to California where I had been working on recording studio installations I was offered the opportunity to travel to Nashville to help set up a new coffee house venue. Nashville was a new page for me and within a month I had met my wife, Sandy. We were both on a healing journey and healing has continued to be central to our relationship. After three years of working in the Nashville music scene, performing and engineering in recording studios as well as booking and mixing live bands, I came to the conclusion that the music industry was simply not a healthy environment for me. The late hours were becoming incompatible with my growing massage practice and helping take care of my two stepsons, so I transitioned from music and audio into a full time therapy business.

Looking back I think, along with meeting the love of my life, it was MFR and not music that drew me all the way from the beaches of Northern New Zealand to the rolling hills of Middle Tennessee – I just didn't know it at the time.

An early clue had come to me on a trip to Sedona in 1992. I remember driving up Oak Creek Canyon and seeing Therapy on the Rocks, John's Sedona treatment center, and it was as if the building was glowing. I didn't get it then, but it was a big noticing. So much so that a few years later Sandy and I were bumped from a flight in Phoenix, given a hotel and a rental car so we elected to take the last flight out the next day and drive up to Sedona. Sandy had never been there and I wanted to share the magic with her. We drove up Oak Creek Canyon a short way past John's clinic and stopped at a parking area that gave us access to the creek. We sat for a while with our feet in the cool water with the warmth of the day blossoming around us. Gazing upstream we realized we were looking at the same scene as the picture above our kitchen table, a photograph of Oak Creek Canyon taken by a friend in California that had been given to us as a wedding gift. We drove back to Sedona and this time instead of passing by John's clinic we stopped and went in.

I wish I could say we met John or something happened that made us immediately sign up for classes. We had some samples of massage cream a friend in Franklin, Tennessee had asked us to drop off at any massage therapy clinics we saw on our travels. The woman at the counter at Therapy on the Rocks was very gracious and took the samples even though, as we were soon to learn, MFR is not done with lotion.

We left the clinic with a positive impression, given the atmosphere and the beauty of the place. The creek below and the red rock vistas and the sound of the waterfall out back had triggered a shift that we were only dimly aware of. Not long after that we had our first MFR treatment and began actively pursuing the training.

One of the defining things about MFR and an important reason that MFR has become the central modality in my therapeutic work is the emphasis placed on the healing journey of the therapist. John says you can only take the client as far as you have been yourself. For me the reason I got into bodywork was my need to relieve my pain and dissociation in order to find meaning and resolution in my life.

I believe we never stop our healing journey throughout our lives. We are continually evolving and healing. The key to a happy and productive life is openness and flow. On a physical level this can refer to the fascial system. Motion is a defining quality of life. Fluid motion is more efficient; less painful than restricted motion. Opening and maintaining the fascia not only relieves physical pain but also emotional blockages. As dance psychologist and dancer, Joan Chodorow states in her book, *Dance Therapy and Depth Psychology*, "Movement reflects the total personality, it draws from both conscious and subconscious sources."

We begin life as fluid entities in a fluid environment. When we are born we begin to feel the effects of force and gravity, perhaps even our birth itself was traumatic. I was born with the help of forceps. My mother tells me you could see the indentations on my skull for several days after my birth. Occasionally I still feel tightness in that area, especially when I am stressed. Although I have had several deep and powerful releases from MFR work through the years, at a recent repeat of MFR 1, receiving a cranial technique, I had another shift along with a minor "healing crisis".

One thing I have learned is that the healing never stops. Patterns diminish so they are no longer pervasive, but there is always a deeper layer. This may seem confusing to some people, after all we are all looking for a cure to whatever ails us at any given time, but in a fluid interconnected system a shift or release in one area can highlight a restriction in another part of the body.

Along with a traumatic birth, I have nearly drowned twice as an infant. One near drowning was in a sludge pond behind a cowshed on a neighboring farm when I was about four. My father tells the story of rescuing me by the hair. It seems funny now to recollect what the scene looked like: me sitting in a truck, covered in cow manure, and stinking to high heaven! I'm sure it was traumatic for my father but it is a dinner table reminiscence that I have no conscious memory of. I do remember having a gag reflex for some time after that and my mother taking me to the local hospital where they found "nothing wrong". That restriction only began to be resolved after John unwound my larynx during a treatment in Sedona.

My list of injuries is long, but no longer than many of my clients. I have been trampled by a horse, broken bones in Rugby, been in multiple motor vehicle accidents as well as suffering other physical and psychological abuse that caused me to dissociate or live an 'out of body' existence.

Many healers, both Western and Native, have helped me on my journey, but I don't think I came fully into my body consciousness until I took that first myofascial Unwinding class. Movement for me was complicated with many layers of force and struggle from contact sport, patterned/controlled movement from dance and theater, restrictions particularly in the pelvic, upper thoracic and throat areas from cultural norms and expectations as well as repetitive activities from driving, work and playing musical instruments.

Before unwinding I was glued in place, my range of motion along with my consciousness was diminishing. For me the very first shift during myofascial unwinding was moving beyond patterned response. I was so well trained in controlled movement, from catching and running with a rugby ball down to the micro movement of fingers on a piano keyboard or guitar, that I found it difficult to allow the energy to flow through me and move me.

The portal to unwinding for me was not the wild drumming music that was being used in the class to spur movement. This particular type of music sent me into left brained musical analysis mode. This realization has since inspired the creation of my own original music for MFR and other healing modalities. Instead of being moved by a beat, which my musical brain translates to dance pattern and performance, I found that stillness was my way into authentic movement and release. Finding the stillness in the moment, the silence in the sound, the thought beyond words, the energy of an emotion: these were and still are key to unwinding for me.

What works for me is resting with the stuck place, not being compelled to move, but rather deeply feeling into a restriction and allowing movement to flow like the melting of ice until motion becomes free as running water. Unwinding is probably the thing that sets John Barnes' Myofascial Release apart from other soft tissue mobilization and cranio-sacral modalities. Motion is life. Without movement or oscillation we cease to expand and begin to decay and decline. As I have progressed in my MFR training I have come to realize that everything we do is a form of unwinding whether the client moves or not.

The very act of applying sustained pressure into the fascia will facilitate motion or unwinding within the layers of fractal connections that make up the tensegrity unit that is the human (or animal) fascial system. The key is to allow for motion in every moment of a treatment, to not use so much force that the system is guarded, but is always open to responding from within.

The paradigm shift with MFR, which makes it a pre-eminent Mind Body modality, is trusting that the human body/mind is inherently self-correcting. Just as water will always flow downhill, unless it encounters an obstruction, so, too, does energy and motion seek to flow in the human body. Continuing with our water analogy, when a boulder blocks the stream, water first dams up, but then it finds a way around the obstruction. Often that one boulder will trap debris carried by the stream, thus forming an island. The stream may be split into two streams. This is similar to a fascial restriction. If the layers of fascia become glued together by a force-induced injury, scar tissue, or repetitive strain, the force and flow of motion and energy will find other ways through and around the restriction.

Motion can become less efficient, more painful, further restricting movement and setting up a holding pattern that is both structural and psycho-emotional. Because the fascia is a web, like a spider's web, a pull in any one part will cause a reverberation through the entire system. The myofascial therapist's role in healing is not so much to fix a problem as to facilitate an improvement in function so the body can reorganize and repair itself.

"...when we treat disease as a concrete entity entirely capable of technological remediation, we lose the notion of an integrated system." – Jean Achterberg, author of *Imagery in Healing*.

Myofascial Release deepens the human element of manual therapy. MFR, at its best, is performed by a fully engaged therapist, one who is practicing the art of centeredness, deeply listening to and shifting with the client's body/mind. The human being cannot be reduced to the level of a machine. The same rationale that fixes a motor has limited applications in healing. We are beautiful beings, alive with potential.

As a therapist I enter each treatment with the goal of facilitating the expansion of that beauty and potential in whatever way the client will allow. The operating principal is 'allow' rather than force. Force always causes resistance and can be counterproductive to authentic healing.

I was drawn to work in a healing profession because I needed healing, pure and simple. The act of helping others has been my greatest comfort and fulfillment.

In finishing, I would like to quote from Dr. Lawrence LeShan, author of *Alternate Realities:*

"Our freedom is so much greater than we have comprehended. We can learn to shift from reality to reality, choosing the one that is most relevant to our needs and purposes at the moment and use our new approach...to nourish our being, love, cherish, and garden ourselves and each other, be at home in our universes, and help save ourselves and our planet."

Ann Udofia, PT, DPT

Washington, DC
Body Connect Health & Wellness, LLC
ann@bodyconnecthw.com

As a young Physical Therapist, I stepped into my professional career wondering what I would offer my patients that was going to be of true value in their lives. I bounced around from various treatment settings yearning for the 'right' environment and the 'right' skill set to allow me to feel empowered in what I still considered true PT to be- 'A healing art'. I was disappointed time and time again with these different settings, and began considering other health related fields that would be more nurturing to my patients and me. This was all until I stumbled into Myofascial Release (MFR).

I walked into the MFR world looking to enhance my hands-on skills as a physical therapist and to help resolve injuries I had as an avid runner. This included repetitive injuries and falls that led to acute hip and knee problems; all unsuccessfully managed by conventional physical therapy. Compared to thousands of patients I have treated over the years, I now consider my concerns as being minor as the immediate issues were quickly resolved once I started receiving MFR treatments.

However, what was most profound to me was that by addressing these orthopedic problems, I was led to the discovery of issues I had overlooked since childhood. It also led to me unearthing emotional tension trapped inside my body that I had no idea existed.

This revelation started with the help of my mentors and advanced trained MFR Therapists. At this time, my focus was to reduce acute pain in my hip and knee related to a running injury while training for the New York City marathon. With their help, I learned and understood more about the mal-alignment issues I had around my hips and spine, and was feeling empowered with daily self-treatment techniques to help keep my muscles loose and pliable. Within a few sessions, I began to notice positive results in the reduction of my pain and was running faster and more efficiently than I ever had. So at this point I was completely sold about the benefits of MFR. Little did I know that my therapists were intuitively picking up something that I had no clue was an issue.

I remember one of my early treatment sessions when one of my therapists intuitively asked if I had any problems with my pelvic floor. I naively responded "no" while thinking to myself; "I don't have incontinence, and I haven't had a child yet, so- no problems down there!" However, later in conversation I casually mentioned the fact that I had always had constipation issues. As a child, my mother gave me enemas about twice a week, and now as an adult I would get pretty frequent hemorrhoids. I was also now aware of urinary frequency and urgency problems, and would urinate every 45 minutes to an hour during the day and 2-3 times through the night. I later found out that normal urination patterns were every 2-4 hours or 6-8 times in a 24 hour period. The most distressing issue was the consistent pain I experienced with sex. This had become a regular occurrence since I became sexually active, but being raised in a home where sex or sexuality wasn't discussed- I figured those moments of pain were only to be expected.

I still remember my therapist's response when I casually mentioned these issues. She quietly said "Ann, this is not normal". She further explained how fascial tightness in the abdominal and pelvic floor muscles could compress the organs in this area causing dysfunctional patterns like the ones I was experiencing. We also discussed how these issues could be related to tightness in my back, hips and legs and my alignment problems. She talked to me about direct pelvic floor work and encouraged me to explore this area of treatment for myself and perhaps consider taking the MFR Seminar that focused on Women's Health.

To say the least, I was amazed. I had no idea that what I had experienced for years was actually "not normal!" Women's health issues was something we glanced over in physical therapy school and the summary of what I felt I learned was- "If you have incontinence, do Kegel exercises; post pregnancy problems, do Kegels." The answer to most issues related to the pelvic floor seemed to always be 'fixed' by doing Kegel exercises. So what was pelvic floor treatment from an MFR perspective really about? She further explained, "We would simply go into the fascial system vaginally or rectally to find and release the tissues that were tight in your pelvic floor, the same way we would anywhere else in your body".

Armed with this new information, I wanted to explore pelvic floor MFR but was extremely scared. I asked myself questions like: "How painful will it be?" "What if some of my buried childhood trauma comes up? How will I deal with it?" So, I chose to sit on this information for months. In the meantime, my running injuries completely resolved, I continued to take other MFR classes, and started a part time position with one of my mentors in a Myofascial Release clinic in New York. All the while, I purposefully avoided the Women's Health seminar and opted not to see any of the patients that came in with Women's Health problems. I remained afraid of what could be trapped in my pelvic floor. I decided to get my OBGYN's opinion on my concerns surrounding my bladder and sexual function, and scheduled an appointment. After a brief abdominal and pelvic exam she gave me a clean bill of health and suggested I should try to relax more during sex and yes- do some kegels! I had enough information and decided that at my upcoming trip to the Myofascial Release Treatment Center in Pennsylvania, for treatment and for my Skill Enhancement Seminar (a 1 week externship), I would sign up to get my first internal pelvic floor session.

It was the evening of my scheduled session and although I was nervous, I had 100% confidence in the therapist I had been paired with who had 20+ years experience as a John Barnes MFR Therapist. She quickly picked up on my trepidation and approached me with such warmth, patience and kindness that put me even more at ease. Even though I was a PT and was knowledgeable about anatomy and physiology, she started by explaining what pelvic floor internal work involved. "This is direct intra-vaginal and rectal MFR to release tight fascia surrounding the muscles and the organs in the pelvic floor", she said. She further explained how common it was to hold tension in this part of our bodies without realizing it. She explained how the session would run and, most importantly, if I needed to take a break or discontinue the session for any reason, we would do so immediately. I felt safe and empowered and ready for this part of my body to begin to heal.

All of my fears were dispelled after that initial session. We found multiple fascial restrictions in my pelvic floor tissues: especially around my bladder and reproductive organs. We also found that my tailbone was significantly out of its proper alignment. It dawned on me how truly disconnected I was from this part of me! Like most people, I referred to my pelvic floor as 'DOWN THERE'. For me this was the part that I felt held the space of deep feminine energy, sexuality and sensuality- all of which I knew nothing about. "Without awareness there is no choice" is a phrase commonly said by John Barnes himself.

If I wasn't fully connected with my pelvic floor and brave enough to strip away the belief systems I had about 'Femininity' that had been trapped here, then how could I fully heal myself? I made the decision that I needed to face the belief systems I had around what femininity meant to me. I believe this was when I started to truly unravel deeper layers of my fascial web.

I grew up a tom boy and although I always admired everything feminine, I seemed to just relate to things masculine instead. I sprinted, played sports, climbed trees, hated wearing skirts and dresses, and felt more connected to my brothers and male friends. My father seemed to always demonstrate leadership, independence, and confidence with everyone he interacted with. So, I wanted to be just like him. My mother was a shy and reserved woman, and unfortunately consistently bullied by other women in our extended family. As a child watching her, I mistook her compassion and restraint for weakness and created a belief system that femininity meant being powerless. This belief system was what became cemented in my tissues, but specifically trapped in the area that represented my own femininity- my pelvic floor.

I continued my journey receiving pelvic floor treatments with my local therapists, and soon thereafter, took the Women's Health seminar. Within weeks of consistent treatments, my bladder function normalized. Within months, pain with sex was non- existent. The incidence of hemorrhoids reduced and my constipation issues improved. What was so powerful for me was how I re-connected with my femininity and was now able to fully embrace this once foreign part of my body. Now as I think of my femininity, I'm reminded of a beautiful creature which I've long identified as my power animal, the Black Panther. In my mind's eye she is a graceful warrior and the epitome of incredibly powerful feminine energy. She is a leader, a protector, a lover, a mother, and simply a force to reckon with!

At 33 years of age, I am very grateful to say that my body now feels whole, complete and powerful. My intention with every patient that I treat is that they take away the experience of feeling fully re-connected and powerful, not only in their bodies but also in their lives.

One such former patient I'm often reminded of is SL. She is a woman who took back her power in such an inspiring way, and I would like to share her story here. At the time I started seeing SL, she was in her late 40's and had been living with the diagnosis of Fibromyalgia for about 10 years. Fibromyalgia is a chronic and severely debilitating condition characterized by widespread pain throughout the body. Her pain was usually much more severe in her neck, and after several years on a variety of unsuccessful treatment regimens, including numerous medications, she began Myofascial Release treatments with me. One treatment I had with her, which she described as the turning point for her, was a session where I was working deeply into muscle spasms in her neck. After several minutes of direct pressure into a particular area, I could tell she was disconnected from her body. I dialogued with her to help her reconnect with this part of her body by asking her to say what she would like to say directly to this area. Her response was "You're hurting me!" I knew this was not directed at me, so I asked her to give herself permission to confront this painful spot using those words. As we continued to dialogue, she had huge emotional releases—she screamed, and cried—connecting more deeply with her body and this pain than she ever had before.

After the treatment, I was honored that she shared what that treatment had brought up for her. She was reminded of the repeated physical and sexual abuse from her older brother as a child. She was often pinned down to the floor with his hand around her throat, and his thumb pressed into the area I was treating in her neck. She realized how despite years of talk therapy, the impact of the abuse was still trapped particularly in this part of her body. She was also aware of powerlessness she felt as an innocent child, and how the same sense of powerlessness was what she currently experienced in her job, health and other relationships. From that point on, she continued to shed the layers of pain and belief systems that no longer served her. She felt powerful enough to confront her brother for the first time, began divorce proceedings for an unhealthy marriage, and began to make other huge steps to move forward in her life.

This was a truly courageous woman, and my point in sharing her story is in the fact that she made that choice to take her power back. This is the possibility that MFR offers people as they uncover the secrets within their fascial web.

So, as I reflect on the person I am today- a vibrant woman, wife, sister, daughter, friend, and business owner- I am deeply connected with the fact that my experience of life would have been very different without MFR. I feel love, joy, gratitude, sorrow and loss at a cellular level and my mind/body has found an authentic way to connect with me and the world.

Life has also now become more exciting as my husband and I will soon welcome our first child into the world! Having tried to conceive for two years, I am convinced that my entire fascial web needed the time to be nurtured with MFR, especially pelvic floor MFR, and other holistic practices to fully embrace a healthy pregnancy. The opportunity of being a powerful mother is the greatest possibility that MFR has helped create for me, and one that I am ever grateful to share with others.

Drucilla J. Likens Pape, OTR/L

West Carrollton (Dayton), Ohio
The Intuitive Body, LLC
dru@theintuitivebody.com

I felt a gentle squeeze on my arm and then felt it release. It felt pleasant. I felt another gentle squeeze, another release. It felt pleasant. Opening my eyes, I saw a clock on the wall. I was warm and comfortable, but this was a strange thing; the squeezes, the clock, the warm blankets. Within the slumber of anesthesia, my heart began to pound. This was no pleasant retreat! This was the recovery room and I had just had surgery for breast cancer! Under these warm covers was a bandage wrapped around my chest. What was under that bandage?

Adrenalin quickly flooded my body, and jolted my already pounding heart. I felt a flood of urgency, whirling fight or flight, pure panic. How had this happened to ME? My name, Drucilla J. Likens Pape, was impressed upon a Loyola University Cancer Treatment Center card! My name was typed on the tabs of medical files and countless forms. My name was connected to cancer! There was only one person with such a moniker, and that was me. No escaping this reality. The bandaged body was mine. I touched myself, just to make sure, half-hoping that I wouldn't feel anything. That would mean I was dreaming, and that would be a good thing right now; to awaken, shake it off, and be anywhere but here, in recovery.

How had I gotten to this point? This was surely the lowest point in my life, right here, right now. Disbelief flooded my soul. I felt a rush of cold, salty nausea with prickles and ringing in my ears, heralding a faint. Can one faint when lying in a recovery room bed? Impossible! The whole scene was impossible, and could not be happening to me. No, absolutely not. No. Not. NO!

My mind rifled its pages, back to before. I had been happy, healthy and quite full of life, and full of myself! If it was fun, I was there in an instant, to add my laughter and love. If there was adventure to be had, without hesitation, I was hanging on the end of a rope, spelunking in Hellhole Caverns! I had a great job, loyal friends, and the best family tree upon which to be a nut! I loved life!

My mind rested there, enjoying treasured memories of the early 1980's, a most lovely nook in the library of years past; warm and comfortable, not unlike my pre-conscious recovery room bliss. That pleasurable pause, like the anesthesia, was zapped with a jolt of reality. I realized that in my chapters of my life, I had skipped past quite a lot of pain and emotional mayhem...half of the 1980's and the entirety of the 1990's!

Spring, 1985: My sister was shocked by the demon of divorce, and, in order to find a job, had to move far away with my two little nieces. I was heartbroken! A few months later, on Saturday, July 6th, I became engaged, and was waiting to tell Momma and Daddy in person the very next weekend. I knew before I answered the phone call; Daddy died of a massive heart attack on Friday, July 12th. Momma left after the funeral, and went to live with my sister to take care of my little nieces. I couldn't even cry. I felt dark and frightened and alone for the first time in my life. I couldn't shake the reality that Daddy was gone, and Momma and my sister and nieces were too far away for me to visit.

I went through the motions of life for the next year. I even got married, albeit in a state of numb, squelched panic. It didn't go well. I had nothing to give, and couldn't receive. So, I worked. I had a full-time caseload as an itinerant therapist working with handicapped children and adults. I was also coordinator for our large group of itinerant therapists, which was a full-time job, squeezed into my already long day. I was exhausted; a numbing exhaustion. My pilot light had gone out. Nobody was home. Hurt circled around in my heart like a cat trying to get comfortable. I was too tired to feel it.

I vaguely remember turning 33, because my friend taught me to say it in American Sign Language. Family hinted that it was time to start a family, then hinted more and more. I felt resentful. How could I possibly add a baby to my life? I felt guilty. My sister wanted to be an aunt, and she deserved to be an aunt. I loved my nieces so much! My husband wanted time with me, and that did not involve taking time away from him to care for a baby. He was starved for attention. He wasn't functioning, either. There we were...two failures, two mismatched head-butting muskoxen, one miserable marriage, with no baby.

I first met John Barnes in February, 1993. He was teaching a series of Myofascial Release courses in Cincinnati, Ohio. I had taken two introductory MFR courses in 1989, and had loved them. I'll admit that I had questions about meeting the powerful-looking man with a full beard and a walking stick, pictured on the brochures. He took people out "on the rocks" for class in Sedona, Arizona. I just couldn't see myself following anyone into the rocks. I decided I simply wouldn't take that class. Cincinnati felt safe enough, so I found myself committed to a 10-day stretch of classes with John F. Barnes.

I felt like a hot mess. I sat in the back of the room, mostly to avoid eye contact if at all possible. At break time, John ambled past me and remarked, "I like your shirt." Oh God, I thought! I've been singled out! I felt like I had been "found out". I felt tired and disconnected. Anonymity would take the least amount of effort. I wanted anonymity. I looked at my shirt; black with a huge, colorful parrot and "Panama Jack" sprawled across the front in hot pink letters. I liked it, too. I realized that my fun self was hidden somewhere inside that shirt after all!

Profound things happened in the grand ballroom of that stately old hotel in Cincinnati; healing things, and wonderful things! I heard the sound of my voice, for the first time in a long time. I will never forget it. My body was physically hanging upside down, shaking. With my ears, I heard a sound that was much like the cry of an animal fighting for its life. It rose to echo throughout the cavernous dome of that rotunda ballroom, and came back down to me. It was the sound of my pain. The instructor walked by, and lightly touched me. I let go even more. My voice expanded to fill every nook of every ornate carving in that rotunda. It felt so freeing. I knew it was much-needed. I began to cry. I cried with the sound of my voice flowing freely, not feeling the choke of squeezing back so many silent tears. I really cried, and this time I heard it with my heart.

During the second class of that 10-day series, I met a sweet woman with whom I partnered for many of the techniques. She, too, felt insecure at first. She carried torturous memories from childhood, and needed to feel forgiveness and safety in her life. We sat, sequestered behind a dusty silk tree in the ballroom. There, she shared intimate details with me. She cried. I cried. We cried, and healing continued. In fact, throughout the progression of those ten days, I began to feel lighter and lighter.

The ten days flew by. I found myself bonding with others who were feeling similar to me, or even worse than me. We didn't have to hide. We shared, instead. We laughed and cried. We looked into one another's eyes and hearts. We treated one another and opened up to healing and learning. I had come to this continuing education series for a much needed break from work, because I felt broken. I had no idea that the series was going to be a personal learning experience for me...for my own healing journey!

I vowed that I would take the next course, and every one after that. I hungered for more healing. I now had my sights set on the course where John took his students out into the red rocks of Sedona, Arizona! I literally endured the months until I could leave for that course.

Meanwhile, I slipped back into my pattern of working hard and long hours. I added more work by starting a little Myofascial Release private practice on Sundays. Very quickly, word of mouth brought more and more clients to my door. Sundays became busier than the rest of the week, and appointments soon began to overflow into weekday evenings, which were already very full. I limped along, giving to everyone but myself. The teapot was really getting empty, and the cups continued to present for filling! I meant well, but life was out of balance, and I was still living in a state of numbness. I was "out of my body", so to speak. The following share is an example of just how poorly I was functioning.

On a rare day off, my husband and I retreated to a quaint town to enjoy the antique shops and a nice dinner. I had taken off my wedding ring and three other diamond rings to put lotion on my hands. I wrapped my rings in a tissue until my hands dried. I held the tissue in my hand, but soon couldn't feel it, nor was I even aware of the tissue full of precious rings. When I exited the car, so did my rings. They were never found. We were even scammed by someone who searched the papers for rewards offered for the return of sentimental pieces and lost pets! As it happened, we were under-insured, but the paltry amount of insurance reimbursement paid my way to Sedona. From that great loss, ultimately came great gain.

Sedona finally came that October, 1993. I had completed all the pre-requisites throughout the spring and summer, and was holding my breath, praying that I would be accepted into this cohesive and comprehensive course. I didn't know what would be taught. I just knew that I had to be there! I recall needing to send a picture with my letter of request. I sent two pictures; one of me smiling brightly with sparkling eyes, the other smiling with "the unhappiest eyes I have ever seen" (the comment of a friend who saw my picture). I was accepted into MFR III.

I took two seminars before "the big one", MFR III. I still felt quite alone, and did my share of hiding. Then, horror of horrors, I missed my ride from the seminar site to my hotel, and had to ask for help! I was truly shocked when someone offered to take me to my hotel, via dinner and a scenic ride up the Oak Creek Canyon! Life was beginning to open up, and I was beginning to feel the sensations of...joy!

MFR III proved to be life-changing. I became part of the MFR family, the Tribe. Everyone was there to learn, and to let go of old messages, old hurts, physical barriers, and educational misconceptions. We all accepted the challenge to "go deeper" and "go higher" in our quest for learning. We grew exponentially as individuals and as therapists, and as a group. I counted the months until I could repeat courses. I loved them all. I loved the work. I craved the time for myself. I contemplated, for a mere heartbeat, of having my husband come along the next time. I quickly squelched that idea. This was my sacred space. I couldn't bear to share it, or to have it desecrated by dragging the dysfunction from home, to my new-found sanctuary in Sedona. I was tired and angry when I was at home. I didn't like myself, and I didn't like my husband either. I pushed. He pushed back. Yes, we were the two mismatched, head-butting muskoxen. It was terrible. The tug-of-war continued between what I was learning through MFR, and the imbalance of what I had created in my life at home and at work.

My colleagues were seeing a shift in me, despite my turmoil! They didn't really know what I was doing while I was in Sedona, but each time I returned from a seminar, I was a little more changed. They lovingly dubbed me "Drubie1Kanubie" after a Star Wars character that was a teacher of sorts. My little light was shining with love for MFR! They knew that MFR was a continuum of learning treatment techniques, as was stated in the brochures which they also received. A few fellow therapists even took an MFR class or two. Yet, my shifts were more personal. My boss asked me when I would be done taking MFR classes. I, for once, felt like laughing, because I realized the answer was, never! I recall having told him that repeating classes was an important part of being an MFR therapist. It was the first time I referred to myself as an MFR therapist. I heard myself saying it. It felt good. My boss was very patient with my requests for time off. I used every one of my 30 vacation days and holidays for MFR courses.

My sister had since moved closer, and I was able to drive the six hours to see her, and my nieces and Momma. It was wonderful! Having been apart for a while, she, too, noticed a change in me. It happened that in February 1994, my sister had exactly one week to do ALL of her studying for the bar exam (to become a lawyer), as she was juggling a full time job, raising my two small nieces and attending law school at night. Appreciating an overflowing schedule, I insisted that she accompany me to Sedona so that she could focus on uninterrupted studying, except for the two treatments that I scheduled for her, knowing how badly she needed it. She reluctantly agreed to take the time from her compressed study schedule. After the first treatment, she was free of the headache she'd had for several years due to a collision with a pizza delivery van. Following the second treatment, she was able to focus and memorize with incredible visual recall of information! She had been sitting outside of the seminar room while I was inside taking class. John walked past her, and saw that she was really struggling to memorize case law. He asked her to close her eyes for a moment, and touched her forehead with his finger. She wondered how long he was going to stand there with her, so she peeked. He was long gone, but she recalled the case law information exactly as she had seen it when John touched her forehead!

My sister passed the bar with flying colors, and went straight to massage school as a means to study MFR. We took all of the classes together. Shortly thereafter, my husband decided to follow suit. He completed massage school and the three of us took all of the classes together. We also began to instruct with the seminars.

Life was improving. My health was not. I had added to my imbalance by adding the intensive study and practice of MFR to my still-packed plate at work, not to mention my responsibilities at home! I knew I was in trouble, when I was walking into a school building one morning. My vision narrowed, my ears began ringing, and I counted the steps to the front office. I then headed to my first classroom, vision narrowing, ears ringing, counting the familiar steps. When had I begun counting steps because I was feeling so ill I was about to faint? I crawled, very nearly literally, through the remainder of the school year, and absolutely could not face the stack of summer students that was being handed me. I met with my boss, and requested to give up my 12 month contract. My boss was surprised, and asked me if I was sure, as that meant goodbye to the freedom of vacation days and commencement of the rigid school calendar. I was so exhausted that the loss didn't faze me.

The first day of my first summer vacation, I leaned forward to look out of the window into my garden. My coffee cup touched my right breast. It burned. I played out all the possible reasons why I was feeling an M&M under my right nipple. Ultimately, there was only one reason. It was cancer.

Y2K preparedness could not have prepared me for cancer! Monday morning, July 17th, 2000 was the date of my confirmed diagnosis. A chirrupy 20-something front desk cicada from the doctor's office called at 11:32 a.m. I answered the phone with a leaden hand, and the familiar ringing in my ears. I confirmed my name, and she confirmed my cancer. She kept saying bits and pieces of unbelievable information, while simultaneously chatting with other front desk cicadas about schedules, calls, and blah blah words that I couldn't comprehend because my brain was only relaying electric jolts of terror.

The New Millennium equaled change, alright. My job had changed drastically, from working 19-20ish hours/day, seven days per week to a medical leave of absence for the school year! Momma said, "Well, you're going to have to change your diet". My sister said, "You're going to have to change your sleeping habits". My husband was mute. I was stunned. Life as I knew it, screeched to a dead halt. The rubber hit the road, and it was time to use what I had given to others for so long; Myofascial Release!

My sister whisked me to Chicago Loyola University Medical Center, where I received my red Cancer Center patient ID card, with Drucilla J. Likens Pape imprinted on it. Surgery removed the nipple that had nursed the world. It was a terrible loss. It was a symbolic loss as well. It was time to do or die; literally.

MFR helped me through surgery. I put a little rock from Sedona into the toe of my compression hose before going into surgery. I had MFR with me, unbeknownst to the surgery team! Following surgery, my sister did energy sweeps to help rid my body of the anesthesia and did thoracic, respiratory diaphragm, and pelvic floor diaphragm releases to help me handle the panic of being under anesthesia while my body was subject to the mistakes of an arrogant surgical student.

Later, MFR again helped me to accept the chemotherapy treatments. I resisted the drugs going into my arm, to the point where they would cease to flow and my arm would spasm. My sister did energy sweeps and releases again, and helped me to visualize a better picture than I was envisioning! When the chemo crossed the blood-brain barrier, a severe headache would ensue. I thought I couldn't survive it, and told my sister, "Boo, I'm dying," She would pull out the heat energy from the headache, and the chemo smell with it.

I hated getting chemo. I hated most of all, walking down the long hallway to the cluster of gray chemo chairs. The hallway was lined with curtained rooms where patients lay in bed for hours, receiving their chemo (remembering the "hisss-shunk" sound of the pumps still gives me shivers). They looked terrible, having lost all hair, their skin gray with pallor. That sight made me more ill than the chemo. Just as I was giving up, John Barnes called me! Like a sobbing child, I blurted out my fear of that lifeless-looking state happening to me. He said, "Dru, picture yourself smiling, happy and in glowing health! Don't identify with those patients." This had never occurred to me. What a positive shift! I also blurted out to him, my utter frustration with my husband through all of this. He wisely said, "Dru, detach, and detach from the outcome. Don't worry about what anyone else is or isn't doing, and focus all of your energy on your own healing." Again, this had never occurred to me! Focus on my own healing, let others be free of my expectation, free myself to free up my energy and make it available to myself for my own healing? I really could do that!

I knew I would heal after talking with John, or rather, after listening to him. I finished my chemo, and went on to the last phase of treatment: radiation. By this time, I was feeling more in control of my body. When the burning started in my armpit from the daily irradiation, I discussed it with the radiation oncologist. I had no cancer in my armpit, and my surgeon said that it would not need to be treated with radiation. The oncologist wouldn't listen. I decided to take a break, or be done. I hadn't decided which. I went to Las Vegas with the MFR group, and received loving hands-on treatment. I treated others. I felt normal. I felt strong, and I felt good for the first time in such a long time. When I returned, the head of radiology was listening, and changed my treatment to a focused "boost", eliminating my armpit from the field. I finished the sessions. I was free!

Twelve years have passed since my cancer. I have made many changes for my health and well-being. I have released my previous jobs, with great love, and have followed my dream that was always "too good to be true". I have a thriving Occupational Therapy/Myofascial Release Therapy practice in Dayton, Ohio, where I now help others to journey back to health and well-being through the principles of MFR. I have had the opportunity to work at Therapy on the Rocks, the Western Myofascial Release Treatment Center in Sedona, Arizona, a dream that I have had since I attended the open house in October, 1993! Amazingly, I have also had the opportunity to assist as a senior instructor with the Myofascial Release Seminars, including being the keynote speaker for the Pediatric MFR Seminar.

Only when I was willing to release what was not working, could these gifts be received into my life. Still, I must be mindful of my old patterns. I know them when I feel that familiar feeling of my teapot getting low. MFR has become a way of life. I am living in balance and in joy!

Thanks to my immediate family and my MFR family, the Tribe, for circling the wagons of love around me. Thanks to my co-workers and friends for loving me as Drubie1Kanubie.

Thank you, John F. Barnes, for being my greatest teacher, the Grand Pubah! I humbly carry you with great love, in my heart, and in everything I do. Thank you for loving me when my world was black, and for holding the space for my growth throughout these many years!

Little did I know, when I received my first MFR brochure that the bearded man with a walking stick would come to lead me exactly where I needed to go, by nudging me to take to the trail under my own power, and with my own walking stick!

Grab your cups…this teapot is full!

Post Script: As so often happens on this MFR Journey, even the writing of my story has brought deepening insight. Looking at what was to be the last sentence, I had a true "aha" experience, and a most humbling awareness!

I realize that a very old belief has been lurking beneath the surface of my awareness; an old program that has been silently and subtly running, and ruining my life. Somewhere along the way, I came to believe that my role in life was to be the longsuffering teapot, duty bound to fill everyone else's cup! As a result, I treated everyone else like a cup, and no one had a chance to help or encourage me, because I was a teapot.

With this realization, I am reminded of John saying, "Where there is awareness, there is choice!"

I will just "be" with this awareness for now. My old pattern would have been to try to "figure it out" right away. My higher self knows that I need to give myself time to let the awareness fully come to me.

My Russian grandmother used to make "cowboy coffee". She always told me that the secret to developing the best flavor is to "Nai opsedyich" which means,

"Turn off the heat and let it rest!"

Drucilla's client shares...

MFR has been a journey of healing for me, empowering me and giving me the tools needed to repair many years of damage to my body. In order to understand the power of MFR, I need to share with you the path of my injury and the deep hole that I was in that finally led to this discovery.

When my son was born, he was a very large baby, so despite pushing for 3 hours, he did not move. My doctor finally asked me if I wanted to have a C-section, and I quickly agreed. Everything went well with the surgery and mother & baby left the hospital fine. But little did I know that over the next 15 years the way the surgery stitch healed, it pulled unevenly on the two sides of my body due to a 5 mm difference in the length of my legs, which was never diagnosed.

I first noticed an issue about 5 – 6 years after the surgery with the front of my right thigh. There was a tight band of muscle that formed and was giving me pain. Next, I had a very tight area along the right buttock and another one in the upper right hamstring. I was given analgesic patches to put on these tight areas, which I did especially when I travelled.

Over the next 5 years, I visited a chiropractor who kept adjusting my right hip, which was rotated and would not stay in place between adjustments. My right thigh became increasingly tight and my feet started to hurt and were becoming increasingly stiff. I kept going through all of these symptoms, getting massages, exercising and using pain patches to get by. Until one day in 2006, I was walking down the hall at a trade show and I completely lost my balance – I felt that I was being pulled over by an uncontrollable force. People at the show looked at me like I was under the influence, but it was the middle of the day and I had not had one thing to drink.

This was a defining moment for me that I knew I was in trouble.

What made matters worse was I could hardly sit in a chair because of pain in my buttock muscles. Not knowing where to turn, I made an appointment with my family doctor who promptly sent me to physical therapy at the local hospital. During the exam, not one person checked my muscles. They watched me walk and set up a program for me. At the end of the six weeks, things had still not improved, so I went to another program at a different hospital. The therapists listened to my complaints of pain and tight muscles and built another program for me.

During all this time, I never had a diagnosis. During this period of time, I became increasingly frustrated with the lack of diagnosis and improvement from these programs. My pain continued to increase and by now, my legs and feet were so stiff, I could hardly walk. I had to tell my boss at work that I could no longer travel due to my condition. When the second physical therapy program did not work, I visited a new chiropractor who x-rayed my hips and spine and showed me the twist in my spine, rotated hip and 5 mm difference in the crest of my hip bones. He put me on a physical therapy program, gave me orthotics for my shoes and adjusted my bones. It was during this time that my physical therapist introduced me to an MFR therapist.

The Road to Healing

During my first visit to the MFR therapist, she checked my complete structure and alignment. Based on this exam, she treated my body using elongating stretches, sustained pressure, and leg pulls. My body responded very well to this treatment, and I felt like I had found the "missing link" in my treatment. I left my visit with some self-treatment exercises to do at home in between visits. After a period of time, this therapist suggested I attend the JFB intensive program at one of John Barnes' treatment centers. I wanted to get better and figure out what had gone wrong with my body so badly that I could hardly get around anymore. I signed up for the two-week comprehensive intensive program in Pennsylvania in the spring of 2011.

I was excited to be attending a program where I could focus on treatment and get an even better understanding of the MFR techniques and how to help myself. The trip to the treatment center was exciting to me...finally I would find out what had gone so wrong. Once inside the facility, my muscles were analyzed for tightness, range of motion was measured and my walking was analyzed. I also filled out paperwork on my medical history, including past surgeries. Armed with this data, the first thing John Barnes did when he came into the room was to go to my c-section scar and examine it. The scar was so tight, that my abdomen was concave from all the pulling. So began my journey of healing with therapy, and self- treatment using MFR.

I left the treatment program and was referred to another therapist in my geographic area who was trained by John Barnes and was also on his staff. She continued my treatment, and also contributed to my understanding of the techniques and tools used to facilitate the stretches. It was most important to keep my pelvis in alignment – not tipped or rotated, and this was accomplished using wedges under the hip bones. All of the muscles in my body that had hardened – my legs and feet – had done so due to the drying out of the muscle and fascia from the stress and injury.

One of my most visible and rewarding successes came as I brought my feet back to their original soft, supple and flexible nature by using a golf ball on the bottoms of my feet. Several times a day, I would roll the golf ball under my feet while in a sitting position, hesitating in one area for several minutes until I did not feel any more muscle restrictions opening up in my foot. Over a period of time diligently working my feet, they were restored back to health, no longer stiff and cold from lack of blood circulation. Releasing the restrictions in my feet enabled the blood to flow and bring oxygen and nutrients back. I realized after seeing these transformations, that I could use the MFR principles on any area of my body where the muscles were, in the words of my therapist, "hot, hard or tender" and heal that area.

The MFR principles I have applied are:

+ Sink into the area of the tissue as far as you can and apply pressure for a minimum of 90 - 120 seconds

+ If doing a stretch, elongate it as far as possible and hold that stretch for 5 minutes, if possible

+ Feel for the areas of releasing while you are stretching, and stretch until the body is finished

+ Once you are done stretching, move to the area that was releasing, and stretch that one, too, as they are connected

+ Be creative and use whatever "tools" are in your surrounding area to do your stretch – for example, if you are travelling and don't have your neck roll, roll up a towel and put it under your neck

+ Most of all, be patient– remember that the injury didn't happen overnight, so the healing process is going to take time. In this culture where we (and I include myself here) expect everything to be done quickly, I could not find a pill or program that was going to be a quick fix. My injury happened gradually over 15 years, so it was just going to take time. The great news is that through MFR, I finally found something that worked, and restored my muscles back to their original tissue memory.

At this point in my journey, MFR has helped my scar to heal, restored my feet, kept my pelvis in alignment, fixed the tight band of muscle in my thigh and enabled me to walk much better. I have now moved on to fix the upper part of my torso that was rotated due to the rotated hip. I am confident that MFR will take me all the way through this journey and completely restore me to the active, pain-free lifestyle I used to have.

The great news for me – and you – is that there is a healing technique called MFR that is able to make sense of the injuries to the body. And, by applying the principles, you are empowered in your own healing process to restore your body and be healthy again!

My hope for anyone reading my story is to know that even when there seems like there are no professionals who can help you, even when you are in the dark hold of pain where it seems there is no way out, there is actually something that works and will not only alleviate your pain, but restore your functionality and your freedom to be active again.

Before MFR, I felt helpless and out of control from the pain and lack of understanding why my body no longer worked correctly. With no professionals who could diagnose me and give me relief, discovering the JFB MFR techniques gave me hope again and is restoring my body back to the way it was before a functional alignment and scar injury took me out of active living.

Nancy Murray, BSN, RN, MA

Wyckoff & Montclair, New Jersey
Nancy Murray, LLC
NLMURRAY@OPTONLINE.NET

As I sit here pondering what to write and look at some of the things I have jotted down over the years, I feel a bit nervous and hesitant. Despite having gone through a linear education, getting my BS and MA in Nursing, my life is now experienced as non-linear and yet there is forward motion. For me, non-linear is a way of looking at life and an acceptance that I don't really know what life is all about. This acceptance has resulted in freedom and has helped my everyday living be more vibrant and flexible. I no longer try to follow some idea about what my life **should** look like. Instead, I engage and enjoy what my life **is** and who I am **now**.

I am an imperfect, incomplete, suffering human being while at the same time I am glowing perfection filled with joy and love. I am checking my own web and finding some places that need some work. Taking a deep breath, I soften, knowing I will visit those places and ease the tightness and the holding, perhaps discovering yet another wondrous aspect of me and my reality. My name is Nancy Murray.

I have practiced the John F Barnes Approach of Myofascial Release (MFR) since 2006. My primary office is in Wyckoff NJ and I also see clients one day a week in Montclair NJ.

"Without awareness, there is no choice". I am hearing the words John Barnes says at most seminars. Strange sometimes how his teachings rise to the surface when I need them. Sometime in the mid to late 1990s I began a subtle, slow, downward spiral. Pain was a constant- all over and ever changing. I stoically carried on putting on the good face, taking Advil often just to plow through the days. Oh, there were certainly some good times mixed in but the pain continued to get worse.

Then, my left shoulder froze. Physical Therapy three times a week- the Spanish inquisition may have been less torturous. I went to physicians, taking drugs that are now off the market due to side effects; I saw shamans, chiropractors, acupuncturists and more. I researched and read self-help books, spiritual books, and medical books. I took supplements and herbs and changed my diet. Sometimes something helped and I became hopeful. The help didn't last long but did, at times, sustain me. My moods varied according to the pain and the pain varied with my moods, a vicious unending conundrum of suffering. While my story goes on for many painful years and is unique to me, I hear similar stories from my clients and my heart aches with compassion and hope that each will find their way with the help of the very powerful potential of Myofascial Release as taught by John F Barnes and his protégés.

Over the years, I periodically saw a massage therapist, a talented woman with soothing hands. One day she asked if I would like to try this "new" thing she had just learned at a couple of seminars. Change and healing didn't happen overnight; however, I knew within two sessions that there was something here that felt real and true, deep in my being. I began an exciting journey of discovery. The answers and help I was seeking existed right there in my own tissue, body, fascial system; in my own being, my own reality. My pain became my informant, opening doors to my inner self and wisdom. As trust evolved, trust of myself and of my therapist, the trapped and buried unconscious traumas, some acknowledged, some just sensed and felt, emerged and released. In time, I began to feel better, happier, engaged in life. Other times, I felt deep despair and depression as many necessary healing crises occurred. Insights, change of patterns and new endeavors gradually, without great effort, happened. Sometimes it was two steps forward and one step back. I never quite knew or could predict what would happen with each session; however, I grew to trust the work enough to know that whatever happened was for my higher good.

Authentic healing is a messy business and definitely a process. We are very complex beings and we choose (consciously or unconsciously) to believe we can heal or not. I wasn't aware of any of my own beliefs about the topic when I began to receive MFR; however, it wasn't long before I became hopeful and then clear that I could heal. I have, and I continue to heal in ways that up until a few years ago were unimagined.

Myofascial Release is potent work *and* it is whatever you are willing to allow it to be for you and your journey. Nothing is ever forced. People who receive MFR, as taught by John Barnes, are given support, space, compassion and assistance with the opening of those trapped, restricted places in their web, allowing for discovery, release, freedom and change all at the pace and the choice of each person. This is authentic healing.

As my own journey progressed, I began to take power back. For most of my life, I looked to others to give me the answers or to fix me. Now I take responsibility for myself and listen to others to see what feels right. I don't drive myself crazy trying to figure everything out. This doesn't mean that I stopped learning or that I don't make mistakes. It just means that learning is now an enhancement to my knowing and not necessarily the absolute answer to my needs or questions. When something feels right to me, I know what to do and no longer have to keep trying to figure it out. And sometimes I knowingly take a risk and, sometimes, it works.

So much has changed for me over the years and the most important thing of all is that I have learned to love and respect myself; something that hadn't happened as I blamed and beat up on myself most of my life. My willfulness has become willingness. I became more centered and grounded. I became less reactive and more responsive. I feel gratitude often. I notice my surroundings and appreciate nature and its teachings every day. Instead of helpless tears, I cry cleansing tears. I no longer take any drugs, and I am able to play tennis several times a week with joy. I forgive myself more readily and easily once my faux pas has been acknowledged. It is great to be alive and I no longer fear death.

Of course, I have my aches and pains and get treated with MFR regularly. Just like most other people, I experience hurt and suffering. The difference is that I flow better with all the experiences in my life. I have learned how to self-treat and use many MFR principles and tools to live my life. And I am honored to share my MFR skills and knowledge with others. My relationships are rich and rewarding, even and sometimes especially those day to day interactions with the cashier, the waitress, etc.

Let's look at some very specific results I credit to MFR. Prior to MFR, because of pain, I had difficulty walking more than a block or two. Now I can walk for miles. Prior to MFR, I didn't even dream of playing tennis. Now I play at least several times per week and my strength, agility and rating have all improved. Since MFR, my eyeglass prescriptions have decreased twice since my eyes improved. Prior to MFR, I wore only sneakers since my feet hurt with other shoes. Now, with the exception of high heels, I can wear any kind of shoe. Prior to MFR, I had severe low back pain once or twice a year lasting 4 to 6 weeks. Now, I don't have low back pain. Prior to MFR, I had a cardiac arrhythmia and took a beta blocker. The arrhythmia is gone and so too the beta blocker.

And while those are all fabulous results, the much bigger result is the easing of the chronic fear and anxiety that ran my life. It is no wonder that my body tightened down when I think of the many fears that were contained and buried in my web. I thought I was fearless- Ha! Now, many fears are gone and other fears that come up are acknowledged and released to the best of my ability. And some fears, like the raising of hackles when danger lurks, are respected, appreciated and listened to. I trust my own red flags now.

Somewhere along the way in my ongoing MFR journey, I put my ego in the backseat. My higher self, higher knowing or essence, or whatever words work for you, took the driver seat. It was a gradual process that I didn't consciously recognize until one day, I just didn't feel like being right anymore and I lost interest in being right. Who cares? There is recognition that all of us are works in progress doing the best we can. And each journey, each being, and each being's reality and experiences are unique. When I fully embrace that uniqueness and let myself be curious, and interested, I am able to enjoy life.

There were many traumas in my childhood. I grew up in a house of dark confusion, inconsistent guidelines, lots of anger and fighting. When I left at 17 years old, I thought I left that all behind. I didn't realize that I continued to "play out" those traumas, adding more to the already thickening layers until all awareness of what had happened became buried. I can easily recall my horror in one of my earlier MFR sessions when I vividly felt the abuse that occurred at an early age. At the same time, I was beginning to be able to embrace that buried child that suffered dearly.

The rich vastness of our individuality continues to astound me. I am amazed at the many profound and resilient ways we cope to survive the early messages of childhood- "Just push through it" "Oh, you are fine, stop crying" "You can't tell anybody or else……" "You don't know what you are talking about" and the list goes on and on. Many of those traumas, minor and major, and the messages that went with the trauma are trapped in our fascial system and play in the background like a broken record while we think we know what we are doing. Then we become adults and live, often unconsciously according to those same messages even when they no longer work for us. As some of those layers are peeled away with MFR, shifts occur. As awareness dawns, choice becomes possible and welcomed. And in time, life becomes much more interesting and joyful. As a consequence of that shift, the physical body begins to feel lighter and freer.

One chronic fear that has eased over time is that of my worry and concern about how others perceive me. Oh, how I wanted to be perceived by others as beautiful and capable and smart. Now, I chuckle. There is this deeper acceptance of myself and a commitment to being authentic that now usually overrides approval seeking behavior. My curiosity often takes precedence when I am with others. I find myself looking for the inner spark, inner light, or essence of the person I am with. I enjoy and am frequently inspired by how each person operates in the world. My compassion and respect for myself and others has deepened.

I remember feeling the love and the light of my higher self when I was eighteen months old and how much I wanted to share that. The light coming through the window and playing with the dust particles in the air was exquisite. I was very confused and disturbed that my mother and father didn't see or feel it. I remember wanting with all of my being to show them the way. Throughout many ensuing life experiences I forgot that feeling. I suppressed my knowing and my feelings and my intuitions. While school was rather boring, I did my best to please others and get a bit of approval which I mistook at times for love. During college and various jobs, I was a fairly well-liked outsider, not really going with the crowd and yet not anti-crowd. I was often agitated and disturbed as I watched the changes in healthcare that impeded the delivery of good care.

Myofascial Release initially helped me to feel without agonizing pain and to tap into hope. I had times of being pain free. As my journey progressed, I discovered and embraced my hurt and buried "little girl." And as the adult me reunited with the child me, I once again fully felt that love and wonder I once had as an eighteen month old child. Now, I feel that every day.

I can hear John Barnes in a seminar saying, "You can only take your client as far as you are willing to go". Well, I have been and continue to be willing to go as far as it takes, whatever it takes, while respecting and honoring the boundaries of myself and others. While I don't really know for sure, I have come to believe that you and I are here to explore, learn, create and connect. For many of us, as we grow older, much becomes trapped in our system- hurts, accidents, grudges, rote and boring behavior, as well as antiquated beliefs and ideas. Add to that a competitive, fix-me based culture, a healthcare system that views us as parts and chemicals and it is not surprising that pain appears. While there are many paths and many modalities to ease pain, Myofascial Release is a comprehensive and non-injurious option that results in authentic healing of the being. Often, too, other options that are pursued are enhanced by MFR – acupuncture becomes more helpful, talk therapy deepens, blood pressure medication reduces or becomes unnecessary. The list is endless.

Another Myofascial Release principle, heard at every seminar is that "You have to feel to heal". For me, I have found that feeling is the key to living vibrantly and exuberantly. Feeling my way through has alleviated much of my pain. Myofascial Release has helped to open the door to my wise, knowing, feeling self and has given me tools to confidently continue an exciting journey without chronic fear and dysfunction. We have all been conditioned to push down our feeling selves and disease has become rampant in our society. It is not our fault; however, it is our responsibility to reverse the trend. That starts with each of us, one by one. If I take care of me, I can help others.

So that's what I do now. I take care of me, and I serve others. For as long as I can remember, I wanted to be a nurse. As with many things in life, the dream and vision do not always manifest as imagined. Through many experiences and bumps in the road, I am honored to have found the way to practice "nursing" at its finest. The art and science of Myofascial Release compliments all the many things I have learned as a nurse and as a human being so that when I work, I am using all that I have gleaned thus far. It is rewarding to witness the journey of others and the discoveries and healing that occur. Always clear that I don't heal anybody, I am blessed to be a helper of others in their unique process and story.

Nancy Murray's client shares...

I had always been a very active person. I wasn't an athlete, but I loved moving and the kind of exertion and exercise that brought exhaustion in the end. I was a sunrise to sunset gardener and a, "Hey, let's swim to the other side of the lake" kind of gal. When I began pursuing my love of dance through classes at a college, I began to become aware that my body's structure and alignment wasn't suited to that type of activity, or subsequently, anything I tried. Gentle Yoga? Not gentle on my body. Tai Chi? Who gets injuries from Tai Chi? Walking it was, but not without discomfort.

I tried many different healing modalities over the years, from those quite common these days to lesser known ones, such as Orthobionomy, which are all fine therapies, but in the end, their effects were temporary for me. I wasn't looking for short term improvement.

In 2008, I sat on my dying mother's bed, my torso twisted to support her body as she ate. As the minutes ticked by, I could feel muscles start to pull and spasm; then the pulling and spasms began to occur in other areas, then in others. I breathed into the pain. When the director of the facility found out what had happened, she gifted me a session with their massage therapist. Since I couldn't move now without discomfort, I accepted her offer.

As the therapist worked, an amazing thing began to happen. My whole body began to relax and spasms stopped. By the end of the session, I walked away pain free. I felt wonderful. This was not any massage I had experienced and I had to find out what she was doing. It was MFR.

Within two weeks of that wonderful session, while handling some extremely challenging situations, I was opening a cabinet door. All of the sudden, it felt like I had taken a bullet in my back. I couldn't move and even breathing was almost as painful. As soon as I could, I crawled to the phone and later that day, I was on my way to another MFR practitioner. After just an hour's session, I was upright and had free mobility. Without question, I was going to seek a practitioner upon my return home.

Past experience had shown that no matter what modality I was involved with, I would at some point be injured. Though my first experiences with MFR had brought wonderful results and I had never given up my search for resolution of my physical challenges, I lacked the trust and faith that MFR would be any different than my past had shown. Little did I know, what was to come.

During the second visit to a local practitioner, I was in pain and so sensitive, the slightest of touches felt extreme and caused muscles to spasm. I felt sciatic nerve pain begin, something I thought was long gone. The therapist did her best to explain that MFR does not cause injury and that my experience was a part of the MFR process of the healing; I would need to feel the pain in order to heal it. I was encouraged to not give up, but I wasn't convinced. I felt that the session had "created" more problems.

I left without another appointment, frustrated and upset by yet another disappointment and went for a walk. Remembering the practitioner had given me a small book titled, *A Patient's Guide to Understanding John F. Barnes Myofascial Release,* by Cathy Covell, I sat down and began to read. As I turned page after page, a remarkable thing began to happen. The sciatic pain began to abate, spasms began to ease, and my doubts, anxieties and fear began to fade. A huge weight fell away and I took a deep breath. This was the beginning of my learning how to allow discomfort and pain to move through me and be released, so true healing could take place.

With renewed faith and optimism, I made another appointment and many subsequent ones over the years. I have never had a relapse, nor returned to a former state. Healing has always moved in a forward direction and my body has become strong and resilient.

MFR is a true holistic form of therapy. It not only allows pain and trauma to be released for good, but opens up a way for emotional and spiritual baggage (which no longer serves us), to be released as well. We don't have to know what the issues are, just partner in the release. Through MFR, I now move through life more relaxed, with greater flexibility and ease. Instead of resisting life, I now embrace it. For this, I am deeply grateful.

- Claudia, a NY Artist

CATHY COVELL, PT

Orland, Indiana
Motion For Life, S-corp
motion_for_life@yahoo.com

My road to discovering the benefits of JFBMFR involved my own physical pain and dysfunction. I know that having my own pain has really helped me become a better therapist because I know what it is like to go down the road of chronic pain. I know the frustrations that come with trying one thing after another in hopes of feeling better to only be in pain again.

Many of my symptoms began to manifest while I was in high school. I began having problems with ovarian cysts and had at least one ovarian cyst rupture each year through my late twenties. During my junior year in college, I had surgery to remove my right ovary and a large cyst. At the time, I was a very competitive athlete and was in the middle of basketball season. Even though I had undergone major surgery, I was back playing again in two weeks. I now know that caused a lot of bracing and scarring.

I have played sports all of my life and led a very active lifestyle, which involved being very hard on my body. I pushed myself to the limits in sports and also rode horses and motorcycles throughout my life, which led to various injuries. I was a high level athlete and pushed myself to excel in volleyball and basketball all the way through college. I was constantly training for, or participating in, organized sports through my early twenties.

After I graduated with my first degree, and before starting physical therapy school, I began having back pain. As my pain continued to increase, I was unable to walk more than a few blocks before I had to stop because of pain down my leg and spasms in my back. During this time, I was working as an aide at a physical therapy clinic and I tried all the different non-invasive avenues that I knew of. None helped so I thought surgery was my only option. At that point, I was in so much pain that I agreed to the major surgery that was suggested. I underwent surgery in May and started physical therapy school in August. I did have some improvements after the surgery. I didn't have constant numbness, but I still had pain, spasms, and occasional numbness.

During physical therapy school, and for the five years after I graduated, I searched for a way to relieve my own pain. I tried everything I was taught in school, with little result, and then started taking continuing education classes. I focused on taking any seminar that had to do with the pelvis or the back. I tried all the manipulations, mobilizations, stabilization exercises, and stretches that were supposed to help alleviate back pain. I also was constantly pushing myself with all the strengthening exercises that were supposed to help with back pain. I was in what most people would consider excellent physical condition, but I was in constant pain and was unable to find anything that gave me more than temporary relief.

Believe me – it was very frustrating to be a physical therapist in more pain than my patients. I know what it is like to be let down by the health care profession, and I was a part of that profession! Since I was a physical therapist and was in excellent shape, the doctors couldn't look at me and say that I just needed to lose weight or that I just needed to do my exercises correctly, so I was given different drug options. I was also frustrated by the fact that many of my patients continued to have pain after receiving treatment. I felt like there was something that I was missing. So, I started trying alternative treatments. I had about every kind of massage available and also tried acupuncture. All produced only temporary benefits.

During this time in my life, my good days were days when I had a constant dull ache; my bad days were when my leg would go numb or I had a knife like pain in my back. I was unable to sit or stand for more than twenty to thirty seconds without needing to shift my weight due to the pain. I was slowly giving up the things I loved to do, like playing sports and riding horses. I was told that my pain was due to scar tissue and there was really nothing that could be done to help with scar tissue. I was frustrated, depressed and angry. I worked daily with people who had been in chronic pain for years and I could see the path I was heading down- pain medicines that would have to be continually increased, a slow decline of my life to the point of disability. It was a very bleak future. Here I was, in my mid- to late-twenties and in constant pain. I didn't even want to think about what life would be like when I reached my fifties. It was very depressing and frustrating.

It was at this time that a therapist colleague offered to treat me using John F. Barnes' MFR. Honestly, I didn't really have much faith that it would help, but I thought I would just go along with it. I didn't have anything to lose by trying. So, I started the treatments. Within three or four treatments I felt a significant change for the better. I will always remember the night I laid down in bed and was able to straighten my legs fully. Previously, I always had to sleep with my knees bent and my trunk turned to the side or else I would have too much pain. My first thought was, "Wow, I can put my legs straight without pain!" Then my second thought was, "Well, we'll see how long this lasts." I was so used to having temporary results that I didn't think these results would last either. Well, I'm still sleeping with my legs straight today!

So, when I have patients who come to me who are skeptical, who have tried it all and really have no faith that this can help, I can relate. I tell them that they couldn't be any more skeptical than I was when I first started receiving treatments. To be honest, I thought it was crap. It looked too simple and wasn't forceful enough, so how could that help? The thing is, the results speak for themselves.

To say that MFR has given me my life back is an understatement. I can honestly say that I feel better now than I did at twenty-six. Not only that, I also have the knowledge to help keep my body in the best shape possible for the rest of my life.

After my first treatments, I signed up to take classes taught by John F. Barnes. I wanted to be able to help others the way I was helped. These classes changed everything. I signed up for the classes thinking that I would learn a nice manual technique that would help reduce physical pain and improve physical function. Little did I know that these classes went way beyond just helping with physical symptoms, but would help with true healing. They would lead me down the path of mind/body/spirit healing.

During these classes, I learned about tissue memory and how the body can store physical and emotional sensations from past traumas in the cells. I discovered that much of my pain came from the past physical and emotional traumas that I had suffered throughout my life. I learned that these past traumas were actually still actively being felt in my body all the time, which was the cause of much of my bracing and pain. How did I discover this? I experienced it! Healing involves feeling and clearing the past traumas and the false beliefs and lies we hold onto. It also involves having an increased awareness that can lead to choosing healthier beliefs.

I was awakened to an entirely different idea of healing that went beyond just the physical. It involved the mind, the body, the heart and the spirit. I began reading books by Don Miguel Ruiz, Caroline Myss, Wayne Dyer and many others who focus on true healing of the mind, body and spirit. These classes and books opened my life up professionally as well as personally. I learned ways to finally help patients heal themselves by walking through my own healing journey. The whole body approach taught by John F. Barnes completely changed the way that I treated as a therapist and the entire way I look at health, balance and life.

I continued to take John's classes, other classes on healing, got treated myself, read books and also participated in a Skill Enhancement Seminar at John's Pennsylvania Myofascial Release Treatment Center. This led to the opportunity to become a coverage therapist there and eventually led to working full time at the Treatment Center for two and a half years. Being able to work at John's clinic was a huge catalyst in both my personal and professional growth. People came from all over the world to receive treatment at this facility. We saw all types of diagnoses. The experience I received helped me gain the confidence needed to start teaching a seminar on treating horses using JFBMFR. Teaching this seminar has been an incredible experience. Every seminar I teach helps remind me of how effective the techniques are and also how easy it is to treat when following John's principles.

In 2007, I returned to my home in Indiana so I could be close to my family and bring MFR to the area. I really didn't know how successful my clinic would be. My hometown is in a very rural area. But, the results of MFR speak for themselves. I did not market. I started treating people and they spread the word. I decided to have my treatment center in the lower level of my house to begin with and see how it went from there. I started out treating 2 days a week and within a year I was there full time.

During this time, I also read several books about people interacting with horses to help with their healing process- including *The Tao of Equus* and *Riding Between the Worlds*, both by Linda Kohanov. The philosophy of these books went along perfectly with the healing philosophy of my clinic, so I started implementing what I call "Equine Facilitated Awareness" at my clinic. The results were fabulous. I found that the principles taught in the JFB-MFR classes are life principles, and that applying those principles to all aspects of life can lead to freedom on all levels. What are these principles? They are: Everything is connected. Everything is unique and dynamic. If you force, you will get resistance. Change takes time. There is a flow to life. Life has cycles. Truth is a felt sense.

I wanted to create a treatment center that could help with all the aspects of healing. Adding the horse sessions was a perfect way to help people become aware of patterns, thoughts, beliefs and attitudes that were limiting their healing. I am continuing to let my clinic evolve so that each person can have the dynamic experience that will help them on their healing journey.

We have created a center where people who are ready to take the steps to heal are helped on their respective paths. We make it clear that it is a participatory process. We will do what we can, and we need each patient to meet us by doing his or her part. This is the only way to help empower people in their healing journey. Too much of healthcare has put the patient in a passive position and has taken the patient's power away. Healing needs to be about *empowering*.

In 2012, my clinic had its five year anniversary. Here at Motion For Life, I currently have two full-time and two part-time human therapists, one office goddess, one horse rehab facilitator, and several four-legged therapists, including horses, dogs and cats. We treat people, dogs, and horses with Myofascial Release. We rehabilitate horses that have had physical and emotional traumas and offer Equine Facilitated Awareness programs. We also hold seminars on Equine Myofascial Release and Equine Facilitated Awareness, and we do comprehensive programs, as well.

Motion For Life is now a vital part of the community. We have become the treatment facility that people refer their families and friends to. They know that each person will get individual treatment that focuses on healing and balance instead of just treating symptoms. We have people come from all over the country and world to receive treatment and to participate in the seminars. This is one of the few clinics, if there are any other, that combine Myofascial Release with Equine Facilitated Awareness.

Also in 2012 I completed my book, *Feeling Your Way Through*. It is a comprehensive book detailing all that I have learned thus far on my healing journey. I wrote it as a way to help myself process and integrate all that I have learned, and also to hopefully help others along their journey.

What does the future hold? I am now converting my house fully into the treatment center. The facility is perfect – on a dirt road with rolling hills, a nature reserve across the road, an indoor arena for the horse activities, and an incredible energy. The treatment center continues to evolve, as I am looking to hire another human therapist and also expand the horse rehabilitation and the Equine Facilitated Awareness programs. I want to continue to be open to providing an inclusive and dynamic treatment program for every individual, in order that each may find their own unique healing path.

As for me personally, in 2012, I also made a big transformation. I took a three week journey to Italy. It started on January 1st, with the intent of really doing some inner work and focusing on what I wanted in the future. It was an incredible trip filled with moments of complete connectedness and also moments of absolute shattering and loneliness. It was a great way to really look at what I wanted, what was important to me, and to see in what areas of my life I was still letting fear control me. To truly be free, you have to be willing to "lose it all," and to let go of all the beliefs, thoughts and lies that are keeping you small. It was a tough journey, but it has been worth it.

I feel that I have reached a place in my life where I am really focusing on freedom – freedom of my mind, my heart, my spirit and my body. It is an exciting place to be that has led me to really letting go of restrictions on all layers. As I have done this, the clinic that I started has also broken free. I do not consider it MY clinic anymore as there is a family of humans and animals that has come together to bring this treatment center to life. I truly feel honored to be a part of the transformation.

Physically, instead of dreadfully wondering what life will be like when I reach fifty, sixty and beyond, I feel excited at the possibilities that I will continue to feel even better and better. As I continue to self treat and receive treatment, my body continues to become even more free. Not only am I riding horses, but I am going on weeklong camping and trail riding trips where I ride every day for two to eight hours and feel good. I was able to complete the plane rides overseas and sleep in different hotel beds without issue. I no longer have to moderate my life because of the pain.

I feel like I continue to connect more fully with my body and will be able to live a much more full and enjoyable life due to freeing up the restrictions in my body. I used to have to plan each day by the amount of pain or limits I would have, and now it isn't even a consideration. Any trip that involved sitting longer than 15 minutes would be painful. Then I would have to weigh out the fun I may experience with an activity against the aftermath I would suffer when done. It's nice to now have the freedom to do what I want!

When you have been in pain for so long, your version of "normal" gets off balance. I feel so good now compared to how I used to feel, that I really start to believe that I am back to "normal." Then, I get a treatment or self-treat and realize that I can feel even better. Looking into the future and now thinking, "I wonder how much better I will be able to feel," instead of, "I wonder how much longer I will be able to stand the pain," is an absolute gift!

I am extremely grateful for John F. Barnes and all of the wonderful teachers that have helped me along my journey. And I am also really starting to appreciate myself and the journey that I have taken. It truly has been up to me each step of the way whether I chose to heal or to continue to spin on the merry-go-round. It is true that when the student is ready, the teacher will appear. My road had many bumps and I know that I have, at times, made choices that delayed my healing, but each delay also led to healing opportunities.

There have been many times that I wanted to give up, that the struggle seemed too hard or impossible, but something kept me going. It is my hope that the treatment center here, my books and seminars, my website, and my story will help others on their journeys. I hope those who feel like giving up will be able to see that healing is possible on all levels. I am extremely grateful that I am able to live my dream with the evolution of the treatment center. As I look back on the road that I have taken, I can see there were a lot of bumps along the way, but each one has led me to become the person I am today and allows me to be the therapist I am, too. I have to say that it's wonderful to feel that the future is full of possibilities!

Two of Cathy Covell's clients share...

Seven years ago, my husband and I bought our first house. After all of the excitement of moving in, redecorating, and holiday parties was over, we quickly realized that we were missing something...we needed a dog! It took several months of calling on advertisements in our local paper, but we finally found the right Labrador Retriever breeder. We agreed on the largest, and only yellow, male of the litter. We were on our way!

My husband and I spent the next two weeks buying all sorts of puppy supplies, puppy-proofing our house, and soaking in as much advice as we could from seasoned Labrador Retriever owners. By far, the toughest thing we did in those two weeks was try to pick out a name. We didn't have any children, so this was the first time we had to give something a name. After much thought, we settled on Bentley.

The first year with Bentley flew by in a jumble of early mornings, early nights (because of the early mornings), crate training, house breaking, a million walks around the block, trips to the store to buy yet another bag of dog food, refilling the water bowl because he'd knocked it over for the thirtieth time that day, constant monitoring to make sure he wasn't chewing on the table legs again, and obedience classes (after finally remembering a piece of advice we were given months ago). Thanks to Bentley we did finally get to meet our next door neighbors one afternoon, because we had to knock on their door and explain that our dog ate part of their fence and was currently in their back yard digging a hole to China!

Bentley grew up overnight. We fell into bed one night totally exhausted from wearing out a puppy so he would sleep through the night, and woke up the next morning to find a laid back dog that very easily fit into our lives. Yes, we had made it through the puppy stage and we were greatly rewarded with a fantastic dog! Over the next four years, Bentley went everywhere with us, did everything with us and was always very well behaved. Bentley had grown to love spending time with my father-in-law's dog, Copper, and running with her through the cornfields near her house. He also loved playing fetch with a basketball in our backyard with my husband and going for walks all over our neighborhood with me. Bentley never met a stranger and was certain every animal or person he came across really just wanted to play with him!

Bentley's injury happened on a Thursday afternoon in December of 2011. I received a call at work from my husband saying that something was wrong with Bentley and I should meet him at our vet's office. My husband said he and Bentley were playing fetch with the basketball in our backyard, just like they did every night. Bentley was sitting waiting for my husband to throw the basketball. When Bentley stood up and turned to chase the basketball he immediately fell back down to the ground. Bentley tried to get back up and chase the ball but instead was only able to get his front legs to move. The good news was that no bones appeared to be out of place or broken. The bad news was that the vet wasn't sure what was causing the paralysis. The vet suggested Bentley spend the night with him and receive a course of steroids shots. I remember the vet mentioning exploratory surgery or possible permanent paralysis. I agreed to the vet's suggestions but requested that Bentley be given something to help him calm down and sleep. Leaving Bentley with the vet that night was hands down the hardest thing we've ever had to do.

After leaving Bentley, my husband and I went home to talk about the hard stuff. We discussed how we felt about exploratory surgery, what it would be like to have a ninety-pound Bentley with permanent hind-end paralysis, and how we would decide when enough was enough. And, of course, we discussed where we would bury him.

Late that evening, we came to the decisions that we would not make Bentley endure the pain of exploratory surgery or permanent paralysis. If we were not able to have Bentley be Bentley then we preferred to have no Bentley at all. Friday morning I received a phone call from the vet that there had been zero improvement in Bentley's condition since the night before. The vet had three suggestions; exploratory surgery, continuing the steroids for the weekend to see if any improvement occurred, or putting him down. We already knew that we weren't doing the surgery but my husband and I just couldn't give up on Bentley yet. I called into work to give my boss, Cathy Covell, an update. Her reply was, "pick him up and bring him here!" I was at such a loss about what else to do for Bentley, there was no choice but to accept her offer. If nothing else, I could get some work done and have Bentley close by.

I picked Bentley up from the vet's office and headed to work at Motion For Life, which is a myofascial release clinic. When I pulled in, Cathy came out to the car, and Bentley WAGGED HIS TAIL!!! I quickly pointed out to Cathy that this was the first movement from that end of his body since his injury. I was so excited for a brief second but then was too afraid to get my hopes up. Cathy checked on Bentley throughout the day, and also showed me some techniques to try on him. I had no idea what I was doing or if I was doing the techniques correctly but it made me feel like I was helping. All of the other therapists at the clinic that day took time out of their schedules to work on Bentley, too. His breathing slowed to a more normal pace and at one point he was even laying flat out on his side snoring! I felt like he was finally getting some relief and comfort. Bentley stayed the weekend with Cathy and she worked on him every day. By Sunday, Cathy was taking him outside to go potty with a rolled-up bath towel as a sling around his belly. Every once in a while, Bentley would slightly move the tip of his tail when the other dogs or cats came around. This gave us all hope.

My husband and I took Bentley home with us Sunday night. We both felt that Bentley was not in any pain but we also recognized that we could not carry his hind end around forever. It was hard to put a specific time limit on how long we could do it, but we both felt comfortable taking it day-by-day. We promised to be honest with each other and not let it drag out for too long. On that Monday, I called to update the vet. Bentley was prescribed steroids in pill form, starting with a larger dose and gradually tapering off. I was able to take Bentley to work with me every day and all of the therapists continued to work on Bentley. My husband and I became obsessed with finding something new each day that meant Bentley was making progress. He soon became able to get himself into a sitting position and I even talked myself into believing that he eventually was sitting straighter than he had been...we looked for anything to keep the hope alive.

By the end of the second week, Bentley was putting weight on his back legs again. It wasn't much, but it was a couple of seconds. Every day, he got treated and was making small progress. During the third week my sister was at my house helping me prepare for the family gathering we would be hosting on Christmas Eve. She was holding the back door open for me so I could take Bentley outside when she said, "Oh isn't that cute, he's moving his back feet like he's walking!" I just about dropped Bentley's hind end on the back porch. I couldn't believe it, but she wasn't lying! I took a video with my phone and sent it to my husband. This was amazing!!

It was obvious at this point that progress was being made, and it was possible Bentley might make a recovery. By the end of the third week (Christmas Eve), Bentley was walking again. Not well, not for long distances, and not without looking like Bambi on ice, but he was walking. It became a matter of trying to keep him contained so that he didn't walk too much or hurt himself trying to get somewhere. I believe this is also when his MFR treatments became a little more physically active for the therapist! My husband and I once again talked about the hard stuff; what percentage of a recovery was good enough for us? We agreed that Bentley could not be in any pain, that he had to be able to eat/drink on his own, and that he needed to continue to not have any potty accidents in the house. As long as these conditions were met we didn't care how much he recovered. As long as Bentley was happy then we were happy.

I took Bentley to work with me every day for five weeks. During those five weeks, he received MFR treatments almost every day. He made about an 85% recovery. We were ecstatic. In all of the years of our vet's practice, he had never had anyone else with such a large dog elect not to do surgery or just put them down except for us. We were so fortunate to have MFR!

It has been exactly one year since Bentley was hurt in our backyard and he is still making progress. He is back to playing with Copper and we're back up to being able to walk for forty minutes. He is able to use his hind legs to jump into the backseat of my car again and just this past weekend he jumped over a puddle of water on the sidewalk! It amazes me that after all this time I'm still noticing things he's doing for the first time again. I don't know if he'll ever make a 100% recovery, but we're very pleased with the recovery he's made and extremely grateful for the extra time we've been given with our beloved Bentley.

My journey started on September 23, 1952. I'd had a difficult delivery and was caught in the birth canal. The doctors argued about a cesarean section, but my mother's O.B. doctor would not allow it. Thus, I was born with torticollis (a twisted neck). At six months old, I was admitted to Hillsdale Community Hospital – where I was born – to have the sternocleidomastoid (SCM) muscle excised from my neck.

Years passed and then, in the late 1970's, I began to have problems. I was working in construction, making apartment buildings and houses. I started having headaches, and the left side of my neck had spasm-like twitching and jerks. My left arm seemed to be getting weaker, and my left leg jerked at night when I went to bed. After seeing a couple of doctors, one decided to do a myelogram. A herniated disc at C-6/ C-7 was discovered. The strength in my bicep and tricep was also weakening, as was the grip in my left hand.

On September 18, 1980, I had the disc surgery and did well for a short time afterwards. Then, it turned out that the disc at C-5/ C-6 was bad. Those vertebrae were fused on June 25, 1981. The doctors tried to excise the other SCM band, but I always felt they were just hoping it would help.

I also had some problems with blood pressure, and there was question as to whether I'd had a stroke, so I was sent to a neurologist in Kalamazoo, Michigan. Several tests were done at Borgess Hospital, including an EMG, CT scans and another myelogram. It was during this time that the neurosurgeon speculated that I had syringomyelia. So, he sent me to the Mayo Clinic in Rochester, Minnesota for a second opinion from the doctors who had trained him. They confirmed the diagnosis, and discussed with me a new test that was being developed at the University of Michigan in Ann Arbor, but that would not be available for several years. I was given medicines for pain, many of which made me feel like a zombie – completely out of it most of the time.

In June of 1985, I was sent to the University of Michigan for an MRI exam. When we got to see the results on the computer, we could see the syrinx. It was from the brain to the C-4/ C-5 level at that time. I was repeatedly told that my symptoms were not bad enough to do such a serious operation, but in August of 1986, doctors operated and put in a shunt at the C-2 level. All of the spinal fluid had to be taken out, and I had the worst three days of my life while the fluid built back up.

For the next two years, I continued to have burning and weakness on my left side. The syrinx extended down the entire length of the spinal cord. Because of my leg problems, a disc surgery at L-4/ L-5 was performed in September of 1988. I was told that I had degenerative disc disease along with all of my other problems. I was also told that I had Arnold-Chiari malformation. I had tried physical therapy at the hospital after surgery, with little success. Over the years, I had also tried a tens unit and trigger point injections, as well as an assortment of medicines which, in the long run, only helped a bit.

We traveled to a renowned clinic in Ohio in 2003 for a neck surgery, and I ended up with a severe Staph infection – MRSA. In 2004, when none of my surgeries proved successful in relieving my pain or helping with my walking or arm strength, a pain stimulator was recommended. That, too, caused infection, and had to be removed. I continued to be followed by my neurosurgeon in Kalamazoo as needed, although he has now retired.

In 2009, I went to step into my van, fell backwards, and saved myself by catching the steering wheel. My wife and I went to Kalamazoo, and the next day I had lower back surgery. The specialist put rods and screws in my back, and I was in a back brace for three months. Things seemed to be going okay until the doctors found that the screws were coming loose. My bones were too soft, and, therefore, the doctors had to operate again. I was in a body cast for three months. I spent five weeks in a rehabilitation facility nearby. Water therapy was suggested, and this helped some. At this point, I was using a walker just to get around, and I slept in a hospital bed at home. The pain never went away. The medicines would take it away some, but they also made me sleep all the time. When my wife would ask me to do something simple, like fold a basket of towels while she was at work, it never got done.

In 2011, we were visiting with family after a Christmas dinner. My sister from Chicago, Judy, brought up John F. Barnes' Myofascial

Release therapy. She had been trying it, and felt that it was helping her quite a bit. My wife, Phyllis, started researching it and we decided to ask my neurosurgeon about it at my appointment in January of 2012. Since we had tried every surgery anyone dared, we presented this idea to think outside the box. He said that as long as there was no manipulation to the neck, where my shunt and fusion was, I could try this.

Back at home, my wife and I researched who might be available in Kalamazoo or Ann Arbor. But, knowing that traveling to either of these places would be a 90 minute trip for each treatment, we decided to look in northern Ohio and Indiana. My wife found Cathy Covell at Motion for Life in Orland, Indiana. It was about 40 minutes from our home, so we decided to start there and see what would happen. Well, I feel like I have won the lottery, because our relationship has been a very successful one.

I believe that I started treatment in May of 2012. At the time, I used my walker outside and a cane inside. My left leg was still dragging some. I could not lift my arm over my head, and could not turn my head side to side, or look up at the sky.

Since starting this therapy, I have cut my pain medications in half. I no longer walk with the walker. I can lift my left hand up to wash my hair (before, I had to use my right arm to help lift the left arm). I do not use anything to walk within the house and use the cane only for long walks, or on uneven ground – and only for safety!!! I can turn my head more side-to-side, and can even lift it up a bit more to see the sky.

Since coming to Motion for Life, I have been changed. I was about to give up. I've still got a long way to go, but I feel like there is hope here. I have had to give up a lot of things that I loved to do – bowling, hunting, and fishing. Now, I have returned to doing some fishing with my wife, doing small wood projects, and playing with my grandchildren. I have just finished a fire truck bed for a little handicapped boy, and am presently working on Christmas projects for my grandchildren. I even have a future project in mind, to try something new.

I have possibilities again!

SANDY WHITCOMBE, LMT

Nashville, Tennessee
Nashville Myofascial Release Center
therapymuse@comcast.net

Profound! I have heard this word so many times through the years, and every time I smile in agreement. Yes, this work is profound. It is powerful. It is effective. I remember vividly my first Myofascial Release treatment.

My husband, Garth, and I had been in practice as Massage Therapists for several years. The chiropractor we worked with had an MFR session with a visiting therapist and was impressed enough to gift us with a treatment. I remember during the postural examination noticing my high shoulder for the first time. During the treatment I was surprised to find myself moving, a completely natural feeling, but then I began to feel uneasy, slightly panicked, which my therapist said was tissue memory surfacing.

This was impressive work! We felt we had found a missing piece to the bodywork puzzle, particularly when Garth's longstanding low back issue got substantially better and I had relief of neck and shoulder pain. We were cautioned to take a John Barnes Myofascial Release course only, as there are many MFR courses offered that are an older form, similar to deep tissue massage. Only Barnes' MFR offers the lasting results we were seeing from our first treatment.

A few months prior to that introductory MFR session we had visited Santa Fe, New Mexico. Returning home we had a stopover in Phoenix, Arizona. Our flight was not yet boarding, so we relaxed next to the gate, eating pizza and watching Oprah. That was when we entered a time warp, suddenly noticing not only had our flight been called, but there were only two people left in line. We rushed to the desk, finding that the flight had been overbooked. Since this was the last flight to Nashville until the next day we found ourselves in Phoenix with a day to explore.

Garth had passed through Sedona on a road trip a few years before and loved its powerful energy and stunning beauty. We drove through desert with tall cacti, enjoying the perfect summer day. Coming into Sedona the whole world lit up with color: red, purple, and orange against blue skies as the canyons opened up around us. We went for a swim in Oak Creek Canyon and sat in the sun, playing hooky and soaking up the magical vibes.

A photographer friend had given us a special picture as a wedding gift, Oak Creek Canyon in the wintertime. We agreed this must be a place we were meant to visit.

Back on the winding road we saw a beautiful clinic perched on the rocks overlooking the canyon. Therapy on the Rocks beckoned, and we pulled into the parking lot. We went inside, curious to see what kind of therapy they offered. There was a huge waterfall through the center of the building, and we were told this was a John Barnes Myofascial Release clinic. We walked through the facility, feeling a lovely connection and appreciating the rich vibrancy of the glowing red rock landscape visible from every room. What a wonderful tranquil atmosphere. We marveled, not realizing the enormous healing effect this special place would soon have on our lives.

Within months John Barnes came to Nashville to teach MFR1. We were filled with anticipation as we entered the building. Outside of the hotel ballroom country music Christmas songs filled the air. Massage therapists like us mingled with physical therapists, occupational therapists, and other health care professionals. We found our way quickly to the front row, not wanting to miss a single second. John entered the room and our MFR journey began, a journey that would lead us into an exciting and profound career and deep personal healing.

Myofascial Release, as taught by John, encompasses a comprehensive understanding of the body's structure, as well as emotion and spirit. None of this is ever truly separate, and in MFR we are always treating the whole person. The fascial system itself is a whole body system, a living dynamic representation of our lives. Fascia is present in every cell of our bodies in a continuous web, giving us shape and support. It is our shock absorber, dispersing forces throughout the system.

John led us through several hands-on techniques, reminding us often to soften, to feel, to stay present and centered in the moment. Each treatment would be different, he said, "This is not a cookbook approach. There are no recipes. Treat what you feel and let the body tell you where to go next. If you know what you are going to do when you enter the room, then you are not doing Myofascial Release."

The assistants were ever present and nonintrusive, gently touching our shoulders, encouraging us to soften and feel what was happening beneath our hands. It was quite unlike any class I had experienced before. There was an abundance of clear anatomical and linear information, a deep education imparted on how the fascial system operates. At the same time the feeling part of us, so often completely ignored in our modern medicine, was gently and firmly validated.

I felt I had come home. I often referred to my massage career as my second life. I had been an X-ray Technician for twenty years before taking the leap. My formative years, in a career sense, were spent entrenched in the medical system with all its technological marvels and its sometimes impersonal and dehumanizing structure. I had struggled with the square peg in a round hole syndrome for many years as my spirituality blossomed and my intuitive sense strengthened. Finally, I left the safety of an established career path for one that fed my soul and nurtured my health in a way that felt right to me.

The lights were lowered as John led us through a scar release technique. Scars from injuries and surgeries can greatly impact our fascial system, exerting pressure into pain sensitive structures and creating havoc in ways great and small. We may see a small scar on the outside while beneath the skin the fascia has hardened and formed tough ropy tissue that can cause pain and loss of range of motion.

Garth began to gently trace my C-section scar, which, to my surprise, was full of sensitive and tender spots. It hurt, but felt so needed, as if I had been held in a straight jacket without being aware of it. Suddenly my heart started to race and I felt an overwhelming panic. I fought for control, knowing I was in a class of medical professionals and not fully understanding why I was reacting like this. I began to shake as Garth asked if he was hurting me. "No," I said. "I just feel such panic. I don't know why. I've never reacted like this before...oh, wait! Never except when I had my C-section!" Whoa!

It all came back in a rush of sensation, the drape in front of my eyes, the joy of the birth of my son interrupted by a sudden intense panic that I could not control. I felt no pain, only a pulling sensation as the doctor expertly sewed the layers of tissue back together. "What is going on?" asked the anesthesiologist. "I'm a little nervous," I gulped, not wanting to be a wimp. "I'll say! Your blood pressure and pulse just went through the roof!"

He began to talk, telling me stories from his life in a calm and soothing voice, and the pulse and blood pressure slowed and normalized. Whenever he would stop talking I would hear the beep, beep, beep of the monitor begin to get faster as my heart began to race again. He talked throughout the rest of the procedure, and I promptly forgot the panic and went on with my life.

Back in class I asked about what had just happened to me. John began to talk about tissue memory and how this work provides the ability to access those frozen moments in time that have become embedded in our tissues, placing a drag on our entire fascial system. "Tell yourself 'I survived,' " he said. I felt a great sense of relief, as if a weight had been lifted. Profound! He went on to explain that to our body and our subconscious mind, surgery is experienced as a mortal wound. Our rational mind knows this is not true, but that understanding is not available to the subconscious mind.

Many times we develop bracing patterns and postures within our bodies in response to this sense of threat that impact us deeply. Our fascia, living structural tissue that forms to support us and keep us functional, begins to harden and thicken into an internal straight jacket, creating pain and limiting our range of motion.

Myofascial Release, by honoring this subconscious information and bringing it to our conscious awareness, returns us to balance and health. "You will learn more of this in the Unwinding class," he assured us. Garth and I looked at each other. It looked like we would be attending the Unwinding class! Neither of us could imagine stopping now.

I have long thought a big part of the genius of John Barnes' Myofascial Release approach is his naming and validation of natural phenomena. Anyone who has ever watched a dog or cat move and stretch has observed unwinding. Children fidget and move and tap their fingers until we domesticate them and force them to be still. In Myofascial

Release we have Unwinding and Rebounding, both the most natural and intuitive of physical responses. When they are named and taught they take on some kind of mysterious power and sound strange, that is until you experience them. Then there is a deep recognition, a sense of coming home. There is a giving of permission in this work, an allowance of the intuitive nature within each of us that knows what we need to come back into balance and heal.

As John is fond of saying, "You can only take your patient as far as you have gone." The Myofascial Release journey is a life journey, and the principles are life principles. We do not force or lead in this work. We hold the space for another's healing and we assist and keep them safe. The unwinding class opened a portal for a deeper understanding and respect for the process of life.

As we were encouraged to let go and allow our bodies to move in whatever way they needed, the miracles continued. Observing, supporting, allowing, we were encouraged to feel into our bodies, to fully occupy our physicality. I was surprised to experience the depth of emotion beneath physical pain when I simply softened into it and allowed what was there to be expressed. Sometimes this is loud, with wrenching screams coming from the gut. Sometimes it is soft, with gentle tears flowing. Sometimes it is funny, hilarious even, the insights flooding my being with the most exquisite understanding.

There are forms of psychology that embrace the mythic. What is unique in Myofascial Release, as taught by John Barnes, is the acknowledgment of the physical, the understanding that our bodies are receptacles not only of our unique life experiences but also our unique conclusions about those experiences. As memories surfaced I discovered deep core beliefs in myself that I had no hope of changing because I was unaware they even existed.

In one treatment with John I was locked into struggle, fighting and pummeling the pillows provided with all my strength. "How would it be to give up the struggle?" John whispered. Give up the struggle? My eyes popped open. "Give up the struggle? No way! That stuff is in my DNA!" At that moment I felt all those hardworking determined strugglers who had come before me, and the impossibility of letting that go filled my being. Struggle? It defined me! "Just be with that," John said softly. "Let your inner guidance bring you insight, maybe now, maybe sometime in the next few days. Don't worry about it. It will come."

The next morning as I woke I was filled with the most delicious feeling. Of course! I am not my DNA! I am so much more than that! Laughing and crying I felt such love, blessing, and release. How did I not see that before?

We are constantly trying to make sense of our world and our place in it. When we find the beliefs that are running beneath the surface of our lives we have the opportunity to shift our perceptions and "upgrade the software." Most of the time we have no awareness of what is running us, and we suffer needlessly, triggered by people and events around us.

Through unwinding, the body-mind will take us into a position in space that is significant to us. In this still point, memories will flood in. We may shake or cry or scream. We may feel frozen in place, as if we will never move again. We may feel our awareness leaving our bodies, becoming spacey and floating, and then with the therapist's gentle prompt, feeling more deeply alive in our bodies than ever before.

Because Garth and I treat each other at least once a week and do self care on an ongoing basis, as well as attending seminars, this teaching has allowed us to gently resolve traumas and live with fluidity, joy and presence. Our first response to injury (unless life-threatening, of course!) is to unwind, to vocalize, to cry or shake, mostly to feel and release.

Once, when observing her two year old child throwing a temper tantrum, my sister remarked, 'I wish I could do that!" Indeed! Our children know what they must do to release disturbance from their body-mind. That same two year old, passionately alive and filled with an uncomplicated joy, is running freely through the house within minutes of the tantrum. Messy though it might be, uncivilized as it might seem, it is to our detriment that we have lost the ability to "do that!"

The memories and the releases come in an order that reflects and works with our daily lives. Big and small events, some long forgotten but important to us in ways we have not understood, surface. Our bodies and minds contain a wisdom that is forever guiding us toward miracles, integration, and expansion.

Following the unwinding class we knew we had found a life teaching, and we continued to study with John, gaining deep friendships with other myofascial therapists and an authentic approach to vibrant health. Each seminar offered flawless technique alongside profound shifts in sensitivity and intuition.

One morning I ran through our kitchen in way too much of a rush. I caught my little toe on a chair and dislocated it. Garth came running as I howled in pain. I could not bear to look at my toe sticking out at a right angle. I hobbled to a chair and he began energy work, thinking I should unwind the trauma before heading out to the emergency room. Soon I began to unwind, my whole leg and then my whole body. I trembled and shook and cried. We noticed that the toe was at a lesser angle than before. The pain had lessened as well, not that I was ready for Garth to touch it yet! Slowly the toe moved closer to its proper alignment, and after nearly an hour he was able to gently traction it. After three hours of treatment it was completely straight! No Emergency Room visit was needed. I had some tenderness for a few days but no residual damage. I will never doubt the efficacy of this work and the value of addressing an injury immediately.

The night before the rebounding seminar was to begin in Chicago my parents made an unscheduled trip to Nashville and stayed overnight with us. My Mom had suffered from Parkinson's disease for several years and was having episodes of dementia. She started to cry at bedtime and wanted to go home. It was so hard to watch her decline and see her slipping away from us.

During the seminar we were learning rebounding, a rocking back and forth motion that rehydrates tissues and softens fascial restrictions. As the motion entered my body I became aware of a tension and bracing. Softening into the gentle movement I suddenly felt an overwhelming grief. "I let go." By now the familiar mantra of Myofascial Release was so deeply ingrained that it was second nature in treatment to simply go with those wrenching feelings and let them carry me where I needed to go.

Deep sobs came from my gut as a whole history of my Mom and I replayed through my mind. At the end I felt such relief and peace, knowing she would always be there with me. Through her transition a couple of years later I was able to more fully feel, grieve and release because this "preview" had happened. The insights received were beyond words, comforting in such a complete way that later I could draw on the feeling and knowing that love would keep us forever connected.

Sedona! Again and again we returned to Sedona to study with John. The advanced studies are masterfully designed to nourish our intuition and take us "beyond technique." I am reminded of learning a musical instrument or learning to ride a bicycle, where movements and techniques are practiced over and over until the soul takes wings and the movement or the music pours through us. We cease to play the music and instead the music plays us.

In the red rocks of Sedona we were powerfully nourished and deeply challenged as therapists and as human beings. So often in life we guard and brace and hold our awareness outside anything that might feel threatening or hard, keeping ourselves "safe" even from our own memories. In so doing we cut ourselves off from our own worthiness and power.

I was deeply spiritual before Myofascial Release. What this work has opened for me is a level of trust I did not have before, an understanding that I am worthy and good, that whatever I need is available to me. No matter what has happened to me in my life, I love me!

MFR, as taught by John Barnes, is an open-ended work that honors the self-correcting nature of the body-mind and the inherent goodness of life itself. It does not attempt to impart a religion or a theological construct. It does not tell the body or the mind what to do. Instead our relationship with our own power and ability to find our way is gently mended and supported. The principles of not forcing the system, of being led by the body-mind of the patient, softening into each barrier, we find both in our physicality and in life itself have become life principles for me.

Indeed, MFR is a profound work, an honoring of the divine and of human nature. It returns us to ourselves, and for this I am eternally grateful.

Laura Probert, MPT

Bethesda, Maryland
Bodyworks Physical Therapy
bodyworkspt@comcast.net

My name is Laura Probert. I grew up in San Francisco but have spent the last eighteen years in Maryland, which is where my career as a physical therapist has grown and my awareness and happiness in life have blossomed. I began my myofascial release journey when I was thirty years old after signing up for MFR 1 in Baltimore, Maryland. I was four years out of physical therapy school and exploring different treatment approaches, hoping to be a better manual therapist and hoping to find a technique that helped people feel better. What I didn't realize back then is what an intense and fabulous leap I was about to make, not only in my career, but in my life.

Looking back to reflect on the last fourteen years of this amazing life, the one that myofascial release has helped to let shine by lighting a spark in my awareness and peeling back the layers of my web, is a complete joy to share. And rather than hoping I help someone decrease pain with a particular technique or exercise, I now hope that if I do anything at all, it is to help someone by lighting that same spark in their own awareness. For it is awareness that is one of the secrets to healing. Being able to share my story with the anticipation that I will light that spark for someone is exciting.

"Without awareness, there is no choice." This is an often repeated quote of John F. Barnes. You will see this multiple times throughout your MFR journey, pay attention. Stuck in my web before MFR were traumas, mostly minor, both physical and psychological: the stones on a path of a child of divorce, a young woman lacking self esteem trying to find herself, a mother surviving birth trauma, and a wife who had lost her voice. I had a life of goal-setting and striving and accomplishment. I was tired and some days miserable, wanting something different but not really knowing what it was. I kept meeting the goals thinking that each next one would make me happy and then it didn't. I did not pay attention, did not allow myself to feel, kept working harder, trying harder, doing more, and so my web tightened. When the price of what had accumulated in my web was too high (sadness, fatigue, conflict and pain), I started a journey toward awareness and release and it has been the best journey of my life. Mind you, I did not say easiest. I did say BEST!

I remember the day I entered that humungous ballroom and John Barnes, the MFR guru, walked in. Quiet enveloped the room, and he was already, from the first few moments of the lecture, holding a healing space for the fifty or more participants there. I learned the crossed hands technique that weekend, and watched someone unwind for the first time. "Oh my gosh," I thought, "What the hell was that?"

I have used the techniques of myofascial release ever since that day in 1998. I have facilitated the healing process in my clients, and I have experienced my own unwinding. The layers peeling off, one at a time, letting me shine through and helping me hold the healing space that my clients need to do their own healing. How cool is that?

Every workshop I have attended since the first one has built on the last. A deeper knowing, deeper understanding, deeper awareness and deeper clarity resulted. These things have given me choices in my life I never saw before. These things gave me my power back. I get to be the driver of my own bus at this point, and I am feeling a flow that seems so effortless compared to the striving for perfection that I grew up with. These things have given me a way to help my children live amazing and joyful lives, and that alone is enough.

I find myself wanting to share the gifts that go beyond physical here, but am reminded that many people are simply searching for pain relief. So make no mistake, I am also here to tell you that the balance, alignment, flexibility, strength and stamina you gain from a session of myofascial release surpasses most traditional physical therapy sessions because first of all it is addressing your whole body, mind and spirit, and secondly it reaches the tissues through your own awareness. This is the part that can be difficult. Your therapist is your facilitator and they have been trained to meld with and listen to your body, mind and spirit so that they can help you release restrictions that are lodged inside of you. These might be physical and they might be emotional. Remember that every physical trauma carries an emotional component. You will be led to the edge, to the barrier of your restrictions, and you will be asked to be there with them, with the pain and fear. This is the moment of opportunity. Right there at the edge. Do you jump? Or do you retreat? I have to admit that many times I myself have retreated. Too scary, too painful, too embarrassing, too something, couldn't handle it. And I was always later disappointed that I didn't jump. A missed opportunity. Your therapist has been there. They have done their own work to face their own restrictions and fear. This is the way they are able to hold that space for you when it is your turn.

During the birth of my son, which included eighteen hours of labor and forceps, I sustained some intense injuries. I had third degree vaginal tears that had to be repaired in addition to an episiotomy. My bladder, uterus and rectum prolapsed as a result. In the years following, I searched for help. I was having pain when I ran. Running was my escape, my meditation, my everything. And I couldn't do it without pain. I tried everything to help myself heal and ended up with a surgeon telling me I would need a full hysterectomy and reconstruction of my pelvic floor. Really? In short, it was myofascial release that helped. It not only helped to normalize the damaged and scarred tissues, "I started to be able to feel when I was anxious, nervous, fearful and lacking self confidence. These emotions had physical feelings in my body, like tightness and pain. All these things went together." (quoted from my book, *Living, Healing and Taekwondo*)

The MFR therapists I saw were trained in Women's Health, a specific component of myofascial release. I will be forever grateful to June and Ann, who helped me to heal the deepest pieces of my trauma with their skills, professionalism, patience and love. I would also like to say thank you to the partners I had in the workshops I have taken in these years. The best kept secret about continuing education (although we have nothing to hide) is that the days you spend learning, you also spend getting treated.

When I attended back-to-back courses in Pennsylvania a couple years ago, I remember another huge chunk of healing. Five full days of MFR, what a treat! We had just finished the first day of Rebounding, a class I highly recommend! The treatment felt profound, brought me to tears at one point, but even more intensely brought me to giggles. I laughed so hard in the session that day that at one point I shushed myself, worried that I was ruining it for the people next to me. It was at that exact moment that one of the assistants came around and whispered in my ear, "It is okay to laugh." Oh boy, did I laugh. And even better than that, I started a laughing wave around the room and everyone was laughing. Or crying. But it didn't matter. We were all in it together. What fun. What healing. What love.

I returned to my hotel room that day after class to change and then meet a new friend I had made in class for a walk. It is really hard not to make good friends at these classes, after you basically have shared your soul with each other. We enjoyed a long walk in a beautiful park just across the road from the hotel. As we walked and talked (boy did we talk) we picked the right side of a fork in the path, thinking it was the way back, only to discover a couple miles later, that we were far from the parking lot. I began to feel a familiar pain that I had only had previously with running, an old, familiar pain from the prolapse. As I walked and talked with my friend a fearful voice began to take over in my head, "What is this pain? Why is it happening again? Could it be from all the rebounding treatment today? This only happens when I run, never when I walk! Will I have to stop and ask her to go get the car?"

I finally told my friend everything, my whole story from when my son was born to my current pain on our walk. She said, "Why don't we stop and just sit a while?" You mean rest? Stop and rest and give myself a chance to feel and breathe and relax and let go? You mean I don't have to keep going to reach the finish? I can rest? And we rested, sat on the grass and continued our conversation and we sat there as long as I needed to. She didn't push me or rush me or suggest we get going. She just sat with me and let me rest. What a gift. We finally started back and found our way to the car. I woke up the next day without pain. In fact I had no remnants of the prior afternoon. I felt better than I had in a long time. Stronger, lifted up, lighter. I also felt good in my body, I liked the way it looked and felt.

The following passage was a journal entry I made during the class and is taken from my book, *Living, Healing and Taekwondo*.

281

May 22, 2011: **Transformation**

Three days of Myofascial Rebounding, one day of Cervical-Thoracic. Back in my room with a different body, one that is beautiful, nice to look at. Shifted. Transformed. What was it that shifted?

Second day of C-T, after a long class, went for a walk with Iveta. A long walk. Kept walking, talking about life. And kept walking. A different body was walking. And a healing crisis in the midst of my walk/talk. An old familiar symptom of the old me body. Dropping out, painful, hold myself kind of ache. But just from a walk, never before from just a walk. How could it be? What was happening? Was I destabilized? Was that Good?

Walked and talked some more. Rested. I never could rest before. Never could say, "Okay, I need to rest." Always pushing on, pushing, striving, running, straining. Never listening, feeling, resting. So we sat on the grass and talked some more, and I rested my core. Let it rest. You have time. I had to get back to the car and part of me wondered if I would have to ask Iveta to take my car keys and go find the car, and come for me. Part of me wondered if I would make it. We walked again and I was okay. And this morning I am fine. What the hell? Am I tight again? Did my body recognize and remain shifted? Yes. I feel open, lighter, less effortful. My core is light, not strained. And it feels balanced. It might need more rest. I can do that. I can ask for that. It is only just what I need. And that is important. My voice. What adventures will be coming, I can't wait to see.

The following poem comes from a place in my heart that opened up as a result of MFR. As my awareness and ability to feel increased I was more and more able to face fear and take action, find my voice and speak up, ask for what I wanted and needed, and try things that filled me up. Horses are one of the things that fill me up. There is a unique branch of MFR that includes treating animals. Treating and learning from animals is important. It is non-verbal. Listening in this way is what is important and what we can take to our sessions with humans. Treating an animal quickly gives you a special awareness. An awareness that all creatures in the universe matter.

Learning How To Fly

Guinness taught me how to fly,
From walk to trot to take off
He knew his job
No matter where my feet were in the stirrups
Or how much I fumbled with the reins,
He lifted me into the sky.

And then I felt the rhythm
And sank into my heels and spread my wings
And we were two spirits alive with each other
One heart together

I was breathless
Not from exhaustion but exhilaration, pure joy
I WAS joy
With my mustang boy
Who nibbled at me in waiting
To tell me that he was a good soul.

I hope to live many more days
To fly this way
In powerful rhythmic breath, only present to the moment
Which is pure delight.

Only knowing that, over and over and over again.

So with MFR, I have learned, healing comes in many forms. A treatment. A cry or a laugh. A walk. The right words at the right time. A journal entry. A horse ride. But only with awareness. I have to show up for the stuff of my life, including my own feelings and emotions, and actually feel them. I might think that analyzing or worrying or planning or organizing will help, but without awareness, without feeling, it's all just noise. Without feeling there is no healing. You now have the idea that myofascial release, I hope from what I have shared, is so much more than a physical therapy modality. It has meant so much more to me that just another continuing education credit.

I cannot tell you what a relief it was to feel hope. To know that there was a treatment out there that would address all of me, my physical pain and my emotional pain. That would take into consideration how these things were connected and help me to release and heal. An approach that blew all others I had tried away in the "caring" department. A practitioner who not only listened, but who I could tell could feel. A place where I could feel my fear and face it, where I could feel my pain, and release it. A practitioner who honored my process, whatever it was that day, and gently moved me toward a deeper awareness. I wanted to be that practitioner. I wanted to give that gift and continue to give it on a regular basis, to light the spark and teach others how to light it. It felt like to me that I was on to something that would heal the world.

I began my career, even back when I was choosing it at sixteen, because I wanted to help people heal. I set that intention, without really even knowing it back then, based on wanting to choose a profession where I could make a good living and help people at the same time. Today I truly appreciate the intention I set back then, and every person, circumstance and opportunity put in front of me that has supported my journey. Being able to practice myofascial release has given me a life filled with purpose and passion. It has given me a job that isn't work. It has allowed creativity and joy to flow through and inspire me. I have turned that goal oriented, striving and achievement kind of life, into achievements that have come from inspiration, from my heart and my true voice. In the years I have been practicing myofascial release my business has transformed, I have published a book about my healing journey, I have an awareness in my relationships I did not enjoy before, and I found a passion for taekwondo that lights my fire like no sport prior. I feel that my heart is full and at my best, I have enough energy most days to shine my light on others. Myofascial release has taught me to care for myself, the only way I can care for others.

Discovering, learning and practicing the gift of myofascial release has been the piece of my life that has made it rich, alive, joyful and true. My ability to live in the moment, and feel happiness with whatever is here for me now has been strengthened by knowing John Barnes and the many people I have met through his workshops. My choice to face fear in my life and let go of things that do not serve me has been supported by everything I have learned and continue to practice through MFR. The awareness of my body, mind and spirit has been enhanced through myofascial release to the point that I can now mindfully listen to my body's messages, give them the attention they need and feel better, both mentally and physically. This is greatly empowering. I recognize the connection of my body, mind and spirit and I recognize not only my web that is made of these pieces, but how mine is connected to all others. The gifts of knowing myofascial release go far beyond feeling less pain. These gifts are constantly being given to me, through awareness, in every interaction, every treatment, every expression of love that I give or receive. I feel immensely grateful for it.

I encourage you to explore MFR. Find a practitioner and get treated. Practice awareness. Feel. Heal. Have fun! Work hard. Work easy. Let go! Find your voice. Laugh. Cry, as much as you need to. Scream. Unwind. Be you. Express yourself. Stretch. Find your limits, and push beyond them. Walk to the edge. Jump!

Laura Probert's client shares...

I'm a 35-year-old woman. I live in northern Virginia and am a paralegal for a personal injury law firm. I've had a desk job for eleven years. My back pain was not caused by a traumatic injury. It was more of a strain in my upper back that spread to other parts of my back and got worse over time. It started about nine years ago when I carried a heavy bag in my right hand for too long while holiday shopping. The next day I had shooting pain in my upper back when I moved or stretched my right arm. I went to a doctor, he did x-rays, didn't find anything, so, he sent me to physical therapy. The main physical therapy treatment was me lying on my stomach while the physical therapist used his hands to mobilize my back and dug underneath my shoulder blade and found a big knot, which was the source of my pain. That was coupled with strengthening exercises using weights. The pain got better and, after two months, I was discharged.

Months later, the pain was back. So, I tried a chiropractor for two months. That didn't help. A year or so later, I tried a new doctor and was sent for more physical therapy. I was in physical therapy for my upper back when my lower back started hurting. I was told my lower back pain was normal and since it wasn't constant, it wasn't a big deal. My lower back pain became worse than my upper back pain. A couple of doctors later, I had a new diagnosis: sacroiliac (SI) joint dysfunction. I still had the upper back pain, but was now focusing on treating the lower back pain. I found a physical therapist that "specialized" in SI joint dysfunction. She gave me new exercises, pulled my legs to get the SI joints back into alignment. But, after two months of that, I still wasn't progressing.

I ended up seeing eight doctors and four physical therapists from different practices over a four-year period. Those eight different doctors came up with eight different diagnoses depending on their specialty. There are so many conditions or injuries that can cause back pain. I think my pain would have been easier to diagnose if I could point to an event causing a traumatic injury.

Besides clinical exams, the diagnostic tests I had were x-rays, MRIs, nerve conduction studies with EMG and a discogram (very painful injection into my L5-S1 disc). My invasive treatment included steroid injections: facet joint injections and SI joint injections. I was also prescribed multiple pain killers, muscle relaxers and anti-inflammatories over the years. My physical therapy treatment included strengthening with weights and machines, stretching, ultrasound, e-stim, TENS unit, and different foam roll and ball exercises, and a TheraCane. Several vertebrae of my upper back started getting "stuck" and wouldn't move. So, one physical therapist actually tried mobilizing my upper back by physically jamming the heel of her hands into my upper spine…ouch.

All of my old physical therapists were stuck on the theory: "You have upper back pain? Then do these exercises…". They didn't examine my body and how it works. An old friend suggested a physiatrist, who then referred me to Laura Probert, MPT. I was a little skeptical at first because she didn't do anything the same way the other physical therapists did. But, I thought, maybe her techniques will work since she's not doing any of the things that didn't work with my prior physical therapists. There was a lot of touching, breathing and mental focusing. There was no strength training with weights or machines. There was no ultrasound or e-stim.

I didn't really know what MFR meant at the beginning, but I experienced the immediate difference. The difference being reduction in pain, increased flexibility, and increased range of motion. MFR deals with the whole body, not just the location of my pain. All the medications I was on only treated the pain, but didn't address the source of the pain. I ended up developing carpal tunnel syndrome during my treatment for the back pain. So, Laura worked with that too. She would release my neck and it would decrease the pain in my wrist.

After three months with Laura's using MFR and one home exercise, my upper back was getting looser and my SI joint pain decreased dramatically. MFR helps mobilize your body. I realized why all my prior physical therapy wasn't working. You have to get the body moving, <u>then</u> use stretching and strengthening exercises to maintain the body's new condition.

I learned how to listen to my body, how to interpret what it's saying, and then what to do with that information. I can now tell when my SI joints are out of alignment and I know what exercises to do on my own to get them back in place. Laura also showed me how to do releases on my own with the TheraCane. I know that if my wrist is bothering me, it probably has something to do with my neck and shoulders tensing up.

You wouldn't think it, but having a desk job can be very destructive to the body! Our bodies don't like being immobile. That's not how we were built. Now, I am more aware of my posture and the angles my arms make while typing or using my mouse. My desk at work is now ergonomically set up, but that's not going to help my immobility. I'm the one who has to remember to stretch often and, more importantly, move.

I've learned over the years that the hardest thing for physical therapists is to get their patients to do their home exercises. We can't see our physical therapist once or twice a week and expect them to "cure" us. You have to do the work too. Even when you are discharged from your physical therapy, you still need to do your home exercise program to maintain your level of mobility. I'm sticking to my maintenance plan on my own, but I still see Laura for "tune-ups".

Wendy Isom, LMBT

Concord, North Carolina
flow Total Wellness, LLC
wendy@flowTotalWellness.com

My story of a broken spirit began long before my body started to rebel at a decibel I could hear.

I was raised in the era of "children are to be seen and not heard". It was a time when I received my cues on appropriate behavior from the pleasing or discouraging looks of my parents. It was the way of life for me as a child and into my teens.

We lived a few blocks away from my Aunt, Uncle and three first cousins and across town from my Aunt and Grandfather. We frequently gathered for holidays, birthdays and any other possible reason to enjoy a meal filled with laughter. The men and boys would sit in the living room watching television while the ladies and girls would gather in the kitchen. Sometimes my cousins and I would play in the basement waiting to be called for dinner but mostly, I liked to hang out in the kitchen and listen to my mother and her two sisters talk. The conversations varied from new recipes, to church, to town gossip and their latest ideas for our next family gathering. The laughter, giggles and whispers that peppered these kitchen huddles kept me riveted.

Oh, I yearned to belong to this tight group of three. Instead, I would sit quietly knowing that if I dared to 'add' to the conversation, I would be shot 'the look' and I would need to start praying that the social part of the evening would last forever. And if I couldn't hold my tongue, later, as the stars came out, just a few short blocks away, I would be reprimanded because "children are to be seen and not heard."

It wasn't too long before I 'learned' it truly was in my best interest to keep my voice silent; speaking if and when I was spoken to and had something of significant value to add. The lesson I learned was that I didn't have much to contribute.

Most would say I was a shy child. I didn't get involved in after-school activities or sports. I rarely had friends over to play and seldom went to their homes. The only exception to this was the time I would spend at my cousins for play-dates and sleepovers. I didn't go away to college as most kids do. I chose a different path. I lived at home so I could attend a private college to earn my degree. It was during those years that I started to experiment with my voice. I played with the boundaries to see how far I could push out. The response those days was not only 'the look' but the threat of being 'thrown out', abandoned for trying to figure out who I was and what I was capable of doing in this vast world.

I want to be clear, I don't blame my parents for parenting this way. It was what they had learned from their respective upbringings. It just wasn't working for me. After college, my only goal was to land my dream job in a state far away from my roots. And when I did, I packed my car and drove off promising myself that one day I would be ME.

I spent the first 40 years of my life believing the lie I bought into; I had little to offer. I stuffed my thoughts, feelings and needs as far down as they would go. By doing so, it's safe to say that I really didn't start living life to the fullest until my body broke and I subsequently found the John F. Barnes approach to Myofascial Release.

Polymyo$#*!...

It was the spring of 1995 and I was exhausted. The pain I felt on a daily basis depleted my energy often before my day began. I knew I was suffering from something other than sleep deprivation. My frustration escalated after each doctor's appointment. It didn't seem that we were making any progress toward restoring my health.

After numerous tests and seeking the help of several specialists, just before I turned 31, I was diagnosed with Polymyositis, an autoimmune condition that affects the muscles. Up until this point, I had always been active. I practiced yoga regularly, enjoyed roller blading and stayed on the go 24/7.

To the outside world, I was living the American Dream. I was married to the man of my dreams. We had just built a beautiful home, had rewarding careers and shared an immense love and devotion to our spirited little boy.

After the initial year of prednisone therapy, I was told my disease was in remission. At least that was what all the diagnostic tests showed. During the next 10+ years, I managed my pain, pushing through the 'flare-ups' and adjusting my lifestyle when my pain managed me.

Life should have been perfect! Instead, I was going through all the motions of life, smiling and laughing as I had been taught, but not really connecting with any true emotion. Deep inside, I felt as if I was dying a slow death.

Then one day, I hit a brick wall. The inflammation, muscle tightness and pain became debilitating. Again, I found myself consulting with specialists and undergoing newer and more sophisticated tests. For months, traditional medicine and therapy offered little relief. Not willing to give up my dream of a pain-free life, I continued to search for hope. I knew that my strong belief system would lead me to the answer I was looking for as soon as I was ready to embrace it fully.

As a Nationally Certified and North Carolina state licensed massage therapist, I had continued to study and earn certifications in additional therapeutic forms of massage, offering my clients a variety of modalities to help them manage their pain. It wasn't until I met John F. Barnes and embraced my own healing journey using the JFB approach to MFR that I knew I could truly live without pain.

I remember that day as if it was yesterday. I was attending six days of continuing education in Atlanta, GA, taking my first two MFR seminars with John. Just before class started, I walked out into the hallway. John was coming towards the seminar room; he walked up to me, placed his hand on my shoulder and said, "Welcome." From the first few moments of class, I knew I had found the modality I had been searching for. It all made perfect sense to me; it spoke to my mind, heart and soul.

After class one day, I received my first 'real' JFB-MFR treatment from a senior instructor. My life changed during that session. I received much more than profound bodywork. I received HOPE! I knew in my heart I had to learn as much as I could and put the MFR principles that were being shared, which truly are life principles, into practice for my own total wellness. Soon after returning from Atlanta, I went to Sedona, AZ, to learn alongside John as he treated patients in his world-renowned western Myofascial Release treatment center, Therapy on the Rocks. It was an amazing experience!

I arrived physically broken. It was difficult to walk up and down stairs and navigating uneven terrain seemed completely out of the question. Mid-week, John took several patients and therapists out into the Red

Rocks. Shortly after leaving the parking lot, I remember my eyes tearing up. How was I going to be able to hike when I could barely walk from my rental car to the door of Therapy on the Rocks? It truly was by the grace of God that three angels on earth were there with me that day. Two therapists, Rob and Donna both saw me struggle and each of them took me under my arm, helping me walk to our destination. I was touched by their kindness.

Nothing in my life, up until this point, had prepared me for the unconditional love and support of a gentleman I had only met the day before. Facing his own fears and healing journey that week, with much on his mind, I'm sure, he offered to carry my water and backpack. It was a simple gesture, yet one that is forever imprinted in my heart. It was the first time someone had ever done something so generous for me without the promise of something in return. That day, early in December 2005, Phil Tavolacci was my personal hero. I remember feeling foolish and uncomfortable with his simple gesture. Instinctively knowing it came from his heart, I accepted his kindness. The message I received was simple: I mattered. Not Wendy the daughter, sister, wife, mother, friend…just simply ME, unconditional acceptance for being ME. This was the true beginning of my awakening.

A month later, I embraced my first week of Intensive Therapy for the Therapist program at John's eastern Myofascial Release treatment center in Pennsylvania. I came home a changed woman, never looking back.

It was during this time that I was introduced to the concept that my own belief systems were possibly holding me back from living the life God had intended for me. I was able to look and feel deep into the beliefs I had grown up with to see how they had, and still were, influencing my adult life. At first, it was difficult to sit back and observe my internal chatter, emotional reactions and behavior to situations, both good and bad. I quickly learned not to label these opportunities of growth and to see them through soft, gentle eyes and an open heart for what they truly were – opportunities to learn and grow.

Over the next 7 years, I experienced active re-occurrences of my disease (dis-ease!), some more devastating to my mind, body and/ or spirit than others. Each of those opportunities forced me to stop and take inventory. The life-principles of JFB-MFR have allowed me to magnify these times in my life, taking a deeper and closer look at what is truly going on in and around me. Has the balance in my life been compromised in some way? What part of my soul have I not fully honored? Am I being creative? Are my family, career, nutrition, spiritual practice and relationships flowing in harmony? Have I engaged each opportunity at its barrier and waited for the opening or have I pushed through with disruptive force, crushing and missing the opportunity to learn and grow?

My JFB-MFR family has consistently held a sacred space for me to learn about ME! They have been there to remind me, when I have forgotten, that being true to myself is the key to unlocking all that has dragged me down for so long. Thankfully, I am more fully prepared to navigate the 'side-trips' or relapses, in my journey than I have ever been.

The next little bit is an excerpt from my journal after receiving one of those calls that required a 'side-trip'.

Friday, July 22, 2011

"510.", she quietly said.
"SHIT!", was my reply. How could this happen, again? It wasn't supposed to happen the first time. The second time was a fluke. The third, this is just cruel.
I'm numb. Angry, rather pissed off! Just numb…not able to even feel the tears stream down my face.

The telltale signs were there. I had been pushing them out of my consciousness for a few weeks. I had justified each and every little nuance with a story in my mind that "made sense", at least to me.

My calves burn. I should stop wearing such high wedges.

My scalp is more sensitive and itches. I guess I should switch shampoo.

My nail beds are red and irritated. I need to ask the nail tech to be gentler.

My balance is off. I'm just tired.

My right bicep feels like the tissue is ripping. That's just odd. Sometimes, I wish I wasn't so in-tune with my body. Hmmm…

Was that bump there last month? Where do we keep the Advil? Why am I so emotional?

Looking back, *all* the signs were there. My energy wasn't lasting into the evening. I was withdrawing from my family and friends, becoming quiet and small, hoping to become so small that I could manage or control whatever 'it' was that was happening.

No such luck.

So tonight, I'm hosting a Pity Party. There will be crying, slinging 4-letter words and stomping my feet. And for a while, I will be pissed at the world and everyone in it. I will question God's love for me and His plan for my life. I will try to feel what it feels like to give up on myself, but, quite honestly…I'm simply numb. I'm operating from a place of fear.

I've been questioning the care of my Rheumatologist and while I'm sure he may be a nice guy, I think my case baffles him. I believe I challenge him and he no longer knows what to do with me. Some would say my case is an anomaly. The first time I went into 'remission' I was told, "I hope I never see you again. People just don't have relapses with this disease." Well, nobody ever said I was normal, and quite frankly who would ever want to be. My brother tells me I'm one in a million. I like to think so. :)

This is the third relapse and once again, I find myself in the fight of my life. Only tonight, I don't have much fight.

The "Pity Party" is over and I find myself alone, confused and pissed-off! I think I know what it will take to fight this fight but I'm questioning if those around me know that the battle is truly just beginning. I'm a different person this go-around and I have different expectations. A few days have passed and I have started to reach out to others, professionals who may know more than I or have contacts, my brother with whom I share everything and a few friends, mostly my MFR family.

Emotionally, I have left the party, yet I sit firmly planted on the step just beyond that closed door. How do I take the first step into uncertainty? Which foot goes first? I feel as if I'll take a face plant if I stand up. I can see the bottom of the barrel...its dark and quite scary. Seriously, how do I do this alone? I'm not alone, but it *feels* like it.

This morning I struggled with even the simplest of things to be thankful for today. I'm grateful for my kids, my puppies, especially Delaney who has not left my side in several weeks. I wonder if she is so tuned in to me that she knew something was up before I knew? She is the joy in my life right now, my only true friend.

Thursday, July 28, 2011

Tonight, listening to The Weaving CD by Denean, an ocean-view room and beautiful sunset at the beach, a warm breeze and the sound of the waves crashing on shore…letting my tears flow and carry my fears out to sea with the tide. If only life were THIS simple.

What if, the feelings I have had for sometime about not living to see my 50th birthday is right on target? What if this is the end? How will I live the rest of my life? For many, who surf through life, never facing a 'life-changing' obstacle, do they fully appreciate their gift of health? Or are they so caught up in their daily routines that they know nothing of the real pain and sorrow of others, especially those nearest? Do they walk with blinders to the everyday challenges and hard doses of reality that others face? Or, do they choose not to see or feel the stirring of their own souls? Hmmm…things to ponder at some point I'm sure but for me, I need to use my energy focusing on 'the plan'.

Friday, July 29, 2011

"The Plan"
Hmmm…Still unfolding…

My time away from my 'daily-life' has given me perspective. I have been reminded how very important it is to have 'me-time' and now, more than ever before, I HAVE to take time for myself EVERY...SINGLE...DAY. Time to get quiet, listen and feel for the answers to my numerous questions. If I stay in my head, I'm stressed. If I allow myself the grace to BE, I can soften into the moment. What I have learned these past few days is that I am frickin' scared to death! I can feel my core shake. As I get quiet, my body starts to rock in an attempt to self-soothe. It's deep within my soul; it's not noticeable to anyone, only I can feel it. Quietly, in my mind, I start to hum, Hush Little Baby.

Sad reality-

I have come to realize that I no longer can be the friend I have been to so many who know where I am in their time of need but are unable to reciprocate the flip side of friendship. I give and give and allow people to take and take, rarely requesting that they make a substantial deposit to my emotional bank. My emotional bank is depleted and now, as sick as I am, I must find the energy and stamina to rebuild ME. To others, this process may seem selfish; to me it's called self-preservation. I pray that I can preserve what and who I am right now so that I have a foundation from which to continue to build the authentic ME. How the heck did I let this happen? No energy or time to beat myself up about it. I just need to remember for the next time...because there is always a next time. Someone will always step up for me to handout free comfort, encouragement and unconditional love. I need to stay true to myself; centered and grounded so I can be a friend to those I love without losing ME.

My shoulders are sore. My arms are tired. My head is full and my heart aches. I've carried the weight of others for way too long.

I'm guessing that those who will be placed in my path for this part of my journey may not be known to me as yet. For this opportunity, I'm excited. For this part of my journey to be successful, I will need to be wise and open to all possibilities. I am quickly reminded of a story John tells in his seminars. To be open to all possibilities, you must be like a helicopter pilot, flying with full awareness. The second the pilot tips the blades of the aircraft, the only possibility available to him is the direction in which he leaned. So, I will fly like a helicopter, remembering not to limit my possibilities by leaning too early. Leaning into my awareness…because, "without awareness, you have no choice."

I love my Johnisms!

Saturday, July 30, 2011

Tonight is my last night at the beach and I'm ready to go home. I really don't like the humid stickiness of summer. I'm sad to be leaving the space that has allowed me to put some perspective on my health situation. I pray that I will be able to stay with the sounds and images of the waves crashing up on shore and taking my worries back out to sea. I pray that the calmness and peace I feel sitting on the patio continue to wash over me as a source of comfort. There's a renewing of my spirit that has happened over the last few days. I thank God for the timing of this seminar and the way He knows what I need to find my secret path back to just being.

Monday, August 1, 2011

Re-Entry:

Re-entry used to be SO stinking scary. Learning the delicate balance of coming off a 'seminar high' and landing back in reality had been difficult at best for me in the beginning. I suspect that my family cringed as much as I did when I walked through the door after being away for a few days or long weekend fully emerged in MFR-Land. Ah, the warm and fuzzy feelings of total acceptance for the crazy lady hanging upside down and half-way off a table would no longer be the norm of my afternoons. Leaning into the wind, digging deep and emerging with a little more clarity of my authentic self is heavenly.

BUT, then you fly or drive home, walk through the door and are met with a multitude of scenarios. The feeling(s) of re-entry can be like a bucket of ice water being thrown in your face. It's the extreme emotion and feelings of the safe space held by John, his instructors and the participants versus the unknowing of your family and friends not on a similar path.

Over time, this re-entry process has become easier for me. I credit this to my ability to stay true to myself for longer periods of time. You see, the clearer I am with WHO I truly am and the more honest I am by allowing my authentic self to grow and shine, the easier all aspects of my life become. It's when I lose sight of such vision that my life becomes small and slow, so much so that a certain death almost seems inevitable in due time. So for my health to thrive I must remain true to feeling and believing and listening to the whispers that are spoken, so I no longer have to be hit with the BOOM of a missed message.

Among the many lessons each of my 'side-trips' has uncovered for me, one rings loud and clear: I matter. My voice is not to be silenced. I have many gifts to share. I no longer need to shrink in the presence of others. MFR has helped me face my fears of rejection and abandonment. It helped me unlock my voice so I can be my best advocate, speaking my truth, from my heart.

When I was first diagnosed with Polymyositis, I didn't know I wasn't present for my own life. I walked and sometimes stumbled through days, months and years doing what was expected of me. My first 'side-trip' I truly was thrown off my center. I had a difficult time understanding what I had done to be dealt such a life-changing disease.

Looking back with clearer vision, I now understand that my body needed to scream *that* loud to get my attention. If it attacked itself, I might hear what it had been telling me all along. "Wake-up, YOU matter!" The burden of not speaking my truth has been lifted. I feel validated and empowered to use my voice for my well-being. Now, instead of being called shy, quiet may be a better adjective. I prefer to listen and learn, taking in everything around me.

Today, my disease is in remission. I give credit to a few significant tools in my basket: first and foremost, JFB-Myofascial Release. Secondly, the care of my new Rheumatologist, who not only listened to my words as well as my body, but encouraged and supported my quest to live pain-free. Lastly, I credit modifying my nutrition. I receive MFR treatments on a regular basis, self-treat with my foam roller and ball most days, actively move 30-minutes a day, eat foods that are good for ME and find time to feed my soul creatively.

We all experience times of difficulty. I believe it is our responsibility to learn and grow from each of these opportunities. JFB-MFR helped me see that I am worth the struggles! Freedom and Joy are on the other side.

Finding harmony and connecting your mind, body and spirit takes courage; it's the most loving thing you can do for yourself!

Wendy Isom's client shares...

"Mysterious faithful river of life, cascading through the wilderness of the wounded warrior, within my forever aching soul and while the torrents of tears flow unabated from my weary eyes, falling without end to the parched earth beneath my tired feet, I am thankful to have gotten out alive with body and mind relatively intact, for I am a domestic violence 'survivor' and victim no longer resides in my vocabulary."

~ Darcy F. Meese (written 25-08-11 and revised 21-11-12)

Myofascial Release (MFR) has been invaluable in treating my Post Traumatic Stress Disorder (PTSD) and Traumatic Brain Injury (TBI). Having been both a battered child and spouse/girlfriend, I have had a lot of 'triggers' that I had assumed were the result of the brain damage I suffered from being three months premature, multiple head traumas and a bout of herpes encephalitis. At one point, I was on twenty different medications, fifteen of them to treat 'ailments' that the original medications afflicted me with.

While pain is a universal fact of life, suffering is entirely optional. Am I pain free? No, and I never have been. But when the pain gets to be too much to bear, rather than drown myself in alcohol, take a slew of pills to combat the side effects of the initial medication, or punish my body by running two or three miles, so that I could experience a different kind of pain, MFR taught me to break free from all of the labels. It taught me to not only listen to my inner voice, but to follow where it led. By doing so, I know that when I reached the deep and dark recesses of my soul that the memories which were contained in the deepest suffering of my cells, I could revisit the silent screams, giving my soul and spirit a voice, a healthy means of expression.

In truth, I have always heard my inner voice, and had my words for expression. I have always loved art and music, both performance and composition, enjoyed dance and have a downright adoration of therapeutic horseback riding, but MFR taught my soul to sing and my spirit to dance.

Right after a session with my therapist and friend, Wendy, I came up with this quote: "If I am lost in thought, come find me and bring me back. If I am lost in the music, let me go and let me soar."

I feel the same thing about MFR. I am the type of person who thinks things to death and then resuscitates them in order to think them to death again. MFR taught me to get out of my 'thinking' brain and into my 'feeling' brain. In reality, a lot of my triggers were blocked and/or repressed memories that traditional psychotherapy could not and did not help.

MFR has taught me how to embrace the theta wave state. It has taught me how to embrace myself, by listening to my inner voice and to discard the negative self-talk that wasn't my true essence. In the mind-body-spirit ideology, I prefer to focus on spirit. For me, spirit is about the determination and drive to move toward wellness. After devastation and depression yield to acceptance, it transitions towards making peace that your body failed 'you' rather than you failing your body.

Your illness is not your fault, it just is. Taking in the negative comments of doctors, family and friends, although they may be well-intended, keeps us stuck and sick. We are only as sick as our deepest secrets and if we have repressed those memories we surely won't get better. Put your energy towards getting better. You deserve it.

If you can accept that you are *not* your diagnosis and do *not* get mired down in letting your treatment modalities define you, then you can and will succeed in managing or eliminating your pain as I have mine.

"You cannot see the world clearly through your tears" (paraphrase of CS Lewis)

I'd like to conclude my piece by saying: Take the time to invest in YOU when going in pursuit of true healing. Too often we get caught up in the professional diagnosis and although usually well intended, poorly timed opinions of friends and loved ones can hinder the process of healing.

The personal commitments and financial investments of MFR isn't an act of self-indulgence. Rather it's the ultimate in the expression of the unexplored soul and its desires and utmost needs. It is within letting yourself "ebb and flow" that you can leave behind those things that mire you down and keep you in a constant state of stagnation. MFR allows each of us a chance to stare into that deep abyss and as it stares back at you, you'll be able to feel the ultimate calm because you are more than what you thought and they said you were. Assimilate that which empowers you and shed those beliefs that no longer and never served you. Be well. Be at peace. You are worth it!

I, for one, am no longer a slave to the 'should have/could have/would have' monster. I'm at peace with being me and that's the first step in healing those ancient wounds that afflicted my mind. Until I found Myofascial Release and Wendy those wounds ravaged my body and dampened my spirit.

Now, I shine from within so brightly, I can't help but be an embodiment of how successful this therapy can be.

Darcy F. Meese

LINDA AILEEN MILLER, LMT, EAV

Stuart, Florida
Linda Aileen Miller Massage Therapy
whoisthatwoman@gmail.com

I arrived here in 1947. There are scattered details of my mom's pregnancy and my birth process, which was mostly normal, unless you count the umbilical cord around my neck.

Developing rheumatic fever landed me in the hospital tied to a bed as I attempted to pull strange things out of my throat. Scared to death as my father yelled at the nurse who couldn't find my veins to insert an IV, the foundation of not trusting doctors began.

In retrospect, I realized that we don't know what we don't know until we do! We tend to move through life as if trauma is 'normal'. Getting knocked down, and getting back up as if nothing has happened was just what you did. The old adage, 'if it doesn't kill you it will make you stronger' was our family mantra.

When I was five years old we lived on the north side in Jacksonville,

Florida. The details of the man who came into my dollhouse in our backyard are sketchy for me. He was our neighbor. I remember vividly he and my dad tying two cats tails together and throwing them over a clothesline, as they laughed watching them fight to get down. Terrified of what that 'nice' neighbor man might do to me, I never told anyone about him coming into my dollhouse or his touch. I buried those memories for a long time.

For nearly forty-five years my body held that pain and sadness in silence, until it couldn't do it anymore! At a holotropic breathwork session, all the physical and emotional pain gushed forth like a tsunami!

That day was the beginning of my curiosity, and later understanding, that our bodies hold cellular memory.

With Holotropic (Stanislov Grof) or Integrative (Jacqueline Small) Breathwork, our cells become oxygenated and open, allowing for the possibility of memory and emotion to come forth. While this work is extremely powerful, it lacks the positional memory component, and the low-load sustained pressure into the fascia which occurs when being treated by a skilled therapist trained in Myofascial Release by John F. Barnes, PT. While breathwork is an excellent modality, my experience has taught me that MFR offers us access to even deeper layers of our cells and our soul.

Ten years later, in my first MFR class with John F. Barnes, PT seeing others go through similar cathartic releasing processes was confirmation it was real. I understood it in my soul. In that moment, I coined the term *truth tears*. Seeing, feeling, and knowing something so real in my gut can bring me to unexplainable spontaneous tears of 'truth', often without logical reason.

Having skipped from my youth to years following my education in Transpersonal Psychology at Burlington College and Soul Studies Institute, Electro-Acupuncture Certification, Homeopathy &

Massage Therapy Licensure I will digress back to the beginning layers of my web, before I knew what I know now...or at least what I think I know.

By the age of six, I had been in two automobile accidents, both of my grandfathers had died, and my favorite uncle had been killed by a drunk driver.

Vividly remembering the police coming to the lake house we shared with friends over Labor Day weekend, telling my father his brother had been killed. I never forgot my first feelings about death.

Days later as Dad drove our maid home from work we went to the gas station where my uncle's crumbled motorcycle remains rested up against the building. The young man that hit Uncle Charles was standing there with his friends laughing. By the grace of God, several people kept my dad from killing those boys that day. I began to learn that making my dad angry was something I never wanted to do. Never.

He was a good man. I have no doubt that he loved my brother and I, though he didn't tell us that until I was fifty-five years old. He also ruled his world with an iron fist...sometimes literally. Life with him was his way or the highway, always.

At sixteen, on an early release day from school in a beautiful black and white '57 Chevy along with my boyfriend and two others, we decided to drag race down a winding road on the west side of town. As we rounded the corner a huge bus turned left directly across our path. My boyfriend, Jeff, slammed on the brakes, which locked, and we spun out of control flipping end over end, three and a half times according to bystanders. Somewhere in there I became unconscious. There were no seatbelts. When I regained consciousness I was still inside, looking up at the seats, the cars wheels up in the air, with the smell of gasoline permeating the air around me. Someone in the back had been smoking prior, and I could hear Jeff's voice calling my name.

Panicked, I knew I had to get out, and get out fast. That's when I saw Jeff's outstretched hand.

Crawling from the car, I began to feel the pain in my left leg which was badly swollen across the front of my shin. My sense was it must have slammed into the dashboard. There was a baseball size contusion down the front, covered in dirt along with minor cuts and scrapes from head to toe from the shattered windows. There was nothing else visible. Nothing glaring like broken bones or things that needed stitching.

Cold and terrified, I remember wanting to go home, wanting my mom. My whole body ached, and slowly more bruising began to appear. I went to my neighbor's house after the police were finished with us. I was terrified. My mom was still at work.

My father volunteered part-time with the Florida Highway Patrol. On that day he was, thank God, in the hospital having back surgery. When my mom got home she drove me to the hospital and made me tell my father what I had done. All I could think of was how grateful I was he was stuck in that hospital bed! If he could have gotten his hands on me there was no doubt he would have beaten my behind for being so 'stupid'!

I could walk, though not without pain. It amazes me now that it never occurred to anyone to take me to get checked out. I'm certain I had whiplash and a minor concussion at the very least. In retrospect, I'm just as glad they didn't.

For a long time, there was pain in that leg. There is deep tender scarring there. I didn't remember much else about what happened. The last thing I remember was seeing the bus, and us beginning to spin. Many years later, there were painful physical pieces of some experience which surfaced during an MFR session, and by then I had re-injured that leg again. The layers of trauma to the left leg continued, so I am not certain which one was connected to what, nor did it really matter. The good news is I still have that leg which took out the headlight of an on-coming car, fracturing nearly every bone in it, the only time I ever rode a motorcycle. For this, I am most grateful!

A 'web' of memories that is nearly 66 yrs old has a lot of components. My sense is to share the good, the bad, and the ugly or as I have come to call it: the muck, the magic & the miracles. There was some of it all.

I studied tap, jazz and ballet, along with baton twirling, and by sixth grade I twirled three batons simultaneously on numerous squads with senior high school girls. My knives, fire batons, and flaming ropes, during solo performances at school, and in Orange Bowl parades and football games, are among my favorite memories of adolescence.

Years later I opted for cheerleading in college, because I loved the acrobatics, tumbling & dance aspect of it and it seemed to me the cheerleaders always got the cutest boyfriends!

During that same timeframe, I also competed in local and state beauty pageants, winning as often as not, wondering silently if I would be 1st runner-up for the rest of my life. The quest for a crown in Atlantic City led me to the parts of myself that hated being on stage, being judged, standing half-naked in a swimsuit doing four quarter turns while a panel of people (most often men) looked us up and down. The judges were comparing us butt to butt, breast to breast, and not seemingly caring about the human inside the skimpy swimsuit. I often wondered if the scholarship money was worth the resulting feelings of judgment and self-worth.

Loving to swim and water-ski, and pretty good at both, I excelled more at physical activities than mental ones. School was okay for me, not great, not horrible, unless you count flunking out the second quarter of my freshman year. Truth be told, I actually 'partied' out more than flunking, though the end result was the same. I failed... again. And even I could see the pattern forming.

Returning home I found a part-time job and took some courses at our local Junior College. The feeling of not being pretty enough, good enough, or smart enough, began to permeate my spirit. Then in the fall of 1968 the feeling of being stupid, stupid, stupid dug its evil claws into the core of my already twisted web.

If you were a young woman who became pregnant in the '60's you simply did not talk about it.

In those days unmarried girls *went away for awhile* to visit friends or family. So that was what I did. I returned a woman carrying shame, and the grief of loss on my shoulders.

My son's father did not want any part of the *mess* we created (his words), and certainly didn't want to get married. Terrified of my own father, and facing the consequences of my choices, I left.

Years later, covering my pain with alcohol and drugs, I realized how much of me truly *left* in order to survive what I wouldn't allow myself to feel or express.

A friend offered me a room in her home, in exchange for caring for her children in Indianapolis, Indiana. I gratefully accepted. *I went away for awhile.* How literal that statement was. I lost a huge part of myself during that process, and giving my son up for adoption. It took me years to find those pieces again.

Five months pregnant, I gathered the courage to tell my parents I had quit my job, was leaving home the following week and why. It was one of the scariest nights of my life.

My son was adopted privately through the doctor who cared for us those last four months. The process of labor and delivery was horrific.

I was promised I would be put to sleep as soon as labor began. That did not happen.

I remember the nurses talking about me as if I were deaf or not in the room. I heard them saying things like 'she'll be back, they always are' and more. Feeling their words penetrating my soul, my last conscious thought was the music playing in the background on the radio in that little room. My body screamed with pain though my voice remained silent, fearful it would be worse if I said anything. "You'll Never Walk Alone" played softly in the background, and it was the last thing I remember before going under anesthesia.

For years I couldn't hear that song without crumbling into a useless pile of tears.

I never felt more alone in my life than on May 14th, 1969 when I awakened after the birth of my first child. A nurse stopped outside my door preparing to bring my son in to me. The other mothers around me all had their children. Another nurse stopped her as I overheard the words, 'NO! *She is giving him away!*" WAIT! What? And I cried in silence.

My lifelong best friend is the only living person I know who saw my child. I never spoke of him to hardly anyone except for her for years. It was a chapter of life that was lost and locked away. One day I realized I had to name him. I couldn't keep calling him "*him*". He had to have a name, and so to me, he became Michael.

My own little brother didn't know about my first son until 1984. My ex-husband and I were going through a very tumultuous time. Most of our marriage was that way. He was extremely jealous of my relationship with my brother and the bond we shared. One evening, under the influence of something, he screamed at me, "yeah, well your brother wouldn't think you were so damn special if he knew about you giving up your first son!"

In that moment, something in me snapped. No more. No more hiding, no more lying, no more shame. I walked in the other room and took my brother by the hand. We went outside, and in the night air on my front porch I told him everything. His response to me was the heart opener that was the beginning of healing for me. My sweet baby brother said, 'I wouldn't care if you were a prostitute on Bay Street in Jacksonville, FL! You are my sister and I will always love you!" We laughed and we cried, and my soul was lighter. The truth does indeed set us free!

It was on that same porch eight years later I told my second born son that he had a brother. I was a newly divorced single mom attempting to teach him about sex and life choices. We cried together, for the brother he never knew he had, and more layers of my own pain and healing evolved.

Slowly and surely the words of that experience and many others stopped being a secret. They stopped catching in my throat and crushing my heart. I stopped feeling ashamed of who I was and who I was not, and having to explain or justify simply being. Over time as I waded through the chapters of divorce, life, death, birth and beginnings, it became easier to own all of me, and to share without shame, guilt, pain and judgment- my own and others.

Thirty-two years as a flight attendant took me all over the world with tons of fabulous memories, along with watching my friend being robbed at knife point in Rome! Six of my friends died at once on Flight 191, which was my weekly route. I was spared because I was in the hospital with salmonella poisoning. For years I felt like I should have died too. Guilt squashes our soul. Once I got good and mad at God I felt better.

After awhile, I began to understand there truly is a bigger plan. I made peace with the God of my understanding, and embraced the concept of forgiveness- my own and others.

I am human. I have survived massive amounts of life and death experiences, including walking through my own brother's last breath with him eight years ago and more death than I can count. These are part and parcel of what has made me who I am today.

I did the best I could based on the information I had at the time, and I survived. We all do.

I met a Myofascial Release therapist from Indiana, named Jeannine, about six years ago who knew the doctor that delivered Michael. She shared with me that he had pancreatic cancer, and was dying soon. She encouraged me to contact him to try to find my son.

I decided a long time ago that I gave up that right.

In the sixties, families didn't often tell children they were adopted. My feelings were I didn't have the right to come into his world, and potentially shatter what he knew as truth.

I sat with her words for quite awhile, and finally decided to call the doctor's office. The receptionist listened politely saying she would check with the doctor and call me back.

That evening I had a voicemail. "The Dr. has NO recollection of that adoption!"

That was it. Period. End of story. The raging anger that surfaced was incredible. Once again, having a part of my heart and soul ripped to shreds as if 'that adoption', my son, my life was simply business as usual! No human element attached to it at all.

Let it go, let it go, let it go, I kept telling myself.

I continue to pray that Michael is happy and healthy.

Over the years with MFR treatments there have been layers and layers of sadness and grief about never knowing my son that unfolded. Some came as anger, though most were simply deep, deep grief. Many years after Michael's birth I wrote and published, for the whole world to read, the following words:

I REMEMBER

I remember the night you became a part of me
And I a part of you.
I can sometimes still feel you there
Deep inside of me.
One being for such a long time
Yet a combination of so many from many, many lifetimes before us.
I was drugged.
You arrived in the early morning house.
I never saw your face or touched you with my hands.
They took you away.
You left with a stranger.
I made that choice
For the time, it was the best choice
For the time, it felt like my only choice.
For over forty years I have ached to see your eyes
To tell you that I made my choice out of love
And to hear you say...
It was a good choice, Mom...I have had a great life!
It is my prayer...that this is your truth.
I remember your feet kicking my ribs...
I remember waking to feel my flat belly
Knowing you were gone...out of my body...out of my physical reality
I remember you every day...with hope and with love.
For though you are not visible, you are forever deep within my heart
I remember no one told me anything about sex...
Its joys or its consequences...only not to do it!
That was the way of the world in the sixties
I understand today that life is about choices

I remember that adoption was a difficult choice.
It never got any easier…just clearer.
Choices based on expectations,
our own or those of society can leave an empty space in our souls
That we often spend a lifetime trying to fill.

In 2009, my friend and fellow MFR therapist, Cathy Covell, invited me to Indiana. She is the owner and therapist extraordinaire of a human and equine healing center in the tiny town of Orland, Indiana.

Cathy was leaving for a week to earn her continuing education credits for her physical therapy license. She asked me to house-sit her wonderful four-legged animals, dogs, cats & horses, and to run her clinic while she was away.

At that time, I had taken all of John Barnes' MFR courses, and repeated many. Cathy, however, saw in me something I had not yet been able to fully wrap my head around. She saw my ability to handle the operation of her sacred space, treat her clients, along with three other therapists, and keep her world flowing while she was away. *She believed in me.*

I arrived on a Thursday afternoon. A dear young man picked me up at the airport and drove me to her home. The first thing I noticed as I stood out back was this awesome field filled with tall stalks swaying in the sunset sky, soon to be corn! Kevin Costner was alive and well in Indiana that week. I later joked with Cathy that he was in that field!

After receiving an MFR session, we walked the dogs, and we had dinner. Familiarizing me with the barn and cats it was an early-to-bed night. The next morning Cathy was gone and I was left to feel my way through the following ten days.

I loved the little town and about half way through that first Friday I was aware that a part of me was looking at each young man I saw… wondering…if perhaps…just maybe…he might be Michael. Here I was in Indiana. Why not? Stranger things have happened.

The week was filled with wonderful opportunities and interactions with both co-treating therapists and patients alike. I continued to marvel on my walks through the woods with Josie and Bandit, her pups, at the places I was stretching myself, moving beyond what would have ordinarily been comfortable for me. Walking in the woods after dark? Yikes!

Stepping out of our comfort zones is a core principle of myofascial release. Nothing happens in status quo. Keep in mind, this is not the old "no pain, no gain" adage- pushing through or past the hurt. It is about giving ourselves permission to touch places we are afraid to touch, feel the hurt that is the deepest, moving beyond where we have rested comfortably in the muck for too long!

All week the therapists took turns treating one another as well as our patients. It was a powerful healing time. On Friday, Anne, a PT from down the road in Fort Wayne offered me a session. Physical Therapists, by licensure, are able to do internal treatments (intra-vaginal or intra-rectal) which are highly effective for any pelvic floor dysfunction. At the time, I was experiencing a lot of bladder and incontinence issues following an auto accident in 2007. I asked Anne if we could do some internal work, and she graciously said yes.

I had received intra-vaginal work previously at Therapy on the Rocks, a John Barnes clinic in Sedona, AZ so I had a sense of what to expect…I thought.

I am also aware we can do massive amounts of therapy around the painful issues of our journey, but, until the traumatized tissue is actually touched in a conscious way, there will always be more to be done. Trust me on this one. The issue is in the tissue!

On that Friday afternoon, I felt Anne's gloved finger gently touch my episiotomy scar and the pain shot straight through my body. She asked, 'are you okay with this?' I assured her that I was. I was just shocked at how painful it was there. It felt like a knife! Both of us quietly settled in, and seemingly from nowhere the memories of Michael's birth came forward along with a barrage of tears.

At some point, I began to share what was coming up for me and how I had a son, whom I gave up for adoption, that was born in Indiana. Being the gifted therapist she is, Anne listened silently and waited. I told her I had tried several years before to find him, against my better judgment, because I knew his doctor was going to die soon from pancreatic cancer.

She calmly looked at me and asked, "Dr. Benson?"

I could feel my breath stop.

"Dr. Tom Benson", she said.

"Yes"...in weak and teary voice I answered.

Softly, still touching the scar left from the scalpel of that man, she replied "he has passed".

My heart once again released one of the most powerful aches I had ever felt. In that moment, in that treatment room in Orland, Indiana seemingly all possibilities of ever knowing who or where or what about my first born son came to another screeching, screaming halt. Anger. Separation. Abandonment. Loss...again...deeper, deeper, deeper.

What are the chances of forty years later a woman who did research with Dr. Tom Benson, the man who delivered my first born child, in a town many have never heard of being my therapist one Friday afternoon, would share this news with me? I may never know Michael face to face, and yet one thing was confirmed for me that day. The

Universe is very small and somehow, someway when we give ourselves permission to be real, magic and miracles happen. **Everything is connected.**

And through it all, I gently gathered back one more piece of my soul.

Through MFR, on and off the table, I have come to trust that there is purpose even in our deepest pain.

I loved my studies at Burlington College, and just a few courses short of graduating I chose to attend Alpha School of Massage. After graduation I studied every possible modality I could find except for Myofascial Release with John F. Barnes, PT. Mostly because I was stubborn. We had an instructor in school who never stopped talking about John Barnes, so I went in the opposite direction. Go figure!

That changed in 2001. Thanks to my dear therapist friend, Jessica, who was studying MFR, we began to treat each other on a regular basis and my life changed. Loving the MFR I was receiving, I finally surrendered, and trekked to Arizona and took my first MFR class.

Thankfully, I have never looked back.

Experiencing back to back auto accidents in 2006 & 2007, which totaled my cars, and gifted me with significant concussions, whiplash and head trauma which affected my vision, speech and memory I knew I needed to be in Sedona for treatment ASAP. It took me the better part of the year and a half between accidents to heal only to be slammed again by a driver who never put her foot on the brakes at 45 mph.

I understood MFR. My left brain, the intelligent, organizing, logical part of me understood it. My accidents and the years that followed afforded me the opportunity to feel the healing of trauma in a more profound way.

What came from every life experience I have had has been the ability to help my own clients walk through some of their deepest trauma, keeping them safe as they unwind the journey of their souls, and feel their most intense life events.

I'm not sure I would consciously choose some of my experiences simply to become a better therapist or a better person, and yet, a part of me believes that at some level we do choose it all.

For in the choosing, I have co-created my challenges, my opportunities for growth, and my gifts in this lifetime.

Through this work I have had what I can only describe as an incredible privilege to be witness to people embracing life at the very deepest parts of their being and climbing mountains they never could have imagined. Some days I almost feel guilty calling it "work".

Then I smile from a place deep in my heart, and I remember.

Linda Aileen Miller's client shares...

Myo what!? You have got to be kidding me! You are going to do WHAT? Are you crazy or just a lunatic? There is no way you are going to touch me! You better not touch me! Yep. She is crazy, or am I? What do you think you are doing? Stop it; I don't want to shake anymore! I don't like it! What am I feeling? I don't feel anything, so, what is this? Just make the pain go way. I can't stand it any longer just make it stop!

It did stop after many difficult, freeing, kind, emotional, painful and loving sessions with the most caring MFR therapist I could have imagined. I am grateful and honored for the gifts she shared during my healing journey. How I learned to trust and surrender to the process of healing my body. How I learned to love what I was given-not as if it was my fault or that I deserved it, but as a way of learning about me and why I am the way I am. To love myself for being ME.

I hadn't realized myofascial release work was about to change my life and body forever!

Don't do that! You are hurting me. I'll be good, please don't tie me up. Please mom, don't let them hurt me again. You are my mom and shouldn't let things like that happen to me. Please mom, don't touch me like that. It doesn't feel nice. I hate it!! I'll be good mommy... I promise! I won't tell anyone!

My body hurts, MY BODY HURTS!! MY BODY HURTS!!!!!!!

I have rheumatoid arthritis and fibromyalgia. I didn't have the strength to hold my head up as my neck was so weak. I shuffled when I walked-just like Tim Conway did when he was on Laugh In and Momma's Family. That is what I was like for years. I was slowly dying.

I meet Linda at a center for personal growth where she had an office and was part of a group of therapists guiding participants gently on a path of healing their minds, bodies, and souls. What a wonderful person Linda is.

I was having a leg cramp, which I used to have a lot and I was afraid of being touched. Linda said "I could help your leg if you would let me touch you." She had such love in her eyes so I agreed to allow her to touch me. I had seen another manual therapist and she didn't touch me for months. She could get close. I would shake and shake and shake so she did most of her work without touching me. Linda helped my cramps that night and the touch wasn't too uncomfortable. Eventually Linda became my regular MFR therapist. YEAH!

My body was becoming softer and less painful and I was becoming able to feel my body. It had been numb for so long. I wasn't aware of being numb as that was how my life had been. NUMB!!!. AND I was feeling and healing my body.

Sometimes my body FEELS pain now and then due to memory, stresses of everyday life or from R.A. I call my wonderful friend and therapist Linda, returning to the place of letting go, opening my body for healing and fascial work. I walk away with my HEAD held HIGH and thank God for MFR.

My name is Pamela.

Now I have a new name and a new healthy body and I love my life!

Thank you!

Afterword

This past nine months has been the most packed and accelerated time of my life to date. When I chose to write and collect stories for this book in September 2012 I wasn't fully conscious of the other large-scale events that were about to comingle with the project. Jeff and I were certainly aware that our townhome lease would be ending March 2013 but we weren't planning to buy another house at that time. We had only talked about renting another home for a while. It seemed the logical, economical, and wise thing to do. Well, lo and behold, we were guided to THE perfect house to purchase (thanks Kathleen!) and simply had to leap at the divine opportunity at hand.

In December 2012 we purchased our current home, the third home Jeff and I have owned together in the last 15 years, and moved into it in early January 2013. If this was the only move of the year it wouldn't be much to mention. However, just three months later in April 2013, I also moved my wellness center. My main clinic was a 2,200 square foot space with three private treatment rooms and a substantial fitness/exercise area. In a nutshell, it was tantamount to moving another house.

I didn't just *move* my wellness center, actually- I made a very conscious decision to simplify and restructure my business. I decided that it was time for me to focus more on what I truly wanted for myself, both personally and professionally. I wanted less financial overhead and burden, less stress, more time for myself and my relationships. I wanted more time for creative pursuits that I've put on hold, like my artwork. I wanted to create possibilities to return to a regular daily exercise plan. I wanted to be able to travel more. I wanted to set up a scenario where Jeff and I could become parents. In short, I wanted to create a more joyful and abundant life!

So, over the last eleven weeks we have converted the large, 2-level, detached garage of our new house into a spectacular clinical space. Dealing with architects, contractors, electricians, HVAC specialists, plumbers, and county inspectors while simultaneously running my business, treating patients, and writing/compiling this book has been a juggling act for sure! Just this past Wednesday I treated patients in the new clinical space for the very first time...and I buzzed.

My point in sharing all of this is that it is highly unlikely that I could have accomplished all of these overlapping tasks in the time span of nine months without having lived an MFR-based life for the past eight years! Physically, I couldn't have endured this past year's challenges if it weren't for MFR. Psychologically and emotionally, I likely would have struggled more with the intensity of the last year if it weren't for MFR. I am passionate about MFR because it not only has given me my life back, it has given me the courage and determination to choose and create a life I wish to live.

In closing, I'd like to thank someone I have never met. I would like to thank Brené Brown, PhD. Roughly when I started writing this book someone had posted a link on Facebook to a TEDTalk called "The Power of Vulnerability" by Brené Brown. I watched the roughly 20-minute YouTube video and was captivated by what this brilliant and articulate woman was relaying. She spoke eloquently and compassionately about how her decade of clinical research lead her to understand that the key to unlocking joy, love, and courage was allowing oneself to be vulnerable. I likely watched that video five or six times over the course of the nine months it has taken to write and compile this book.

When the voices of "You're sharing too much, Phil" and "Are you sure you want to put THAT out there for the whole world to see?" cropped up, I was guided to listen to Brené again. When the thought crept in repeatedly of "This isn't ENOUGH Phil- it's just a book of stories", I'd pull up the video again. Currently I'm reading Brené's book, "Daring Greatly", and loving every page of it.

So, Doctor Brené Brown, thank you! I hope that my book finds its way to you and that we might meet one day so I can thank you in person.

Although our fascial webs might physically end at our skin, I believe that they energetically extend vast distances beyond our flesh-bound bodies and allow us to connect with others in this great web of life. Therefore, I look forward to connecting with everyone who chooses to read this book via the unseen web of life.

Much Love & Light-
Phil Tavolacci
PhilTavo@gmail.com

Myofascial Release Resources

Books by John F. Barnes, PT:

Myofascial Release: The Search For Excellence
Healing Ancient Wounds: The Renegade's Wisdom

John F. Barnes based Myofascial Release and Stretching Books:

Comprehensive Myofascial Self Treatment, Your path to authentic healing and pain relief
By Joyce Patterson, PT

Myofascial Stretching, A Guide to Self-Treatment
By Jill Stedronsky, MS, OTR and Brenda Pardy, OTR

Books by Cathy Covell:

A Patient's Guide to Understanding John F. Barnes Myofascial Release
A Therapist's Guide to Understanding John F. Barnes Myofascial Release
Feeling Your Way Through

Myofascial Release DVD's:

Fireside Chat, by John F. Barnes, PT
Myofascial Release- 2 DVD set, by John F. Barnes, PT

Dr. Jean Claude Guimberteau DVD's:

Strolling Under the Skin

Muscle Attitudes

Interior Architectures

Helpful Websites:

www.myofascialrelease.com
www.guimberteau-jc-md.com (French & English options)

Made in the USA
Lexington, KY
25 August 2016